ECHOES OF THE UNDERGROUND

A Footsoldier's Tales

By LEE HARRIS

COMPILED AND EDITED BY HICHAM BENSASSI

BARNCOTT PRESS
LONDON - AMSTERDAM - PARIS - NEW YORK - KATHMANDU - CAPE TOWN

Echoes of the Underground

© LEE HARRIS 2014

ISBN-13: 978-1484986882

Cover drawing by Anonymous Street-Artist, Amsterdam.
Back cover photograph by Karel Kanda.
Production by schmoo.
Published in print and ebook editions by Barncott Press.

CONTENTS

Dedication & Thanks	3
Introduction	5
BUZZ BUZZ WITH THE FUZZ	7
Harry Shapiro interviews Lee Harris	9
Soweto	23
Apartheid Buster	26
South African Holiday	29
Anslinger's Assassin of Youth	33
The Beat Generation (1): A Season In Hell	39
The Beat Generation (2): Journey to the End of the Night	46
The Beat Generation (3): The Decline of the West	52
Introduction to Allen Ginsberg	61
Extracts from Buzz Buzz	64
REALITY FREAKS vs SPACE CADETS	75
Theatre of Change	77
The Great Penis Question	81
Theatricks	83
Sex and the Theatre	85
Hair Roots	88
Notes on Love Play	92
Love Play	94
Moving Statics	98
The Fletcher File	99

Arts Lab Split	101
Meat Sculptor	106
LSD and the Mind Alchemyst	112
Demystifying Human Violence	119
Quo Vadis Israel?	123
When the Flowers Wilted in the Winter	127
Tangier Journal	146
Gandhi: His to Love and Behold	160
Ah, But Your Land Is Free	163
ALCHEMICAL CHANGES	165
Tales of the Portobello	167
Seven Years of Alchemy	177
Komix Kudos: The story behind Brainstorm Comix	178
Thoroughly Ripped with Gilbert Shelton	181
The Home Grown Years	187
Danny De Souza writes…	192
Home Grown Replies…	194
At the Magnetic Centre of the New Stoned Age	199
Decades of Dope	211
Interview with Martin of the Rusland	218
Coffee Shop Amsterdam	222
Home Grown Editorial	229
Ginseng: the Root of Being	235
A Footsoldier's Tale	239
Afterword	245
About The Author	246

Dedication & Thanks

I would especially like to remember my beloved wife Brigitte, who is no more with us, who was my anchor and gave me thirty-three years of love and happiness.

I would like to thank my daughter Amira, who transcribed the tape-recorded Harry Shapiro interview and my son Deben and daughter Edana for their support and love.

This book is dedicated to my late younger brother Mervyn, my soul mate who was a journalist of great repute and was always there when I needed him.

The task of digitizing the text was undertaken by Hicham Bensassi, a poet who was too young to have lived through those times and came to it with a fresh and eager mind. Like a sorcerer's apprentice, he selected and edited the material, which is presented here for the first time. I thank him for his mammoth effort.

I would like to thank Chris Sanders of Barncott Press, a fellow counter culturalist for publishing the ebook and this limited edition paperback. A special thank you to Mark Addis for proof-reading the typo-riddled manuscript.

Finally, thank you to the many people who touched my life and to those whose lives I have touched, without you this book wouldn't have existed.

Lee Harris 2013

Introduction

This is a collection of my writings, interviews and play scripts, mostly written, published or performed in the nineteen sixties and seventies. It is about people and events that were very influential in my quest through the counter-culture underground.

I saw myself as a participant observer of the passing show, in those momentous decades where I discovered an underbelly where new crazes and ideas took root. I got caught in the spirit of the times and was lucky to write for the underground press for a brief period, mainly *International Times*.[1] The new ways of looking at things had an alternative viewpoint, which I expressed in some of my articles

My journey as a 'footsoldier' has touched many diverse areas, from drugs, sexuality, avant-garde theatre, the beat generation, South Africa in the apartheid era, Amsterdam in its heyday, the 'Summer of Love' and the Portobello Road in West London.

Through many memorable events; from the *Congress of the People* in South Africa in 1955, the *Congress on the Dialectics of Liberation* at the Roundhouse in 1967, the *Legalise Pot Rally* in Hyde Park that summer, *The Alchemical Wedding* at the Royal Albert Hall in 1968, to the first *International Cannabis Alliance for Reform* (ICAR) conference in Amsterdam in 1980.

I was able, during this creative and chaotic time, to capture some magical moments and interview many interesting underground poets and writers. The three 'Beat Generation' chapters, originally written under the name 'Angel-Headed Hipster', are based on much that I learnt during those times, as I fictionally put myself in New York in the early Beat years among my heroes.

In the seventies and early eighties, I published and edited a cannabis magazine, *Home Grown*, and many of the articles here come from the ten issues that I produced in those five years. I could write

---

[1] Back issues of *IT* can be read online at the *International Times Archive*.

what I liked and about what interested me, like I had previously in the underground press. For the most part the writings that appeared in the early underground press *IT*, *OZ* and *Other Scenes* in New York, were faded original press cuttings as they were published and printed before the computer was on hand, and had to be transferred to the digital realm. There were also a few articles that were online, documenting the counter-culture as it evolved, and I have decided to add one or two previously unpublished articles that are of interest in the context of this book.

Lee Harris, Portobello Road, London, 2013.

BUZZ BUZZ WITH THE FUZZ

*"No good rushing about.
It gets you nowhere fast."*

Harry Shapiro interviews Lee Harris

Recorded in the Summer of 1998:

HS: I noticed in that press cutting back in the fifties in South Africa that you were an early advocate of legalisation. What was the situation with *'dagga'* in South Africa at that time?

LH: In my early days in South Africa, as a teenager growing up in the early fifties, it was quite political. The only thing I knew about *'dagga'* was as the 'jungle cigarettes', the terrible dangerous weed, of Reefer Madness. It was used by the white motor mechanics called *'Jollers'* which means fighters, and it was often associated with violence. I remember seeing a newspaper story about an African woman who was kidnapped and given these jungle cigarettes, and then raped. *'Dagga'* had a terrible fear attached to it so I did not know about *'dagga'* from any personal experience, only later when I came back to South Africa in 1967.

HS: So that press cutting of you as an advocate?

LH: It was taken towards the end of 1967 when I went back to South Africa, to see my mother who was ill at the time.

HS: You were in South Africa. Why did you leave?

LH: I left at the age of nineteen because I was politically involved in the Congress movement and I had a sort of spring awakening. The *Congress of the Democrats* was the white wing and there was the A.N.C (*African National Congress*), the *Indian Congress* and the *Coloured People's Organisation* for people of mixed race, which were all separate. I was working in a clothing factory and was from quite a poor Jewish family. It was also a personal liberation, from an unhappy relationship with my stepfather and an unsettled home life, I could not wait to get away, and England was the obvious place.

HS: Did you have to leave or did you want to leave?

LH: There were police raids and I knew I would have my passport taken away, I was getting involved in anti-apartheid things, like painting slogans on walls - 'police raids, police state' - late at night, then going to the factory at six-thirty in the morning on the bus, and everyone standing up and seeing the letters that we had painted. So the first things I learnt at eighteen was that police raids represented a police state, and I learned to hide away books that were banned.

HS: Did you mention Nelson Mandela as well?

LH: That whole episode was one of the most exciting periods of my life. I came into the Congress Movement through a cousin and a discussion group, which was on a Friday night where great speakers would attend, introduced by a friend, Dr. Ronnie Press.

They were organising this great conference at Kliptown on the 25th and 26th of June 1955, called the *'Congress of the People'* to proclaim a *'Freedom Charter'*, and in going to meetings, handing out leaflets, and visiting offices, I went with Ronnie to the downtown office of two lawyers called Nelson Mandela and Oliver Tambo.

I was only eighteen and I dared not open my mouth so I sat there taking it all in. I met Father Trevor Huddleston, an Anglican priest, and went to his farewell party at the *Bantu Men's Social Club* in downtown Johannesburg, because he was being recalled to England by his Order.

He was the priest of Sophiatown, a lively and multi-racial area near the city which was being demolished. I went to the townships on Sunday morning with people to talk to the Africans about coming to the conference, and everywhere I would go, plain-clothed police would say in Afrikaans 'these fucking Jews'.

I went for the two days to the Congress at Kliptown and on the second day was sitting there with many illustrious people. Trevor Huddleston stood up on the platform in his cassock and said, "Can we all please be calm, we are surrounded by armed police."

It felt like a movie, I looked up and everywhere there were cops - two hundred police with rifles. As the Chief of Police walked through this gathering of three thousand people towards the platform, the whole crowd stood up and sang the anthem *'Nkosi Sikelele Afrika'* 'God save Africa', which was one of the most emotional and powerful moments of my life. Hours later I was being photographed and searched by the police.

I was just a young man of eighteen selling political newspapers, *'New Age'* and *'Fighting Talk'* which were edited by Ruth First. Her husband was Joe Slovo (who led the armed struggle in exile, and was later a minister in Mandela's government). Tragically Ruth First was later blown up in Mozambique by a parcel bomb sent by 'BOSS' the South African secret police. She was a magnificent woman.

So there were lots of very interesting people there, it was a great awakening to realise there are bad laws, because they used to sing the song:

'In nineteen fifty one, when defiance was begun, mounting oppression is the cause for the defiance of unjust laws, and the Minister of Justice did not know what to do'.

We were aware that people were for direct action, coming and sitting with black people, often academics in a white tearoom at the Zoo Lake, until police were called and people would be arrested. It was very bold.

At that time I met Dr. Yusuf Dadoo, who was the head of the *Indian Congress Movement* and a great friend of Nelson Mandela. He is buried next to Karl Marx in Highgate Cemetery and was honoured by the *African National Congress*. I also met Sally, the daughter of the head of the *A.N.C*, and Zulu Chief Albert Luthule through Trevor Huddleston.

It was a very exciting time, and that was the first time I came across 'dagga'. On Saturdays with a friend, I would sell 'New Age' in the poor white area of Johannesburg and we would often go into these empty shops into the back-rooms where there were usually five or six Africans sitting round in a circle. This was 1955, when men wore broad-rimmed hats and suits. I could smell this pungent scent as they were smoking these cigarettes. Though most of them couldn't read, I'd often manage to sell them the political magazine *'New Age'* as I was very committed. Only in retrospect did I realise of course I was in the 'dagga dens' I never saw anything wrong and looking back they were very nice to me. *Dagga* was cheap and available on every second street corner. *Mutta* or *Mutti*, as it was sometimes called, was feared and known as "jungle cigarettes" to middle class white boys like me.

HS: It was the sort of thing you would do if you wanted a bit of a walk on the wild side?

LH: Yes, but from my background, I do not think I would have come into contact with it at eighteen or nineteen, though I had been born in a big city and been brought up in Johannesburg, but I had been a serious political person, and then I came over to England at the beginning of 1956 thinking I am free, free, free, I can do what I like in life, I wanted to be an actor, so I went to drama school for two years here, at the *Webber Douglas School of Dramatic Art*. During that period I discovered the dives in Soho, because at that time in the late fifties before the *'Street Offenses Act'* came into being, outlawing soliciting on the streets, the West End was full of about a thousand prostitutes, you'd find them all round Piccadilly Circus, in Wardour Street and Brewer Street. There was the coffee shop revolution, the 'gaggia' shop[2] and the Italian spaghetti houses. Soho was at the centre at places like *The Two Eyes, Heaven and Hell* and *Act One, Scene One* in Old Compton Street and the *Artisan*, which was the left-wing coffee bar, and the *Nucleus* in Monmouth Street which was a jazz dive, and the little basement clubs in Wardour Mews where I'd go with my friends after midnight.

I was twenty, and the music was amazing, the dances were utterly intoxicating and all the girls were on the game, and a lot of the men were the pimps who looked after them. I first knew of a 'drug raid' when I read in the papers that the club I frequented was raided for 'Indian Hemp'.

The music scenes then were the Skiffle and the Trad clubs, short for traditional Jazz or Dixie music. The men would dress up in their waistcoats and Victorian clothes and women would dress in black lace-up shoes and dance in a certain way. I was at drama school mixing with arts students and weekend bohemians. We used to go down to coffee shops and wear polo-neck sweaters or T-shirts and jeans and go sit and drink coffee and talk Camus or angst, phenomenology and Sartre, which was part of the scene there, and of course Elvis.

HS: Presumably you did not get involved in the black community in the way that you did till some time later?

LH: I broke from the South African political scene and pursued my studies at drama school while doing menial work six nights a week like washing dishes in the West End. I was a great lover of the gutters and I went through a period when I had to go through what felt like a Hades' Hell, sort of inferno, I had a vision that I would have to go through seven years of dark nights, at the dives, and the hell holes of society, and explore them.

HS: It does not sound to me as if it was that much of a trial for you, it sounds like you enjoyed every minute of it?

---

[2] Gaggia is an Italian expresso machine manufacturer.

LH: Yes I did. I discovered Jean Genet's *'Thief's Journal'*, which was banned in Paris in 1959. It is a stunning book, and in a way I wanted to soar into the sky and feel ecstasy, and I wanted to grovel in the dirt, almost wanting to emulate Genet. For I had no self-esteem myself throughout my orphanage years and my unhappy childhood, and felt drawn towards the seedier (demi-monde) side of life. I saw a guy who had lost his leg from fixing in a cafe in Brewer Street. So I was conscious all through that period that there were heroin addicts. There's something about it, there has always been a low life.

HS: So you suddenly saw an entirely different scene?

LH: Yes, suddenly all these kids from the ages of fifteen to seventeen, with short hair cuts, the girls had their hair short too and looked like the boys, which was the first hint of the unisex thing. So already by the early sixties there was the beginnings of this whole new scene. I had left drama school, had done some acting and I was doing some writing.

HS: Right, you were living in the West End?

LH: I was living in Earls Court, and I had become a nightbird, I would arrive in the West End at ten at night, leave at five, and sleep during the morning. I was exploring these areas. So I came across this mad scene, there were hundreds of kids milling around outside the mod clubs in Wardour Street in the early hours of the morning, drifting in and out of the dives and I noticed that they were all chewing gum with big dilated pupils. I found out that they were taking purple hearts pills, they were sometimes taking eighty or ninety in a weekend at sixpence a time and had comedowns and amphetamine psychosis afterwards. Amphetamine is a perfect stimulant if you want to dance all night, the clubs would end at five o clock in the morning and these kids were all stoned out of their heads with nowhere to go, it was a huge scene, which was the beginning of the mods. I met the MP Ben Parkin, in Paddington, who had just exposed Rachman[3] and his property racket, and he said he would raise questions (about drug psychosis) in the Houses of Parliament.

HS: Is this something you thought was a genuine problem?

LH: I had met Ronnie Laing then too, who had written his first

---

[3] See the 'Tales of Portobello' chapter for more on Rachman.

book, *'The Divided Self'* - he said to me 'you are a moralist'. I'd also met this young guy Johnny, a pep pill addict who was having psychosis and getting very paranoid. A lot of the kids were starting to get paranoiac; seeing insects and spiders on the walls. Then I got a call from Anne Sharpley who was a top investigative reporter for the *Evening Standard*, who did the royal tours and was a Beaverbrook protégé - we had become great friends. She said 'Would you like to show me around the West End' so I said that I would.

Johnny would take about a hundred pep pills over the weekends and grind his teeth while he talked, and when he talked he had the golden gift of the gab. I had written him as a prototype in my plays as he allowed me to tape some of our conversations.

So I introduced Anne Sharpley to him, he bubbled over and we did a magnificent late night tour of Wardour Street, we visited all the clubs and she saw all these young people buying pills from the dealers. That Monday it was on the front page of the *Evening Standard*, with the headline, 'I See Soho's Pep Pill Craze' and it was the biggest story of the week, it blew the scene wide open and that Monday night the West End clubs were deserted.

HS: Oh were you in this article?

LH: No, I was the stringer.

HS: I didn't think so.

LH: I had not taken any drugs at that time; it was one of the biggest exposés in the press.

HS: That's quite ironic really considering the sort of career path you went to afterwards?

LH: It actually hit me later when I looked at the *Misuse of Drugs Act* and I thought 'Oh God' I was one of the main people that helped to bring forth a law which had rebounded on my friends.

HS: Well it was a craze apparent?

LH: Yes, it was coming.

HS: It's probably just as well your name wasn't in the paper?

LH: Exactly, except in the South African papers, I gave an interview in which I mentioned the questions raised in the Houses of Parliament. I'd seen these kids in a terrible state, I decided I did not like pep pills, but I loved the dancing and Rhythm and Blues music in the mod clubs. Coming from my background I needed to rebel in every way possible, so I suppose it was inevitable.

HS: What was your interest in the Christine Keeler case?

LH: I became obsessive about the drugs and sex scenes and the Keeler thing encompassed both. I had a big *Grundig* tape recorder in 1963 where I lived in Bayswater, so I decided that I would record some interviews with prostitutes. One was a call-girl who lived in Chelsea Cloisters, and I talked to her in between clients, who would come to her room and cry. One was a lesbian, who had been beaten in torture chambers, she had been abused terribly as a child and sold her virginity four or five times. Another was a street girl from Gerrard Street in Chinatown. She had been abused by her brother in Cardiff, and the father had gone to prison for five years for sleeping with her. I used this as research in the book I was writing, which I was going to call *'Living for Kicks'*. It was a Genet inspired piece, about the low life, of seedy London.

HS: Do you think the Keeler case had something to do with the growth of the use of cannabis?

LH: Might well have done, Christine Keeler used to go off from Stephen Ward's pad and smoke cannabis with Johnny Edgecombe, her West Indian boyfriend, which they obtained from the late night café *Eldorado* in Westbourne Park Road.

HS: Did the smoking cannabis bit around Keeler get publicity as well at that time?

LH: I think there was.

HS: Was that part of the scandal?

LH: Well I would have to research it. The cannabis thing was very big, first among the West Indian community, in the dives with white women who went with them, but it was not open to the general public.

HS: So people were now smoking dope?

LH: I wanted to try cannabis so I decided to take my big *Grundig* tape recorder and record a group of friends smoking grass. It was a great disappointment, not only did I not get high, but all I got from the recordings were these two girls giggling. How disappointing, because I thought I would capture an amazing drug experience. Only a little later in the West End in Oxford Street did I actually get high. By the early sixties, cannabis culture was beginning and was very much linked I suppose with the young West Indians and the mod culture in the West End with the artists, students, and the people who went to the coffee bars. I often think 1963 was a defining moment; it was the beginning of swinging London and the permissive society. 1967 was the next great defining moment for youth culture though I was an older, participant observer.

HS: So how did things develop for you and your involvement in the scene, we are into the mid-sixties, you wrote this play didn't you?

LH: Yes, a one act play called *'Buzz Buzz'* about the mods and pep pills with some of the tapes of people I had known in the West End. It was about the first kids I met who were living for kicks, they would outwit everyone, making life a hustle, dealing drugs, and had a marvelous lingo. The next play was called *'Love Play'* which is written in hippie language based on the rhythmic speech of the sixties.

HS: So it was really building into quite a big underground scene?

LH: Yes, I gave up my job as a housefather at a remand centre after the *Beat Poetry Incarnation* at the *Royal Albert Hall* in June 1965 attended by over seven thousand people, which was quite liberating.

Then in February 1966 I had my first LSD trip, which came in a sugar cube, from one of the guys I had met in the West End. Suddenly everything exploded, we were all talking at once and bubbling over each other, we couldn't feel the difference between an hour or a minute. I went down to the dives in the West End, and it was an extraordinary night, with the narcotic squads and all these weird characters. The West End was full of undercover police stopping and searching.

I went into this coffee shop and I sat next to this black heroin addict who said "I feel as hungry as a horse, but I feel as if I've been eating a horse all my life", and I remembered marvelous phrases like that for the plays you see.

At that time, I was also working with drama groups, so I decided I'd let them read *'Buzz Buzz'* and they all loved it. We entered it for the *Association of the Jewish Youth Theatre Festival* in Toynbee Hall in the East End and won the star certificate. I was invited to the *National Union of Youth Clubs* conference by the adjudicator and I met the playwright Lord Willis, who said 'send me your plays and I will put you up for an Arts Council Bursary'... then one day in 1966 I had a call from Sean Day-Lewis at the *Daily Telegraph* saying I'd won an Arts Council bursary!

So I had my biography in all the quality newspapers, they wrote on the drug play which had been performed at *Toynbee Hall* and at the *Unity Theatre*, where in the audience were Dr. Holden from the *Tavistock Clinic*, Morty Shatzman, Joe Berke and all the people who worked with Ronnie Laing, because I suppose a lot of my influences were also from mixing with the circle of R.D. Laing at Kingsley Hall in those days.

HS: Tell me about the Congress at the Roundhouse?

LH: The *Congress on the Dialectics of Liberation* was a Congress to demystify human violence and all the greatest minds were there from Herbert Marcuse, Gregory Bateson to Stokely Carmichael, Danilo Dolce, Ernest Mandel and Allen Ginsberg.

HS: Were there many philosophers?

LH: Mainly philosophers, academics, poets and creatives brought together by R.D. Laing. This was in July 1967.

HS: The Black Power leader Stokely Carmichael was there?

LH: Yes, telling the hippies "If you believe in peace and love then come with your flowers and put them in the barrels and stand in between the police when they are shooting us." So it was a strange get together with a sense of revolutionary thinking. Marcuse was my great hero, I'd read 'Eros and Civilisation' in 1965 and to this day a lot of the ideas he put through on the pleasure principle run through my mind. So when he gave his talk at the Roundhouse there was a great deal of preparation. There was a Maoist slogan draped on a wall saying 'Pass the liberation' and joints were passed around during his talk.

HS: Was this particularly aimed at Marcuse because of what he'd written?

LH: I think so, I think specifically him, because he'd mentioned that in the time of the Paris Communes, people had arrested time, they used to throw stones at the clocks to try and stop time. He was conscious of a great revolutionary moment; he taught the young black student activist Angela Davis at Brandeis University. To me it was like seeing and listening to one of the greatest thinkers of our time.

HS: Wasn't that 68?

LH: Well throughout 67 the scene was so bad, that when Ginsberg came over for the Roundhouse event, he was in Piccadilly Circus and he said 'get rid of speed freaks, they destroy'. There were too many people taking too many drugs, with methedrine as well as cannabis, so there was a backlash. In September of that year you could not walk through a place like Earls Court or anywhere without endless stops and searches.

HS: Do you know why that was? That was because of the 1967 *Dangerous Drugs Act*, which I was looking at the other day, which for the very first time allowed the police to do stops and searches just for drugs. And that was the first bit of legislation which allowed them to do that.

LH: That's why it also helped make it political, because once people are persecuted it becomes political, it's a personal act, because I feel a lot of people were politicised by the ruthless action of the police. People were locked up ... also when 68 came, some of the hippies developed into the radical Left and there was a schism because they were far too puritanical, the 'angry brigade'.

There was the great *Legalise Pot Rally* in Hyde Park that summer. I was wearing a kaftan and I had thorns in my hair. I walked from West Kensington and kids were shouting, 'hello Jesus, or Julius Caesar'.

I had dark glasses on and my friends were pissing themselves laughing. We arrived at Hyde Park and there were thousands of people with the most beautiful painted faces and hair styles. We were all the beautiful people, it was amazing, it was like a fancy dress party of thousands.

Then we all walked to the *Albert Memorial* near the *Royal Albert Hall* together. Looking back it was very dilettantish - the underground was very upper middle class and public school oriented, full of American refugees from the draft of the Vietnamese War.

HS: This is another interesting point, because if you like, the sixties were happening in London, but do you think that if you had lived in Ipswich, or Bristol or Birmingham or Hartlepool would you have found the 'sixties'?

LH: I think so. By then there was a whole burgeoning movement and the hundred thousand people who smoked dope came from all over the UK not only London. I had travelled to South Africa and Israel during that period, when suddenly all my cousins in South

Africa, who would not have dreamt of it a generation before, had all taken cannabis. So it was worldwide.

In Israel it was very big among intellectuals and young students. It was not only political but it was spiritual because it could lift you to awakened heights, it can centre you, and make you aware and loving, but I did find out coming to South Africa and meeting smokers there with long hair, that suddenly if you mentioned 'race', you'd find there were bigots like anywhere else.

HS: You said earlier you sensed the end of the 'Acid Dream'?

LH: Yes, the *'Summer of Love'* was a fickle summer it was such a short, split second in history, and then there was a backlash. There were the casualties of the 'Love Generation', people who did not quite take to acid, who were smoking far too much, smoking chillums. People were lost for purpose and a lot of people who took acid became spiritual. I published the *'Alchemical Almanac and Handbook of Herbal Highs'*.

A lot of people at that time were going on the hash trail to India. You could go and get a passport, and someone who had done the trip came with a manuscript which I published called the *'Overland Guide to the East'* which is an amazing book. He was one of the first disciples of *Rajneesh* and the *Orange Order*.

I was 35 then, nothing seemed to make sense. I did not know how to earn a buck as I'd lived in such an airy-fairy underground. I had become a drop out, it was no fun, I never went on the dole, and friends helped to support me. Free-wheelin Franklyn of *'The Freak Brothers'* comix said 'Dope will get you through times of no money, better than money will get you through times of no dope.'

Well in a sense I think I found that a very dark period, my mother died in 1968 and it hit me hard. I went through terrible guilt. I had blown the little bit of money I'd been left at *Phun City* which was the last of the great festivals, which Mick Farren organised at Worthing. It was a terribly chaotic festival, there were a lot people tripping, running about naked.

I am a veteran of all the festivals, where I traded, so it was natural for me to land in Portobello Road when a stall came up. I'd gone through this mid-life crisis and I discovered the ginseng root from a Chinese shop. So I found this very expensive herb which cost nine pounds. After taking some I felt rejuvenated, and felt myself coming out of the depression, so I started *Alchemy* in 1972, inspired by the *'Alchemical Wedding'* which was at the *Royal Albert Hall* on the eighteenth of December 1968.

Almost everyone I knew was coming back from India, bringing all these exotic objects like chillums, balms, patchouli oils and incense. I was used to trading at festivals, with my cloth out, and my shawl off, laid out to sell, like I'd started off in the West End before as an anarchist trader selling psychedelic posters in the late sixties. I published *Brainstorm Comix* featuring the work of the young and talented Bryan Talbot and I then wanted to hire the Roundhouse and do something called *'Ten Years Later'* or *'Ten Years On'* with *Quintessence*. The magazine was going to be the programme for the event.... it turned out that I dropped the event and focused on the magazine instead because Michael Hollingshead suggested contributing something and Heathcote Williams brought Dave Solomon and George Andrews, who were the great drug writers at that time.

David Solomon was going to review a book for me, but two weeks later on March 23rd 1977 he was arrested in *'Operation Julie'*. I've got a letter from him in prison, to get in touch with Mailer and all sorts of people to help him. This became *'Home Grown'*, Europe's first dope magazine, which I published and edited for the next five years. Everyone was doing their own thing.

HS: That kind of assembled into the Stonehenge free festivals, it all kept bubbling along?

LH: Yes and there were many festivals happening all over the country where you were lucky to partake - but you knew you would be stopped and searched to get there. You lived in a sieged state if you smoked cannabis. It was a very difficult time, it was a 'downer' in many respects.

I then settled down and started the head shop. What sustained the hippies or the cannabis culture during the eighties was the Rastafarians and Reggae. They were the ones who smoked the Ganja in their spliff as a holy act of peace and love, they were persecuted. I was on the 'front line' as I had an office on All Saints Road for nine years.

HS: Did you notice the shift between what you might call the person coming back from Afghanistan with his/her little bit to smoke or sell a few pieces, with something that became a lot more organised?

LH: It was subtle because it came in different stages. In 1979 the coup in Afghanistan, which was followed by the Russian invasion, cut off the overland route, which was the main hash trail to Katmandu. Then people had to fly and they couldn't bring little bits back over with them. I think there was always an element of big dealing i.e. Howard Marks with his heyday in the seventies. Then Thatcherism came along with the yuppification, it was big business, somehow the criminal fraternity had become part of it.

HS: But you think the trade in the country was mostly Moroccan?

LH: Yes, it became standardized with 'soap bar' which is the most inferior sort of cannabis, then came the revolution of new technology and the growing of your own, which was the coming of 'skunk'. It was a world-wide phenomenon, from Canada to Amsterdam, because in the early eighties people wrote about the first batch. Over here it started with the guerilla growers growing small plants which then meant you could get a small piece and get twice as stoned as you could from the older variety, because it's been genetically engineered or what I called getting 'zapped' or 'nuked' so cannabis had a new element to it, which it had not had before.

HS: What about the riots in Brixton?

LH: Do you know this happened before the 1979 St. Paul's riots in Bristol? I was working on the last issue of *Home Grown*, I'd moved into a shop next to *Ceres*, and I had all the growers' guides in the window and I had all the marijuana books in the Portobello Road.

I was in the shop and I heard a clicking sound coming from someone's jacket and I said to the guy who I shared the shop with, that's a plain-clothes policeman, so I blew their cover, and they searched me and found nothing.

I was taken to Notting Hill Gate police station, where I was charged and all I could see were plain-clothes policemen bringing in black people for cannabis offences. I said to this policemen, there are going to be riots in this country, and he said 'You're joking', I said 'Yes, there's going to be riots here'.

Suddenly my case was coming up at the Old Bailey. I was charged for allowing the premises to be used for the supply of ten grams of cannabis, found in someone's pocket. I had to be on a four-week waiting list as the courts were clogged up dealing with cases of arrested rioters. You had to be on stand-by for twenty-four hours before being called to court, which is a terrible tension.

Four weeks passed, then another four weeks, and everyday you have to wait. I did my best under that pressure, feeling like I was a Jew in Nazi Germany, and I was eventually found not guilty by a jury. In a sense the attack on cannabis in the late seventies and early eighties directly caused the riots.

In *Home Grown No.10* I write in the submission to the *Royal Commission* that, from the Brixton to the Bristol riots, Cannabis was involved. Cannabis was mainly identified with the Rastafarians and there was terrible persecution. Both riots started off with a cannabis incident. So I think that cannabis was at the forefront of the drug war.

I think cannabis was at its most political in the late seventies, early eighties because it was used as a way to stop and search. Then Bob Marley was stopped in the late seventies with cannabis in his sock, whilst being driven through the Ladbroke Grove; he was convicted and got a fine. It was quite ridiculous, but what happened in the eighties was subtle and quite amazing. This happened throughout the *War on Drugs*, instead of cutting it down, they funnelled and fuelled it.

At the beginning of the nineties, I couldn't believe it, all around me was a whole new generation of kids in every village and town who were smoking cannabis. There were no magazines, there were no public run organisations, there was no legalisation, a movement of any sort was gone. The culture had hidden itself underground, that's what repression does. So what happened is suddenly you look round and everybody's sons and daughters were smoking it in every part of society. It was quite extraordinary because it was really the biggest explosion of cannabis use, which came after *'Home Grown'*.

Soweto

'Other Scenes', Volume 1, No. 6, New York, September 1968:

I am white; Bethule is black. Although we lived for four months at the same address in a suburb of Johannesburg, we were only vaguely aware of each other's presence. Bethule had rented a small room in our backyard, illegally, as Africans who are not employed as servants in the house are barred from living in white Johannesburg.

There we were, two human beings estranged from each other by the conditioning of a system that separates people on the basis of colour alone. Johannesburg is white; Soweto is black.

Although they work side by side, the white masters and the black workers, I had not come into contact with a white person who had ever been into Soweto, the largest black ghetto in South Africa. Soweto, which stands for South Western Township, is eighteen miles outside the city of Johannesburg and houses a vast dormant reservoir of labour, feeding the commercial-industrial complex of the city.

More than 450,000 whites live in the sprawling metropolis, in suburbs that stretch for miles. In Soweto alone there are over 750,000 Africans, from a half-dozen different tribes. Due to the Group Areas Act, there are smaller, separate enclaves beyond the city that house the Coloured (of mixed blood) and Indian peoples. This race classification is known as Apartheid.

My only contact with Soweto was through the pages of the *'The World'* the daily newspaper for the Africans. Its content is a curious blend of urban violence and social chitchat. It is written in a jazzy, simple style, creating romantic folk heroes out of the gangsters caught in ambush by the gun-toting cops.

Soweto conjures up a picture in the minds of the whites, of a violent, seething mass living at a comfortably safe distance from the orderliness of the city, under the constant, controlled vigilance of a ruthless police force. Although it is illegal for a white person to visit Soweto without a permit, I arranged with Bethule to drive there one Sunday.

Bethule and I had become friends and I enjoyed listening to him talking animatedly, with humour and sadness, about the plight of his people. Once, he visited the Chief Bantu Commissioner of Soweto in order to obtain a house for his wife and young child, and was told, "A snake lives in a tree, go and live like that."

Like many young Africans, he had come from a kraal to Johannesburg to seek work and had gone through the bungling bureaucratic apparatus, known as "petty apartheid," which entails getting a pass-book, permission to live in the area, and a license for a specific job, among other things. He was treated like an alien in the land of his birth.

I will never forget that Sunday, driving through the endless streets that link the various zones of Soweto. We drove through Diepkloof, zones 1-4, Orlando East and West, Dube, Meadowlands, Phiri, Mapetla, Senoane, Naledi, Mofolo, and so on. Thousands of uniformly drab two-roomed houses, situated side by side, like a gargantuan army barracks.

The air was heavy and smoke-laden from the myriad little chimneys, as the authorities have not bothered to install either gas or electricity. Africans are not allowed to own property in Soweto, so incongruously one comes across large American automobiles parked outside a few houses. They are invariably second-hand and due to their size, make good taxis. There is only one swimming pool for the entire complex, and a few cinemas that show films that, the government thought fit for Africans. It is shockingly lacking in social amenities.

Soweto at the weekends is like a nightmare. Murder, rape and robbery with violence, are all too common. Gangs of marauding 'tsotsis' roam the wastelands and the stations, preying on the wage earners. The word 'tsotsi' is derived from the American Negro phrase, zoot suit. They often board the densely overcrowded trains that leave the city on a Friday night, working their way from carriage to carriage, taking whatever they can get hold of at knife-point. Most of them have been refused permission to stay in Johannesburg, and are prohibited from working by the law. Their only method of survival in the city is by criminal activity.

In contrast to this, is the mushrooming of the African Christian movements, of which the *Church of Zion* is the largest, with a membership of over a million. On Sundays they dress in their white and green robes, singing hymns of praise to the lord in a variety of African tongues. It is an odd blend of Christianity passed on from the white missionary fathers who came to spread the word, while the Empire-builders conquered their land.

With urbanization came detribalisation, the steady breakdown of custom and ritual revered for so long by the *Zulu, Xhosa, Basutu, Pondo* and *Mapedi*. In Soweto there is inter-marriage between the tribes or nations, and there are divorces. With the migrant worker, parted from his family, came prostitution and homosexuality. To control the illicit flow of skokiaan from the shebeens, the residents now have municipal-controlled beer halls.

The older Africans discreetly smoke their *dagga* (pot) in the veld; the young generation now smokes openly. Barawanath Hospital, a sprawling, ugly complex of adjoining buildings, is situated on the outskirts of Soweto and caters for its medical needs. The wards are pathetically overcrowded with patients bedded on the chairs and floors. The pediatric wards are full of babies with congenital deformities.

Before leaving Soweto, Bethule and I stopped to watch some members of the Mapedi tribe celebrating a wedding feast in an open field. The sky was grey with smoke in the approaching dusk, the women pounded oil drums rhythmically as the men danced with a jagged monotony, letting out shrill sounds from the flutes in their mouths. Every now and then, one of the men would break out into a solo dance, beating the dust into the air and then return to the ritual formation of the other dancers.

As we drove off, I remembered Kliptown, a few miles to the South. It was there in 1955 that I attended the historic *Congress of the People*. Three thousand of us, mainly Africans, had gathered for a two-day conference to draw up a *Freedom Charter* proclaiming that the land is for all who live in it. At the close of the conference we were surrounded by two hundred armed police, who systematically searched and photographed us. Not long after this the five-year 'Treason Trials' began. Then there was Sharpeville in 1960. Today the African nationalist movements are outlawed and Soweto is a symbol of the frustrations perpetrated against the blacks by the whites of South Africa... *Mayibuye Africa!* Come back Africa!

Apartheid Buster

Scene Magazine, London, 1963:

The play that stunned South Africa opens at the New Arts Theatre this month. Lee Harris, a friend of the author, explains its background.

The makeshift theatre occupies the third floor of a dusty building in Motor Town. It has a pint-size stage, no wings and the three small dressing rooms open directly onto the stage. Only one of them has a window.

This is the theatre which gave birth to the African musical *King Kong*, and in this shabby area of Johannesburg another play has been brought to life, a play that challenged the whole concept of apartheid. In September 1961, the *Union Artists Theatre* staged the very first South African play in which a white man and black man appeared together on the same stage.

The management were prepared to have Atholl Fugard's work. 'The Blood Knot' closed by the police after the first night. The multi-racial audience was stunned by the four-hour production with the message rarely heard in South Africa - man must live with man, colour or creed regardless. The critics unanimously acclaimed 'The Blood Knot', even the Afrikaans critics, although one of them misconstrued the whole point and said the play was good because it showed that black and white should not mix.

Perhaps because of the same misunderstanding, the authorities did not close down 'The Blood Knot'. It played to full houses on a tour of the major South African cities.

Now it has come to London, opening this month at the *New Arts Theatre*, starring Zakes Mokae, a brilliant young African actor, who plays the part of a black man who has a white brother. The white brother returns to their mother's home after a long absence. The action of the play deals with the anguish and the hope which the two brothers go through in their ambition to buy a small farm. In South Africa, the author played the part of the white brother. Fugard, who looks like D.H. Lawrence, says his writing influences are O'Neill and Beckett.

'It was not often realised at home that the play is not only about a black man and a white man,' he says, a bearded, intense man who is passionately dedicated to the theatre as the outward expression of man's inner life.

'There are more dimensions than that. There is me and another face on earth. We are different. I feel guilty and responsible for it.

In the play there are mugs on the table with water in them: there should be wine. There is bread, chips and sausage: there should be more. There are beds for the brothers to sleep in: women should be there, too.

'Everywhere there is want, want'. Fugard, born of mixed Dutch and English parentage, is thirty. He studied philosophy at Cape Town University for three years, but gave it up because 'I was thinking too much and feeling too little.' He hitchhiked to Cairo, joined the all-Malayan crew of a cargo ship, and went home to become a lifeguard, a motor mechanic and a journalist.

'One must have an inner life', he says. 'It makes no difference whether the outer one is exhilarating and high-powered, or quiet and withdrawn.'

'I was fortunate to have a woman who said, if you want to write, write.'

He has written two other plays, produced in Johannesburg with limited success. Zakes Mokae had a walk-on part in the first. Fugard recognised his talent and wrote a special part for him in the second. He plays in London opposite Ian Bannen. Fugard's theatrical apprenticeship was spent playing small parts and stage-managing in gruelling one-night stand tours of South Africa.

'I reached a stage where writing ceased to be separable from living to me.' He says 'I needed solitude but people are very reluctant to let you alone when you need it. Writing swallows you up. I became conscious of the enormous hunger and appetites that make one man. I've learnt to love better. In theatre, one must learn to see and feel with the heart. In active writing there is active exploration. As Stravinsky said, the miracle of mistake and accident.'

It took him a year to produce *'The Blood Knot'*. Six months thinking and planning and six months of eight-hour days writing. To relax he went bird watching. Speaking about the London opening, Fugard says he has nothing but admiration for producer John Berry. He says; 'It has been an important experience for me working with Berry. With the play he has made a statement in terms of staging. I get the feeling he likes it. Feels it is beautiful.'

Fugard doesn't like London. 'I don't belong; I'm very local, especially in my feelings.' After the first night he will return to the union, back to his intense, self-chosen life of creative meditation. Back to the third floor theatre where on the first night, a Sunday, of his play, Fugard felt 'Something happening to me.' He says: 'We didn't know what was going to happen, and then after about ten or fifteen minutes we realised we were talking meaningfully to the South African audience, and that is something.'

South African Holiday

International Times No. 26, February 1968:

Sure, they're transplanting hearts in Cape Town, sapping the glorious holiday sun in Durban, and Johannesburg is booming in its eightieth year. European immigration is on the increase and the Prime Minister Vorster tells us we are a stable country, in an unsettled world, which may be true.

There are rumbles, but nothing to get excited about. The Afrikaans laager is gently splitting up into two camps. *Verligtes* (Enlightened Ones) and *Verkamptes* (the Cramped Ones). Is like having two right feet. Vorster's new "outward looking" policy has brought diplomatic relations with one of the Black states - namely, Banda's Malawi. Just ripples dissolving into nothing.

But there is another land in this land. An island within an island, teeming with Black milling masses. A gargantuan depersonalized majority controlled by White Africa: a necessary crutch in the labour structure of Economic man. All ideals bend at the will of the god Mammon. The Blacks migrate to the industrial centres, there to be swallowed by urbanization and to pick up the crumbs of white civilisation. They are mystified by a vast network of laws and regulations too numerous to even contemplate. These controls are known as "petty-apartheid", frustrating and violating the spirit of the blacks. They are so notoriously anomalous that they have become hackneyed, such as the separate facilities on trains, and in post offices etc.

Social contact between the races as we know is a law with the sanction of a taboo, so it becomes extremely difficult to find out how the African lives in the vast government-controlled townships that abound outside the limits of the cities. One has to have a permit and specific business before entering these zones. The only contact is economic, on a master-servant basis in the industrial and domestic complex. Johannesburg has a population of 450,000 Whites and 750,000 Blacks, yet it is a White man's city, with very few restaurants, cinemas or dance halls catering for the blacks, though they may shop at the stores in the city, putting their wages back into the masters' pockets.

This is a conformist society, frightened by any signs of change. *The Beatles'* music has been banned by the propagandist *South African Broadcasting Corporation*, who refer to them as "arrogant young men" on their Current Affairs programme.

Even the hippie movement has come under sharp attack by ministerial departments and the Church. Dr. Winkler, of the Department of Social Welfare and Pensions has stated that the Government was well equipped to deal with a hippie cult should it spread in South in South Africa. Hippies would be firmly dealt with under the *Children's Act* and the *Retreats and Rehabilitation Centres Act*.

Dr. Voot Vorster, actuary of the *Dutch Reformed Church*, stated recently, "The church is becoming very militant about this movement. We are going to do everything we can to stop this sort of thing."

He speaks with the voice of authority, for not only is he the brother of the Prime Minister, he is also the country's foremost Communist baiter, and at the moment, the twenty-one year old editor of *'Varisity'*, the Cape Town university student magazine, is facing charges of blasphemy because of a report on a symposium dealing with the "God-is-dead" theological controversy.

In this stifling climate of no free enquiry, the study of the rise of Nazism and Fascism has been dropped from courses in recent history. A group of pupils at a high school in the little town of Cornelia, in the *Orange Free State*, sent a Christmas card to Rudolph Hess, Hitler's former deputy who is in Spandou Prison:

> "We did it because we are convinced that an innocent man like Hess, who has spent 26 year of his life in jail, needs some moral assistance. We are convinced too, that Hess deserves a Nobel prize for peace because he flew to England to try to convince the British leaders of the stupidity of the war between Britain and Germany. Did circumstances, as they developed after World War II, not prove that the German was the correct one?"

In white Africa, they pride themselves on their closed attitude. A headmistress told me that she believed that education was a privilege for the few and that it was best to keep most people illiterate because they are happier that way.

Consequently the Transvaal matric results showed a record number of over 12,000 White matriculans, while out of a total 2,034 non-white students who sat for this exam, only 796 (30 percent) managed to get a pass or a school leaving certificate. Are the Africans that stupid or is this the result of one year's implementation of the *'Bantu Education Act'*, overcrowded schools, and no free compulsory education?

There is a pop group in Johannesburg called *'Freedom's Children'*. For their first single they had to change their name to *'Fleadom's Children'* and the word "Freedom" has been altered on their billboards by order of the of the police to *'The Freed Children's Band'*.

Such is the symbol of pathology in South Africa, While most Western countries are bringing in liberal homosexual law reforms, this republic is drafting a bill to curb homosexuality and lesbianism. I can't think of another country that has legislated against lesbianism, but nothing surprises one anymore, as they've even banned that harmless titillator called *'Playboy'*.

Who are the ruling junta in this horror-comic fantasyland? They are the Afrikaners - an inbred compassionless lot. To show mercy is a vice to them, unless one is part of the "*Volk*".

A magistrate said to the accused, a coloured (mixed race) youth, in a recent court case:

> "I ask you, how far was the door from the wall. You are not entirely a baboon, you can hear what I say..."

Law and order abound but not justice or mercy. Where are the African resistors to the system? For the time being they've been crushed and broken by torture, banishment and detention without trial.

Take the case of Robert Sobukwe, the former leader of the banned *Pan Africanist Congress*, who is detained in terms of the general *'Law Amendment Act'*.

Sobukwe, who is a B.A. graduate and former lecturer in Bantu languages at the University of the Witwatersrand, served a three-year sentence for incitement during the anti-pass campaign in 1960.

On expiry of his sentence he was immediately detained in terms of a provision, which gives the Minister the power to hold certain people after their sentence if they are "Likely to advocate, advise, defend or encourage any of the objects of Communism."

Meanwhile, life goes on in white South Africa as if motivated by death. And all I know about Soweto, a vast native township on the outskirts of Johannesburg is that there were only eight murders during the long Christmas weekend, this is a comparatively low figure, even for a "non-holiday" week-end.

Anslinger's Assassin of Youth

Home Grown Magazine Vol 1 No.6, 1980:

The history of Marijuana in America is a fascinating one. It is the story of repression of minority groups by the zealous efforts of one man, the late Harry J. Anslinger, Commissioner of the *'Federal Bureau of Narcotics'* for thirty-two years, who wielded a cunning power throughout the years over the lives of countless Mexican immigrants, blacks, jazz musicians, beats and hippies. He was the man who invented the myth of Marijuana, the assassin of youth.

In a new book out *'Reefer Madness'* (The Bobbs-Merrill Company Inc. Indianapolis, New York) the author Larry Sloman charts the efforts of Anslinger and his bureau in their crusade to discredit the weed and all who used her.

At the age of thirty-eight, Anslinger assumed control of the newly formed *Bureau of Narcotics* in 1930, at a time when concern over marijuana was just beginning to have a national impact. Born of Pennsylvania-Dutch Calvinist stock, he was a bureaucrat whose career included a spell as a consul with the diplomatic service assigned to the Hague, Hamburg, Venezuela and the Bahamas. Before taking up his new job he had worked briefly for the Treasury Department, trying to enforce the prohibition of America's favourite drug; Alcohol.

If history is the juxtaposition of people and events, then the stage was set. Here was a man who had a traumatic experience as a boy of twelve that would affect his judgments in later life. He had heard a neighbor's wife, who was a morphine addict, screaming in terrible pain. Then her husband asked the boy to go and fetch a packet from the drug store. When he returned the woman was given her dosage and her screams subsided.

Anslinger was never to forget those screams, or the fact that the morphine she required was sold to a twelve-year-old boy. This incident would later give way to a morbid interest in lurid and violent case histories as exemplified in the pulp, war-against-crime fiction of those times; it was an interest that would be given full vent in the course of time.

The smoking of marijuana in the United States first became defined as a social problem in the early part of this century. Used by Mexican 'wetbacks' who came to work in the beet fields of the Southwest, among the first Americans to adopt its use were the blacks of the South. The first cities to perceive it as a problem were border towns like El Paso and New Orleans, attributing its use to "Prostitutes, pimps and a criminal class of whites."

Although state after state enacted some form of marijuana prohibition, it was still perceived as a local problem until the early thirties when sensational accounts of it's use began to appear in newspapers in many parts of the country and pressure mounted on the Bureau to act.

The Vipers

This was the era of depression, the lean years, and as the hysteria grew the small deviant reefer-culture of sailors, jazzmen, circus people, entertainers, gangsters, the odd cowboy, along with the blacks and Mexicans, formed a native mythology around the weed. It was known as gage, shuzzit, muta, loco weed, Mary Warner, tea, muggles and reefer, by the "Vipers" who smoked it.

Out of the depths of Harlem nightlife, fusing with the unique vocal scatting style of Louis Armstrong and "Mezz" Mezzrow, the Vipers came into being with a mode that encompassed Jazz, language dress and choice of intoxicant. "Light up and be somebody" was the slogan of the day.

By the early 1930s more and more whites were sojourning uptown to the Harlem scene to pick up on good music, the fine dancing, and the righteous bush. Part of the scene's charm and power came from its exclusivity. It was through a secret inner-city code that the "tea pads" and "rent parties" could be found.

Contrary to popular myth, there was no real attempt to proselytize the virtues of the weed outside their immediate circles. If marijuana was anything, it was a psychic equalizer that would confer status and dignity on an outsider while at the same time provide a sensual treat that could allay the heaviest of depressions.

The Gore File

Meanwhile back to Harry Anslinger, who was poised to launch his campaign against this weed that grew wild in many of the states. With a strong following that included many highly-placed pharmaceutical executives, right-wing newspaper editors and some influential Congressmen, he devised a strategy to arouse public opinion on the marijuana issue. He would link it with crimes of violence, rape and murder. His agents would collect cases that he could use in his gore file, however tenuous the link with marijuana use. Usually there were racist overtones, and a fair share of sexual depravity. Anslinger was gearing up for the *Marijuana Tax Act* of 1937. Here are some tit-bits of horror from the Gore File:

- Two Negroes took a girl fourteen years of age and kept her for two days in a hut under the influence of marijuana. Upon recovery she was found to be suffering from syphilis.

- Coloured students at the university of Minnesota partying with female students whilst smoking and getting their sympathy with stories of persecution. Result pregnancy.

- In Texas an oil worker, good character, smoked a cigarette, raped his six year old daughter. When his wife returned home in the evening, she found him lying across the bed in a stupor, and the little child torn and bleeding. He couldn't remember. Was sentenced to death.

- In New Jersey in 1936, a particularly brutal murder took place, in which case one young man killed another literally smashing his head and face to a pulp, One of the defences was that the defendant's intellect was so prostrated from his smoking marijuana cigarettes that he did not know what he was doing. The fury of the murder was apparent. Not content with killing his friend, he tore out his tongue, his eyes and so mutilated him that the hardened Coroner had to turn his eyes away from the gruesome sight. This from a man who had never smoked a joint in his life.

Anslinger had found his theme and a slick gutter style of presentation. He knew what excited the mass media and aroused public emotions. But there was one case, that of Victor Licata, which became Anslinger's favorite and a cause célèbre that was widely reported in the popular press of the time.

Anslinger's files would later sum up the case: A twenty-year-old boy in Florida killed his parents, two brothers and a sister with an axe while under the influence of a marijuana "dream" which he later described to law enforcement officials.

When the slaying occurred in 1933, over three years before Anslinger became aware of it, the local paper reporting the story first mentions marijuana a good few paragraphs from the beginning. In the same paper the police chief vowed: "Maybe the weed only had a small indirect part in the alleged insanity of the youth, but I am declaring now for all time that the use of this narcotic must stop and will be stopped".

The consequences of the growing stream of hysterical propaganda, about the crime-causing properties of the weed, was that any and every two-bit hoodlum began pleading insanity due to the ravages of those *'mutas'* that they had smoked before committing the crimes. It was in this paranoiac era that the "dope fiend" emerged, smoking his "devil-weed" and corrupting innocent high school kids.

Anslinger was able to protect his concept of marijuana from any scientific assault until 1944 when the long-delayed *"La Guardia Report"* was finally published. It was a bombshell, exploding the myths so earnestly perpetuated by the Bureau. This prestigious report stated that the use of marijuana did not lead to physical, mental or moral degeneration and that no permanent deleterious effects from its continued use were observed. The Bureau with its stalwarts of women's clubs and religious groups and the right wing press railed against the findings, and the new strategy against the weed was devised.

The Cold War

By the late forties another, more sinister drug emerged on the scene - heroin. Some soldiers had come back from the war and had caught the habit, and it was spreading. America was in the grip of the Cold War, and what better excuse than to blame the whole heroin epidemic onto the much-maligned marijuana plant.

A new myth was about to engulf the nation; that smoking

marijuana leads directly to heroin addiction. It would serve Commissioner Anslinger well for the next twenty-odd years of his crusade. But it was in the fifties that the draconian penalties associated with the drug laws were enacted amid an atmosphere of controlled hysteria. McCarthyism and rabid anti-communism was the order of the day, and drugs were sinisterly linked to the "Red Menace". Anslinger had succeeded in convincing the American public that there was a grave new narcotic problem, which could be contained only by a strong punitive approach.

However by the end of the forties a new group of young white intellectually inclined jazz devotees began experimenting with the weed. They would later become known as the 'Beat Generation', and through the writings of Burroughs, Ginsberg and Kerouac, they would throw light on the experience of marijuana as a catalyst in re-examining other social attitudes. Even up until 1960 most of the users of marijuana were still non-white, and invariably those at the bottom rung of the social ladder. The turbulent sixties would see all that change as Mary Warner left the ghetto.

Counter-culture

The early sixties saw changes in many directions, and chinks began to appear in the Bureau's armour. The UN *Single Convention Treaty* regulating narcotic drugs throughout the world was passed in 1961 and although Anslinger was a prime mover behind the convention, a last-minute move to dilute the strength of some of the prohibitions meant that the United States did not become a signatory to the treaty at that time.

In 1962, President Kennedy used the mandatory retirement clause to get rid of the Commissioner, who had reached the age of seventy. But the old man was far from powerless, still representing his country on all its international United Nations dealings, a vantage point from which he would be able to gain his last move against the burgeoning marijuana movement that was gathering pace. In May 1967, the *Single Convention Treaty* was passed by the Senate after a one-day hearing.

As the sixties progressed marijuana would become a vital part of the armament in a counter-culture that sprang up manifesting itself as a full-frontal attack on the social and economical institutions of America. Pot was politicised, its powers embellished, its myth enlarged and its use further ritualized.

As early as 1964, Allen Ginsberg and some friends formed the first pro-pot lobby called *'LEMAR'* (Legalise Marijuana). Its use spread around the white middle-class youth on the college campuses and it became linked with the anti-Vietnam war lobby of the new left, and together with LSD, was the great rallying point of the hippies and 'Flower Power'.

Dope busts rose to a phenomenal half a million a year, the majority being young citizens for simple possession. The *Drug Enforcement Agency* superceded the old *Bureau of Narcotics* and the number of agents employed in the battle against drugs dramatically increased from four hundred when Anslinger left the bureau, to over ten thousand agents scattered throughout the world. In 1975 at the age of 83, Harry Jacob Anslinger died and an era was at an end. Marijuana was to be decriminalised in state after state as more than 20 million Americans were smoking it on a regular basis.

The Beat Generation (1): A Season In Hell

Home Grown Magazine Vol 1 No.8, 1980:

The New Vision: It was summer of 1944, the place, New York in wartime. A seminal sub-culture was emerging from the dark depths of the city's night haunts with its attendant mixture of hustlers, hoods, sailors, whores and jazz musicians. You could score anything around Times Square; it was a hustler's paradise. I came on the scene when I was eighteen and in the full flush of youth. I had been laid off a Merchant ship having done a stint as a galley boy, and was naturally drawn to the scene although I was a wild-eyed innocent adrift in a strange city but I soon got the hang of it and learned to hustle my way about.

It was the beginning of my great voyage of self-discovery, my search in the big city for kicks and excitement to experience the depths of my being, the instinctual urge of spontaneity. The great 'American Dream' had spewed a lot of us up, the under privileged, the so-called spiritual and sexual cripples who couldn't fit into the wholesome picture of what life was about. We were the ones who didn't quite make it into their glorious war, but were affected by its consequences; there were plenty of us around and it was a great scene, if you were hip to it.

Down in Harlem there was a cool, complicated jazz coming out of a club which reflected the spirit of the times, hitting you in a strange speedy way, man, you had to dig this new Bop and the cats who were playing it were so cool and detached with their berets, dark shades and goatee beards. Monday nights at *Minton's* young black musicians would drop in for a jam and the place would swing.

There was the high-smiling Charlie 'Bird' Parker on saxophone, the mystic Thelonious Monk on piano, the great John 'Dizzy' Gillespie on trumpet and Kenny 'Klook' Clarke on drums, among others. The music was intense and poured with emotion, something quite different from Dixie and Swing and the music of that skinny crooner Frank Sinatra that you heard on the radio and the Nickel-Odeon.

This new Bebop was the music of the hipster who was evolving as an entity within the night-world of the city smoking reefers of grass, speeding the night away on Benzedrine, and sometimes being caught in the hazy grip of Heroin or Morphine. Everything was available, if you knew how to get to it.

Out of the psychological rubble of America, out of the bowels of this hustling bustling city emerged the 'angel-headed hipster', ushering in what Norman Mailer later called 'the first wind of a second revolution in this century, moving not forward towards action and more rational more equitable distribution, but backward toward being and the secrets of human energy'.

I had met up with a crowd who hung about at the West End bar, mainly students at Columbia University just across the street. They came from well-to-do homes on the whole. There was Lucien Carr, an amazingly beautiful young man with blonde hair and slanted green eyes with a lithe sensual swagger that turned men on as well as women.

Although Lucien was only nineteen, he had a sophisticated worldly outlook and a sharp, cynical wit that belied his tender youth. He was often accompanied by a tall red-bearded friend about ten years his senior, Dave Kammerer who you could see was madly in love with Lucien and there was William Seward Burroughs, a strange kettle of fish, if I ever saw one, somewhat cool and aloof, ordinary-looking like a shy bank clerk, but well-groomed with steel-rimmed glasses, sandy hair and thin-lipped. Bill was about thirty and was working as a bartender in the Village, although he was living off a trust fund from money inherited from his family, part of the Burroughs business machine company.

The three of them hailed from St. Louis and it was through them that I met this skinny Jewish lad from New Jersey with big ears and horned-rimmed glasses and burning eyes whose name was Allen Ginsberg. Allen, who was seventeen, had a room opposite Lucien's on the Columbia campus. I enjoyed listening to them talking about literature and books, as I had not bothered much with reading.

Bill was the sort of big brother of the group putting us on to Spengler and Yeats and a host of others. There was a girl Edie Parker who used to sit there taking in all this intellectual claptrap. To me it was an awakening to new ideas, which seemed strange and rather exciting. Around June Edie brought her boyfriend, who had just come back from a sea voyage, to meet the crowd at the West End. Jack Kerouac was his name, a dark-haired athletic type who wore a sweatshirt and a dark leather jacket. He was somewhat different to the others, coming from a mill town in Lowell Massachusetts; he had won an athletic scholarship as a footballer to Columbia and then dropped out and got his seaman's job in the Merchant Marine. Jack, who was twenty-two, seemed to take to Lucian right away, attracted by his talk of Nietzsche and his dazzling good looks. Both of them wanted to be writers and together with Allen, who wasn't sure whether he wanted to be a social worker, labor union organizer or a poet, they would discuss the greats of literature. Allen had just finished reading Rimbaud's Season in Hell and quoted the line, "Now is the time of the *Hashishins*".

It was around that time that I first smoked grass; I had heard that it got you high and I had a friend whom I had met at sea who could score some for us. The first time it didn't seem to have much effect and I was a little surprised. I had read all these articles in the newspapers about dope fiends and expected something weird and kind of depraved; instead I had this light dreamy feeling and was real hungry afterwards. I had taken Bennies before, as they were the craze and was once up for three days and nights. I knew about morphine and heroin through a few friends who'd acquired a junk habit.

Most of them spent their time around *Bickford's* on Forty-second street, an 'all-nighter' which attracted me with its endless comings and goings of hustlers and whores. Quite a few of the male hustlers on the street were doing it to support a habit, though you had to know a doctor to get hold of any. One night we were all at Edie's apartment on 118th when Allen arrived with a twenty dollar box of grass and we all got high together, a lot of crazy antics and clever ideas were buzzing around and Bill Burroughs had us in stitches with his takeoff of the laconic private dick, Sam Spade.

That summer was steamy hot. Jack and Lucien were making plans to go to sea and Dave Kammerer could see that Lucien was slipping from his possessive grip. He was acting kind of strange of late, not saying much, just continually staring at Lucien who would naturally feel uneasy. Once at Bill's apartment in Bedford Street, they both grappled with a chunk of steak trying to tear it apart, another time Dave, who was becoming a pain in the arse, tried to strangle Jack's cat at Edie's place. I sensed that something could get out of hand, and it did, on the night of August the 13th.

That night I saw Lucien and Dave having a drink at the West End. They hardly noticed me, as they were engrossed in a heated rap. At closing time they took some beer with them and went up to Riverside Park nearby, ostensibly to get some cool air and to continue their personal wrangle.

Something happened between them that went out of control and ended with Dave lying there stabbed to death with a pocketknife by Lucien.

I later heard that Dave tried to have sex with Lucien but he wanted no part of it. He was pawing all over him and Lucien was trying to push him off. He said he'd kill Lucien if he didn't fuck with him, somehow Lucien stabbed him three times in the heart, panting and sobbing he tied the hands and feet of the body with shoelaces then tied rocks to it with pieces of his shirt and pushed it over the side into the Hudson River.

Afterwards he went over to Bill's apartment and told him what happened, Bill listened coolly to Lucien who was frightened out of his wits that he'd get the 'hot-seat' for what he'd just done, and advised him to get a lawyer through his parents who were well-off and give himself up to the cops. He could plead self-defense against rape, an honour slaying.

Instead of doing what Bill told him, Lucien went over to Edie's place and woke up Jack to tell him what had happened. He was dry-eyed by then and was ready to give himself up. Jack came out with him and kept watch while Lucien disposed of Dave's glasses and the murder weapon.

His buddy was in trouble and he had to try and help him. They then went to have a last drink together, Lucien going over the incident repeatedly, telling how Dave lay there dying in his arms. Then you wouldn't believe it, they took a cab to Lucien's psychiatrist, borrowed five dollars and went to see the movie 'The Four Feathers'.

They then wandered round Times Square, had a drink, visited the museum of modern art and late that afternoon, Lucien handed himself in to the cops.

Self-Ultimacy

The whole thing shook us all up, everyone was talking about it and Jack and Bill were booked as material witnesses to a homicide. Bill got bailed out by his family, and went back to St. Louis, but Jack couldn't raise the $5,000 bail bond so he was carted off to the Bronx city jail, known as the 'Opera house' because of the stool pigeons.

THE BEAT GENERATION (1): A SEASON IN HELL

He and his girl Edie devised a plan and a week later with special permission and under the watchful eye of a cop they got married at City Hall. A little later Edie's parents posted the bond and Jack was allowed out and the couple left for Edie's parent's home in rich Grosse Pointe, Detroit.

Only Allen was still around but I didn't see much of him, as he was sick with hepatitis. In October, Lucien having pleaded guilt to manslaughter was sentenced to one to twenty years in reformatory, although he served just over two years before being paroled.

By the end of the year Jack and Bill were back in town but things weren't the same as before. The Lucien affair hung heavy over them, their talk was doom-laden and they were getting caught up in Benzedrine, removing the pads of soaked paper from an inhaler and swallowing it with cups of coffee.

I bumped into Allen one night and went with him to the apartment on West 115th Street where he was staying. It belonged to Joan Vollmer, a tall, attractive girl who was also into bennies and she let her friends take rooms in the large apartment. Allen had just been expelled from Columbia over breaches of discipline, culminating in the dean finding him in bed with Jack, a non-student. So they were now staying with Joan.

It was in December that I saw Bill again in a bar along Eighth Avenue, he had a list with cryptic notes about gamblers' bars, fag bars, old queen bars and cheap liquor lounges, and we went to his apartment on Riverside Drive. Bill liked and respected me because I could hustle the street; I was a character of the underworld.

Bill, coming from an upper-class background and Harvard educated, was intrigued by the whole junkie, sex-hustler and thieving set that hung around some of the bars. He was a low-lifer by choice, seeking out the weird and wonderful in the gutters of life, but somehow seeming aloof from it, like an invisible intruder. Bill had got hold of some morphine syrettes and a sawn-off shotgun and wanted to get rid of them. I knew a guy who could arrange the deal, so I put Bill in touch with him.

Later I went with Bill to this apartment on Henry Street. There were these two guys who had just come off a ship, and I could tell had junk habits. The nervy little one, whose name was Herbert Huncke, thought Bill was the heat, he looked so straight and sort of out of place. The other one, Phil 'Sailor' White, looked him up and down and slowly said, 'Maybe we can get a taste of him,' We sat down at the kitchen table, someone went into the other room and brought

43

back some grass, and rolled a few joints for us. Phil asked Bill how many syrettes he had. Several gross of them, was the answer.

Some guy had ripped them off a drugstore. He then took a handful of syrettes from his pocket and flung them on the table. It brought a gleam to Sailor's eyes, who was just dying to shoot up. Bill gave them a taste, and as they cooked it, he decided that he should also try some. It was his first time. I decided against taking a fix, and just went on smoking a joint.

He took off his suit jacket and rolled up his sleeve, watching intently as Herbie and Sailor shot up. Now it was his turn, he was rather hygienic about it all, rubbing alcohol on his arm and cleaning the spike, drew some blood and then took it out. The tourniquet was too tight so he loosened it and peered down as morphine shot into his arm. He closed his eyes and after awhile said, "Well that's quite a sensation." He opened his eyes and nodded, "That's very interesting", as if he was appraising the situation scientifically. So that was Bill's first fix. The next day the deal was done with Sailor, and him and Herbie started seeing a lot of Bill. They had a common interest in the sweet taste of junk, the bright neon lights of Times Square, and the predators and prey of the city of night.

January 1945, out of the blue, Bill suddenly married Joan Vollmer, and moved into the apartment at 115th Street, although we all knew he preferred the young mavericks of the street. Edie had returned to join Jack, but they soon split up and she went back home. Allen was getting rather hung up on Jack, who didn't know if he should give in to his persistent demands. Jack was getting into a heavy bennies thing, often sitting up all night scribbling in his little notebook. Joan was speeding around the place trying to keep a semblance of order. I would drop in quite often.

Sometimes Sailor and Herbie Huncke would be sitting around. Bill used to meet them at the *Angler Bar*, or they'd be hanging out at *Whelan's Drugstore*, on Seventh and 47th. Jack would tag along, as they'd roam through the motley crowd of hoods, drag queens and other zombies of the night. I often saw them at the Greyhound Terminal, or in one sleazy bar or another. Sometimes Allen could be seen wandering about dreaming visions of the night. Here was life in the raw, spontaneous and vibrant with primitive animal energy.

They were seekers of souls, the street wanderers of the night, sensually exploring their emotions with an obsessive zeal, seeing in the rejects of this most abundant society, festering maggots that would bring the whole edifice crashing down.

THE BEAT GENERATION (1): A SEASON IN HELL

Herbie Huncke, the hip Professor, led the way into this crazy twilight zone as if it were a triumphal processional, a holy place for saintly sinners. Bill had developed a devouring junk habit to match those of Sailor and Herbie. He was able to buy morphine scripts from a doctor on 102nd Street, but it was not enough. He and Sailor, who was an adept at picking pockets, 'Worked the hole', rolling drunks down the subway. Jack had turned pale and gaunt from endless nights on Bennies; his wiry physique now resembled a bag of bones, with haunting eyes staring from his hollow face. Benzedrine intensified his awareness and made him feel clever. But it was a revelation into the self, a look into the dark corners of the mind, a struggle for identification in a world gone mad, the beginning of a new vision that would make them soar above the night, bursting with fresh imagery and apocalyptic flights of poetry.

> "I saw the best minds of my generation destroyed by madness, starving hysterical naked. Dragging themselves through the Negro streets at dawn looking for an angry fix.
>
> Angel-headed hipsters burning for the ancient heavenly connection to the starry dynamo in the machinery of night,
>
> Who poverty and tatters and hollow-eyed and high sat up smoking in the supernatural darkness of cold water flats floating across the tops of cities contemplating jazz....
>
> Who pass through universities with radiant cool eyes hallucinating Arkansas and Blake-light tragedy among the scholars of war,...
>
> Who got busted in their pubic beards retuning through Laredo with a belt of marijuana for New York,
>
> Who ate fire in paint hotels or drank turpentine in Paradise Alley, death, or purgatoried their torsos night after night...
>
> Who chained themselves to subways for the endless ride from Battery to Holy Bronx on Benzedrine until the noise of wheels and children brought them down shuddering mouth-wracked and battered bleak of brain all drained of brilliance in the drear light of zoo,...
>
> Visions! Omens! Hallucinations! Miracles miracles! Ecstasies! Gone down the American river!"

From *'Howl'* by Allen Ginsberg, 'Howl and other Poems', City Lights Books, 1956.

The Beat Generation (2): Journey to the End of the Night

Home Grown Magazine Volume 1 No. 9, 1980:

The winter of 1945 was icy cold and New York was a mean place for a hungry hustler. I was feeling weary and worn out from the incessant drift from one night-haunt to another. After a while, the scene sort of draws in on you and you feel trapped by your very own devices. Everybody looks mean and ugly after several nights up on Benzedrine, a nightmare of ragged characters all on edge.

I was hooked on observing it all, lapping it up with compulsive zeal until I felt whacked and satiated. For some, it was a time for whooping it up. The war was over in a big mushroom cloud and it was the dawning of a new era of American progress and prosperity. The G.Is were back home, all rearing to go after the bitch-goddess that lures with dreams of money and success but for me there was nothing but the daily grind of hustling to keep both body and soul together.

Where did the good times go, the mad people that burn themselves out, those that are beat and gone? What happened to that close bunch of buddies that filled my days and nights with such gleeful joy? When you're down, you look back and it all seems to glow, you get flashes and insights, fleeting glimpses that warm your soul.

So much had happened this year, so many changes to ring out the old and usher in the new. We seemed to have just drifted apart, gone our separate ways due to chance or circumstance. By that summer the communal apartment on 115th street had broken up in a shambles. Things had just got out of hand. There is nothing like an impending bust to get everybody jumpy, and that's the way it was.

Old Bill Burroughs, caught in his junk trap, was starting to feel the heat catching him up. The world of junk is full of informers, and in no time they were on to Herbert Huncke, and then Bill.

To get him out of trouble, Bill's parents had suggested that he move down to Texas. He found a small holding near a little town called New Waverly, about fifty miles from Houston, and moved down with Joan and her little daughter, Julie, with the intention of growing marijuana to sell on the New York market.

Allen Ginsberg, who had worked in a a ship-yard and enrolled in the Maritime Service Training station, shipped out as a mess boy on a tanker heading south, and Jack Kerouac split back home to his parents' apartment in ozone park, where his father was dying of stomach cancer.

The Benzedrine had been too much for Jack, and by December he had developed thrombophlebitis in his legs, and was in the veteran's administration hospital in Queens with his legs up on a pillow swathed in hot compresses. Looking back on it all in calm recollection, it was our journey to the end of the night.

In a way, we were all licking our wounds, lying low in fallow, for there is almost nothing time cannot heal. Winter is always followed by the spring. I had heard by telegram that my father had died on the third of May 1946, and by some strange coincidence, Jack's father had died on the very same day. I didn't see much of Jack at that time, as he was staying at home writing a book, incorporating some of his experiences.

So it was time for me to leave New York for my father's funeral, and to comfort my mother and young brothers and sisters back home in Philadelphia, where I spent the rest of that year. At first it was great to be back home, the prodigal son returned to the fold. My mother was hoping I'd had enough of my 'gutter-snipe' days', as she called it, and that I'd meet a nice local girl, get a steady job and just settle down like all the rest of the people she knew. Sooner or later I knew the game was up and I'd have to return once more to Times Square, with its hustle and bustle and all it entails.

Having paid my filial dues to my family, I arrived back in New York fresh into the new year of January 1947, with a neat stash of dollars to see me by until I got a job as a soda jerk or bartender. Those few days I felt like a stranger as I wandered into the *Angler Bar* and *Whelan's*, looking for familiar faces.

I soon bumped into Vicki Russell, a real character who was a seasoned hustler from way back, into the junk scene and doing tricks. She was a tall girl who managed somehow to retrain her wide-eyed innocence and vulnerability, despite the active life she led.

Through her old friend Herbert Huncke, we'd all met her and spent many crazy nights in her company. Once, when Jack had become pale and thin from the bennies, she applied pancake makeup to his face so that he wouldn't feel conspicuous while travelling on the subway. It was through her that I learned what had happened in my absence, who was still about, and what they were doing.

First of all Lucien Carr had recently come out of prison on parole. On New Year's Eve, she and Lucien, Jack and a girl named Celine has gone to the movie, *Crime and Punishment*, and then went on to some socialite parties getting crazy drunk. Allen had gone back to Columbia to study, but was still very much on the scene, experimenting with drug-induced poetics, and Herbie who had taken a fall for possession of a five-dollar bag of heroin and done six months on Riker's Island, had gone to sea but was now back again. Of course, Bill was still in Texas, though Joan had turned up the previous fall, but too many bennies had sent her to Bellevue Hospital psychiatric wing. It felt great to be back on Times Square.

It was around this time that a new character entered our lives, to lift us back into pulsating life and energise our rather beat existence. His name was Neal Cassidy, fresh, vibrant and bounding with animated excitement, and a sort of primitive sexual magnetism unrestrained by social convention. We heard talk of Neal from Hal Chase, who stayed at the apartment on 115th street and was also at Columbia. Hal had known Neal in Denver, his home town before he had come up to Columbia to study philosophy, and on retuning on vacation, had told Neal about the mad gang in the big city, whetting his appetite for more thrills and kicks.

It was at the West End bar that I first caught my first glimpse of Neal, sitting in the next booth. I could hear this insane giggle of glee from the next table, and this torrent of words bubbling over excitedly as Neal got into his rap. Eventually my curiosity got the better of me and I edged up to the next seat next to Hal, nonchalantly introducing myself to him and the honey of a blonde who was hanging onto him. I found out that she was called Luanne, and turned out to be only fifteen. Bright-eyed and fresh-looking, with loose curls of hair, she sat starry-eyed taking Neal in.

Neal was two years younger than me, at twenty and really enjoying the New York scene. Soon we were talking about Pool, both Neal and I had a hankering after Pool haunts. Neal had spent many an hour gracing the pool tables of downtown Denver with his presence.

He was mad about cars and acquired his learning experience at the age of fourteen when he engaged in a compulsive game of joyriding.

From then until he was eighteen, he had "borrowed" by his own count, some 500 cars, been arrested 10 times, convicted six times and spent fifteen months in reformatory. He was then working as a parking lot attendant at the hotel New Yorker on 34th street, moving cars around, swerving in and out of crammed spaces at a bouncy speed and handling the wheel with magnificent ease.

That was Neal, full of go, baring his adventured in a racy onslaught, randomly picking up crazy scenes from the past that gripped me with awed excitement. In the strange and lonely world of Times Square, I'd met the weird and wonderful, each with his or her own story to tell of a broken home, not being wanted and left to drift like garbage around the gutters.

With Neal I felt a strong rapport. He called himself the "unnatural son of a few score beaten men", as at the age of six, he'd gone to live in a bum skid row hotel with his wino father, washing himself in the mornings in a common bathroom stinking with vomit and filth, surrounded by sad old derelicts sprucing up for a days begging.

His experience and acceptance of situations, his open-faced candor and innate instinct for the beat of life, touched me quite deeply. Hal had already brought Jack over to the cold-water flat in Spanish Harlem where Neal and Luanne were staying; it was an inopportune moment, as Neal opened the door to them stark naked, erection at half-cock, with Luanne jumping off the couch and out of view.

Soon the seeds of a great friendship were sown. In Neal he saw a brother-sufferer, "a wild yea-saying over-burst of American joy" that made his heart pound faster. Neal was thirsty for intellectual knowledge, having ready a few shelf-lots from the reformatory, and admired Jack's knowledge and understanding of some of the great classics of literature, eagerly engaging him in great debate.

Jack told Neal about the novel he was writing, *The Town and the City*, which figured different aspects of himself put into the sons of a family. As Neal and Jack became friends and went out, Luanne was left back at the flat more often. On one of these night outs, I ran into Neal and Jack at the West End, and we had a drink. I was going to Vicki Russell's apartment in the East Eighties to smoke grass, or to get high on some tea, as we called it. Neal had not smoked marijuana before and was eager to get high. They were to have picked up two coloured girls in a diner, but had been stood up, so we made our way up to Vicki's rather small studio apartment.

She let us in with her dreamy eyes glassed up and shining, the sweet smell of tea catching in our nostrils, and bop blowing from a horn on the radio, and who should be sitting on a stool, puffing on a water pipe, with his large dark eyes staring up at us? None other than Allen, whom I'd not seen since my return. Neal had met Allen briefly when Hal introduced them at the West End, but they'd not spoken much. Of course they knew quite a lot about each other, through their mutual friendship with Hal.

Allen lit up the water pipe and we soon got nice and high. Neal and Allen just connected, and charged each other up. Neal just sitting there, his eyes gleaming in the half-light, his head bobbing up and down, exclaiming "Yes, yes and "that's right" as Allen opened up to him. Jack just sat back watching the two of them getting off on one another, ranting and raving on, getting higher and higher and more carried away. I could see Neal's features change, his face softening in moments of repose, and then he was off babbling away, a wicked know-all glint in his eyes, arms flaying in the air in bursts of hyper-manic exaltations. Jack likened them to the "holy con-man with the shining mind, and the sorrowful poetic con-man with the dark mind".

The next morning we wandered off, still high and in exuberant spirits, Jack and me tagging along behind the two of them.

During the following weeks Neal, who was working at the parking lot during the day, divided his time in the evenings with Luanne, three nights of love-making and fighting, Jack, two evenings in rapt intellectual conversation with Allen; two nights staying up all night, seeing how far they could go before they bugged one another, nobody but Neal with his abundant energy could have done it.

Late one night Neal and Allen and some friends ended up at the tenement apartment I shared with a friend on 104th Street. As it was late, they stayed the night. There weren't enough beds, so Neal and Allen shared the same bed, and although Neal only seemed interested in making it with girls, he pulled Allen to him, and they became lovers for the first time.

Though roughly the same age, Allen being nervous and self-conscious, was overwhelmed with Neal's lack of inhibition, and confident ease in sexual relationships. He fell in love with Neal, and they swore vows of love the following week. There was a great emotional bond between them, each filling a need in the other. As Allen got hooked on Neal, he in turn became more highly charged sexually to Jack but nothing came of it, and the three of them spent a lot of time together getting high on tea, drunk on beer or speeding on Bennies.

Meanwhile Luanne, who had had enough, retuned to Denver in a huff. Before she left she told Neal that the cops were looking for him because he was buying too much of that marijuana. A short while later on the 4th of March, 1947, Neal Cassidy left New York for Denver on a Greyhound bus headed west, wearing a dark pinstriped business suit that he'd bought to impress the boys at the pool hall. Allen and Jack had both gone to see him off. They planned to meet together in Denver in summer, and who knows, they could go to Bill Burroughs's ranch-type place in Texas and introduce Neal to Bill.

Then Neal was gone, and as I huddled up against that bitter March wind, New York seemed tight and cramped, lacking in life and lustre. I thought I kept hearing Neal's voice yelling my name from behind when the wind blew and howled, laughing madly in my ear "He-he-hee-hee-hee", like the holy goof he was.

> "... The only ones for me are the mad ones, the ones who are mad to live, mad to talk, mad to be saved, desirous of everything at the same time, the ones who never yawn or say a commonplace thing, but burn, burn, burn like fabulous yellow roman candles exploding like spiders across the stars and in the middle you see the blue centre light pop and everybody goes 'Awww!"

From 'On The Road' by Jack Kerouac (Penguin Modern Classics).

The Beat Generation (3): The Decline of the West

Home Grown Magazine Volume 1 No. 10, 1981:

I often thought of Neal Cassidy after he left New York for Denver in the spring of 1947 and knew deep down that it was only a matter of time before I'd see him again. I heard news from him soon after he'd gone. He wrote Jack Kerouac a letter, which he showed to Allen Ginsberg and me. Jack called it "the great sex letter", a drunken rambling story describing two hilarious and horny sexual encounters on the long bus journey home.

Neal's scrawling letters with their bad spelling and full of street talk, had an ease and flow that Jack and Allen dug, Jack was doing quite a lot of writing himself, sitting at the kitchen table of his mother's apartment in Ozone park, burning the midnight oil, trying to reach the halfway point in the novel he was working on, his literary knowledge inhibiting him from writing with Neal's spontaneous urgency.

When he arrived in Denver I received a letter from Neal begging me to send him two overcoats in his size so that he could sell them and earn some bread. He knew of my penchant for gently removing coats off the stands at certain restaurants and cloakrooms. He needed them in a desperate hurry, putting this heavy obligation on to me, but he moved around quite a bit and I was never sure if they would get to him.

I saw one of the many letters he wrote to Allen, who was profoundly moved by the love and need they expressed. Neal knew how to open himself up if he wanted to, displaying a gentle loving side that needed to be wanted and desired. To Allen he poured out in great flows of honesty the woes in his heart, his unsettled being fluctuating between the hassles of making ends meet, convincing Luanne to stay with her mother and trying to tie the emotional knot with Allen.

Meanwhile Allen was preparing to join Neal that summer to cement their deepening friendship, and Jack was planning to meet up with them in Denver on his way to join an old school chum in San Francisco and become a seaman.

Before Allen left in June, we spent a night together roaming around our favourite haunts on Times Square, and spent the early hours of the morning at the Pokerino, watching the nightly drift of men who had nowhere to go and nothing but time on their hands, Allen had written a story in which he described the joint, and showed it to me. He sure had a way with words: "...beat, absolutely beat characters... tea heads from everywhere, hustlers with pimples, queens with pompadours, lushes with green faces, fat dicks with clubs, cherubs with sycophants, wolves with adenoids, faces with blotches, noses with holes, eyebrows with spangles, old men with the horrors, bums with the stumbles and some squares with curiosity or just passing through to catch a bus..."

We wondered what had happened to Herbert Huncke, now that he was away from the scene, staying with Bill and Joan Burroughs in Texas helping them grow marijuana and oriental poppies. We laughed as we recalled the time he'd blown marijuana smoke at the cockroaches so they wouldn't mess around with his bread and jam. Allen was looking forward to introducing Neal to Bill in Texas after they had spent some time together in Denver.

While Allen departed by greyhound bus to Denver, Jack decided that he would hitchhike to San Francisco, spending a few days in Denver en route.

One evening at the apartment in Ozone Park we sat poring over maps of the United States, and on a road map there was one long red line called Route 6 that led from the tip of Cape Cod clear to Ely, Nevada and there dipped down to Los Angeles. Like the pioneer settlers one hundred years before him, he would blaze a trail of adventure as he crossed the country with the setting sun in his eyes heading west to California.

After his mother had gone to bed, we sat in the kitchen high on Benzedrine rapping about all sorts of things, He let me read a few pages from the novel he was working on called 'The Town And The City', a sprawling tale about a family and their five sons.

Jack had an amazing memory and in poetic images had captured the yearnings of a youth growing up in these times. He kept journal notes of odd incidences and events that he'd witnessed, and had put some of his friends into the novel like Lucien Carr, Allen, Bill and Dave Kammerer, though he'd kept the stabbing out and romanticized it as a suicide.

THE BEAT GENERATION (3): THE DECLINE OF THE WEST

It was on this night that we realised we shared a common sorrow, both our dads having died on the same day just over a year ago. Now at the age of twenty-five, having been a failure in his father's eyes for his lack of material achievement, he felt free to make his odyssey of self-discovery and in the process, discover America.

His mother, who was possessive and clinging, was resigned to the fact of his leaving, and in July he was gone. I could picture him walking across the land, strange and ragged like a prophet.

It was not long before sporadic accounts of what was happening in Denver filtered their way back to me, sometimes from Neal himself in a jumbled note on Allen's typewriter. Allen described this period as the 'Denver doldrums' and no wonder.

Even before he arrived, Neal had met up with a beautiful blonde who was studying at the University of Denver. Carolyn Robinson was her name, a Bennington graduate. Neal was quite stuck on her and somehow she produced a sense of peace in him when they were together.

He was still seeing Luanne on the quiet, as they had a strong sexual thing going between them, and there was Allen trying to resume their love affair in Neal's six dollar a week basement room. But Neal seemed to thrive on these endless emotional complications, rushing from one to the other and engrossing them in his marathon monologues as proof of how much he loved them.

Allen felt dejected, as if he had ben duped and manipulated by Neal. He was hurt and confused as he sat in the basement room trying to compose sad and heavy poems, waiting for Neal to turn up, often hours later than he promised. Then they would screw, take Bennies and talk and write poems throughout the night.

When Jack arrived, that was the situation he found. Allen took him down to the rooming house where Neal was banging Carolyn. He knocked on the door and Neal opened it stark naked and greeted him with genuine excitement, and later the three of them spent many hours together like old times in New York, but soon Jack ran out of money and after wiring his mother for more, set out on his journey to California in August, while Carolyn left to work in San Francisco and the divorce papers with Luanne were being sorted out. Neal and Allen decided that the time was right to go and pay old Bill a visit in Texas.

Well, I heard all about the Texas escapades from both Neal and Huncke when they came back to New York that autumn. Bill and Joan, who had given birth to a baby boy that July, had a cabin with some land in a sparsely populated area some fifty miles from Houston.

It was beautiful bayou country and quite remote, as you can imagine. It beats me how they and Huncke made out during that period, hunting down supplies from all the drug stores in every town within a radius of fifty miles so many times that people were getting to wonder what was going on.

Huncke and Bill were buying paregoric, sometimes in half gallons and all the barbiturates they could get hold of, and a constant supply of Benzedrine inhalers for Joan, who went through them in no time. They also regularly copped marijuana from a coloured connection they had made in Houston, often smoking joints with the man and his old lady.

Sometimes Huncke would score a young seaman and take him back to his hotel room to get stoned and then have sex. Bill had his jeep, which meant Houston was within easy reach, and sure as he said, Bill has this homegrown patch of marijuana plants that grew very tall by the late summer. Bill was thoroughly enjoying playing the country squire, practicing his shooting with guns from a collection he was acquiring.

In August Allen and Neal arrived and at first Bill didn't quite take to Neal, as Allen would have liked, thinking him a conman. Then the sleeping arrangements were not to Allen's liking. He tried with Huncke's help to build a mutual bed out of two army cots for him and Neal to sleep together in, but it sagged in the middle and the whole thing was a miserable failure.

Neal couldn't stand Allen touching him, and the more Allen tried, Neal found himself shutting off from him. Huncke would play his Billie Holiday records on the porch in the hot afternoons, but Bill would request him to play Viennese waltzes on the tinny phonograph.

After a week of rejection, feeling emotionally shattered by Neal's behavior, Allen left to ship out to sea on a freighter carrying wheat to Dakar in Africa. The voyage took two months and the monotonous routine and isolation of the long sea trip made him feel introspective and brought about "The Dakar doldrums".

That fall Bill, Huncke and Neal drove to New York in a jeep filled with mason jars of marijuana that they'd just harvested, ready to sell on the streets. Joan and the kids followed by train.

In a matter of days I bumped into Neal and Huncke who were trying to fix up a connection to sell the tea. They'd tried a bellhop at one of the hotels but he wasn't interested because it was green and hadn't been cured. I took them to this chick's place in the Village and we tasted some, as Bill had given them a sample, and although it made me cough and splutter, it sure got me high.

We all sat on the floor listening to records and blasting as Neal kept rolling them up. He was rapping to this girl who was nodding in response, murmuring "That's cool" to everything Neal was saying. Later she gave a whole pile of her records to him, as she saw that he could really get into the sounds. I had a headache, which the smoke completely cleared it was so good.

A couple of days later I made a connection and Bill, Huncke and myself went up to do the deal while Neal stayed with the jeep and the jars of tea. After a bit of haggling we sold most of it for a hundred dollars.

Of course the moment Bill hit town and had found a cheap hotel room, he made contact with an old junky friend who turned him on. He hadn't had any junk for about six weeks, except for the paregoric he'd melted down, and he got very spaced out.

I took Joan out on Times Square one night so she could get a can of milk for the baby, though I was a bit embarrassed by the straggly dress she was wearing. Nobody else seemed to have minded in the cafeteria, and in fact, most of them dug her, as she was so flipped out.

Then Bill's parents came to see the baby, and they installed him in one of those exclusive beach clubs out on Atlantic beach. He lent Neal the jeep and we'd pick up Joan and drive out there, about thirty miles, to get it to him. Soon Neal became restless and a bit tired of the running about, and managed to hustle fifty bucks from a friend of mine, promising to pay him back and all that, and left for San Francisco to join Carolyn, with the pile of records that the girl had given him. Ironically, shortly after he left both Allen and Jack arrived back in New York from their respective trips.

As the winter of 1947 grew dark and cold, I felt a deep yearning to see my mother and brothers and sisters again, there were seven of us, and decided to put my pride in my pocket and go back home for a while to rest my weary body from the frenzied pace of my Times Square existence. I'd had enough and felt that I was going round the bend. I needed to be back in the fold, cosseted and protected from a cruel and cold world, to feel the warmth and care of the mother I had left as soon as I was old enough. I stayed at home in Philadelphia that Christmas, bathing in the warmth of family togetherness, eating proper meals for the first time in ages.

I worked that winter as a warehouseman packing orders of kitchen utensils and crockery in a wholesale goods depot. By the spring of 1948, I was on the high seas again having shipped out on a cargo vessel bound for Marseille, working as a mess-man. I did that one trip and was glad to get back to New York once again, to be part of the scene with renewed vigour and fresh energy. Huncke was the first one I ran into and we had a good time together spending my hard-earned money until it ran out. Bill and Joan and the children were now living in Algiers, a town just outside New Orleans in Louisiana. They had purchased a hundred acres of land within easy reach of New Orleans where Bill could obtain drugs in the seamy French Quarter with its beguiling mix of gamblers, drifters, seamen, tourists, whores and homosexuals, just like his New York habitat. Earlier in the year, when he was still hanging around Times Square, he had voluntarily committed himself to Lexington Narcotics Farm in Kentucky, and had undergone a cure, but left when the withdrawal symptoms had eased and stayed off junk for four months. Since Jack had come back from his cross-country trip, he had hardly been seen around, and by the summer had at last completed 'The Town and the City'. It was a thousand-page novel, written in a batch of student notebooks, which he carried around in a shabby leather doctor's bag, so he could show our crowd sections of it. I happened to have read some of it and was filled with admiration, wanting to read on and on.

He seemed to be quietly pleased with himself and enjoyed the warm reaction of friends. He had been in correspondence with Neal who was living with Carolyn in San Francisco and working as a brakeman on the railroad. Neal was going to be a father in September, and Luanne was going through with the divorce, so that the baby could be born in wedlock. She was now also living there and had a fiancé who was a seaman. Allen hadn't quite got over Neal since his return.

That spring he was back at Columbia and living by himself in a dark and narrow cold-water flat in a slum tenement in Spanish Harlem.

During the summer vacation he was working two hours a day as a file clerk and spending his time aimlessly idling about or just brooding on things. To make things worse, his mother was going through one of her periodic bouts of madness and was in the Pilgrim State Hospital. I would visit him in that dingy apartment and we

THE BEAT GENERATION (3): THE DECLINE OF THE WEST

would end up seeing the utter futility of life, Allen like "an eccentric dope in a world of mechanical supermen."

In July of that hot summer of 1948, Allen was lying on his bed reading the poems of William Blake having just masturbated for no love over Neal, his "ultimate psycho-spiritual sex o-cock jewel fulfillment", when he had a visionary experience in which he heard Blake's illuminated voice and felt that he had been chosen to experience a vast cosmic consciousness. Here he was, all of twenty-two years old, becoming aware of a deeper, real universe, penetrating the surface of things, and perceiving the living hand that had placed it all in front of him.

He understood Blake's dictum that "The eye altering alters all". A sensation of light permeated his body and he awakened to experience what Blake saw, "Eternity in a grain of sand/Infinity in an hour". In his heightened state of awareness, with a sense of cosmic awe, he completely lost all sense of his body, normal time, and normal consciousness. When he looked out of the window at the old apartment buildings opposite, with an altered state of perception, he became transfixed by the craftsmanship of the cornices of the tenement, the intelligence of the workman who laid the bricks, the architect who had thought of it, the man who had smelted the piece of tin to make a cornucopia, the miner who had dug it out of the earth, the earth that had gone through eons of preparing it, the little molecules that had slumbered, and out of all this he had a breakthrough from ordinary habitual consciousness into seeing heaven in the cornices of a building.

For the next couple of weeks Allen was in an exalted state of mind and the visionary feeling came over him once again when he was reading a volume of Blake in the campus bookstore. He perceived that everybody was completely conscious, but that the fixed expressions that people have, the habitual expressions, the manners, the mode of talk, are all masks hiding the consciousness. But it was difficult trying to explain all this to his friends, some of whom thought he was going crazy. Why, who has visionary experiences in these modern times? He was seeing a Reichian analyst at the time, but was kicked out of therapy for smoking marijuana.

Allen threw a party at the apartment one evening and a whole crowd of us came. I spoke to Jack, who was getting into beer and having a ball. He was hoping that Neal would be able to make it to New York, or he would hitch-hike out to join him in California. The manuscript of his novel had been sent to a publisher, but had been turned down and was now at another publishing house. He was toying with ideas for a new book and finally decided to write about his trip across the country. It was going to be called *'On The Road'*.

The late forties were a strange time, a crazy time for us and America, which was in the grips of the Cold War that permeated an atmosphere akin to paranoia. We were the guardians of a free world fighting against the insidious menace of Soviet-dominated world Communism, Patriotism, that last refuge of the scoundrel, was rife with ardour, fuelled by the new technocrats, men who had too much money and controlled too many things. The ruthless power and looney fanaticism of the military mind held sway, bringing with it a stifling conformity in the name of God, the progress of technology, the family and cleanliness and order.

Mass Society emerged giving birth to 'One-Dimensional Man' who was encouraged only to consume, never to decide. What Allen Ginsberg called the 'Syndrome of Shutdown' began, moving towards a closed society where all decisions would be secret, no final authority, rule by Nobody.

This was the era that gave us that greatest of modern inventions, sliced bread in vacuum packs, along with the plethora of plastic products that would make us part of this planned obsolescence. It seemed as if the Second World War and the Atom Bomb that ended it, had so traumatised the post-war American psyche that only fear and loathing existed, soothed by mass conditioning through the media.

Never had the desire for security been so strong, and never were people more insecure. To play against the system with its air of general anxiety about so much of no real avail, took a great deal of guts, for almost any action or aberration that was not considered commonplace took a disproportionate amount of courage to enact. It was in this climate that we experienced America, seeking the rebellious imperatives of the Self, a burning consciousness of the present through ecstatic states of being, be they madness, visions, sexual explorations, or just getting high on marijuana, booze or junk.

It was in this scenario of mayhem that I existed in the bowels of night city life, digging the freeflow beat of bop whilst high on tea, feeling the pulsating rhythms of New York in all it's frenzy. I was an angel-headed hipster adrift in an eternal nightworld that seethed almost beyond the reach of the law.

Being a seasoned hustler on those mean and moody streets taught me a lot about people that I couldn't have picked up elsewhere. I got to know so many of the characters that hung about, the whores who'd scored a John and were flash with their dollars around the bars, the cool black pimps in zoot-suits, who strutted about as if they owned the streets, the fly-merchant dope dealers that were here today and gone tomorrow, always out for a fast buck, the junkies in alleyways, endlessly waiting for the man to show up.

Somehow we all seemed so interconnected, part of a scene. If marijuana, or tea, wedded us together, the child was the language of Hip, which gave expression to abstract states of feeling, which we all shared, at least all who were Hip.

In the infinite variations of the new black jazz that stirred the soul and gave voice to our feelings of sensual pleasure, through the languid flow and spontaneity of bop, and the cool musicians who played it, we felt a deep affinity with the black man and the cultural dowry he brought with him, an ability to survive on the street with cunning and a consummate mental alertness so attuned to his surroundings that it must have derived from the art of the primitive.

Here I was, in my early twenties, almost a deft hand at street survival, picking up the nuances and cadence of a scene that I felt irresistibly drawn to. I lived through these years, and recall the events that took place as part of this Hip way of being, for a new breed of white urban adventurers drifted out at night looking for action with a black man's code to fit their facts.

Introduction to Allen Ginsberg

At the Megatripolis in Heaven Club, London, 19th October 1995:

It was on the 11th of June 1965, over thirty years ago, that I first heard Allen Ginsberg at the *International Poetry Reading* at the *Royal Albert Hall* in London. We turned up in our thousands to hear some of the best poets of the Beat Generation. When Allen Ginsberg stood up to read his poems you could feel an electric charge in the air. There he was, like an Old Testament prophet, with his long dark hair and bushy beard, his voice reverberating with emotional intensity. Never before in that hallowed hall had such outrageous and colourful language been heard. Someone shouted out from behind me, "Go back to the gas chambers". I saw a couple scurrying out with their children. Hearing Allen that first time was a revelatory and illuminating experience.

That event and his presence in London that summer, helped kindle the spark that set the underground movement alight in the mid-sixties.

But it was ten years earlier, on the 13th of October 1955, in San Francisco; at the first public reading of 'Howl' that Allen Ginsberg achieved fame and notoriety. Michael McClure, one of the poets reading that night, later told Allen that 'Howl' was his "metamorphosis from a quiet brilliant burning bohemian scholar, trapped by his flames and repressions, to epic vocal bard".

A decade earlier, during his student days, at Columbia University in New York, he formed life long friendships with Jack Kerouac, William Burroughs and Neal Cassidy. During those early days in New York the seeds were planted that would influence the literature and life-styles of young people for years to come.

I next saw Allen Ginsberg in London during the "Summer of Love" in 1967, when the flower children were in full bloom, at two memorable events; the *Congress of the Dialectics of Liberation* at the Roundhouse in Chalk Farm, and at the *Legalise Pot Rally* in Hyde

Park, where a policeman stopped him chanting and playing his harmonium, as it broke park by-laws.

Earlier that year, in January 1967, Allen together with Timothy Leary chanted mantras at the *Human Be-In* at the Golden Gate Park in San Francisco where thirty thousand people assembled for a "Gathering of the Tribes", with music supplied by *The Grateful Dead* and *Jefferson Airplane*. Allen Ginsberg was accepted as an elder statesman of the 'Counter-Culture', one of the few older people the hippies thought they could trust.

It was purely by chance that I went along to hear Allen and his long-time lover Peter Orlovsky, at the Roundhouse one cold November evening in 1979, and was touched by Allen's spiritual warmth and gentle serenity. I came away with two books that would lead me on a great voyage of discovery. One of them was *'As Ever'* the collected correspondence of Allen and Neal Cassidy, dating from the forties to Neal's tragic death in the sixties. The other was *'Indian Journals'*, Allen's notebook writings, dream fragments and night thoughts written during his trip to India with Peter in 1962/3.

As you can imagine, it is a great privilege for me to help bring Allen to *'Megatripolis'* in *Heaven*, and introduce him to a new younger audience, here in the heart of London, a short distance as the crow flies from the street where his beloved William Blake wrote *'Songs of Innocence'*, two hundred years ago.

I shall always remember Allen's rendering of *'Who Be Kind To'* at the Royal Albert Hall in 1965. Let me quote a fragment of the poem: "Tonight lets all make love in London as if it were 2001 the years of thrilling god. *Bom Bom Mahadev!*"

Welcome Allen Ginsberg.

Afterword:

"If you missed this event, you missed a moment of history[4]. Ginsberg was in fine form at the tail end of a hectic visit to London. The place was packed, the audience mixed (mostly NewGen with a representative sample of Beats, Post moderns, and media Notables), and the atmosphere electric. The question-and-answer session - held upstairs after the

---

[4] YouTube clip of Ginsberg reading at the event (from DVD): http://www.youtube.com/watch?v=rlJWIKvapzA

formal reading of poetry - was filled to overcapacity, temperature hitting fainting level... and what was originally scheduled to be an half hour stretched to an hour, ending at the stroke of midnight, both Ginsberg and the audience transcendent.

A film crew captured the evening's action (tentatively to be broadcast on Channel 4), and Anne Cosentino handled the live Internet coverage. If you missed this live, don't miss it on the wire.

Henry W. Targowski (in *Mark/Space*, Friday 20 October).

Extracts from Buzz Buzz

A one-act play in 7 scenes. Performed at The Unity Theatre, Oval House and Toynbee Hall, London, 1966:

Scene One

A derelict site in Soho, It is early evening, two old tramps are talking.

Man 1: I put a bob each way on Rufus in the 3.45.

Man 2: Good horse that.

Man 1: Stood at the post though, it did. Bad day for Rufus.

Man 2: Good horse that.

Man 1: Came forth. Last time.

Man 2: Fine horse, Rufus.

Man 1: Good horse that, twenty-to-one. Good outsider.

Man 2: It's the luck of the game that counts.

Man 1: This geezer I knows, he tells me it cant go wrong.

Man 2: Stood at the post, Rufus did.

Man 1: Stood at the post, Rufus did.

Man 2: Either you've got it you haven't.

Man 1: What?

Man 2: Luck.

Man 1: It's all in the game. Me, I'm a sport.

Man 2: It's the only thing to be.

Man 1: Always have been. It's my way. Don't believe in quibbling, like. You know what I mean?

Man 2: You're straight, you are.

Man 1: It's the only way to be. Always have been straight as they'll let you be. There's no other way for me.

Man 2: Got a fag?

Man 1: Not like them scrubbers.

Man 2: Fag?

Man 1: Scrubber, slags, call them what you will. They're all the same underneath.

Man 2: Paddy, fag?

Man 1: Brasses, scrubbers, slags, all in the same boat, like.

Man 2: Painted with the same brush, like.

Man 1: Ay! What?

Man 2: Like you says, all in the same boat. That's right, isn't it? It's what you were saying, isn't it?

Man 1: If you're talking of scrubbers, you might as well classify them what-you-call-its as well.

Man 2: In the same boat, like?

Man 1: Just as bad.

Man 2: Them what-you-call-its?

Man 1: Yes, them what-you-call-its, I mean them thing-a-me-bobs. You know them sorts

Man 2: I must know them. You mean them, uh...

Man 1: Yes, them uh...

Man 2: Them uh... scrubbers is in the same boat, like?

Man 1: Exactly!

Man 2: Them prostitutes.

Man 1: What?

Man 2: Them uh... like you says... them girls... them scrubbers. In the same boat like.

Man 1: I said them scrubbers, didn't I?

Man 2: All alike.

Man 1: I mean them Conner's, them blags, them ponces.

Man 2: I've got no time for a ponce, me, myself, like.

Man 1: It's not straight.

Man 2: Fag?

Man 1: Them blacks too, with them hats.

Man 2: Them new hats.

Man 1: Them's the kind alright.

Man 2: Fag, Paddy?

Man 1: The whole lot of them will sell you down the river. No time for that lot.

Man 2: Paddy, fag? Fag, Paddy

Man 1: What?

Man 2: Paddy, fag on you? Fag end? Run out of them, you know. Got me own papers though. Baccy, bit of baccy is what I need.

Man 1: Fag, you say?

Man 2: Bit of baccy, to roll in me papers. Got me own. Like Oh yes, never without me own papers.

Man 1: Let me see (Puts his hand in his coat pocket) Fag, you say?

Man 2: To put in my papers.

Man 1: (Pulls out a handful of cigarette ends) Fag? Sure, I got tobacco here. (Carefully rummages through stubs, handing three over).

Man 2: (Taking them) It's good baccy, you got there. Good stuff.

Man 1: I don't take them if I don't think the tobacco is good, like (he picks the biggest stub out for himself, putting the rest back in his pocket).

He takes out his papers. Filling one of them with the tobacco from the end given to him. He does this with care, making a thin cigarette.

Man 1: Weather's breaking, like.

Man 2: Rain's what I don't like. Makes you wet.

Man 1: Good for the earth, on the roads, like. Good for them grass in the parks.

Man 2: Oh, its good for them grass, alright. It waters them. It's the rain I don't like.

Man 1: They needs them rain in the country. On the farms, like. The land needs them rain.

Man 2: Too much for me. It pours, like. This country has too much rain. The trouble is we don't know what to do with all them rain. It's not right.

Man 1: It's not like abroad, though.

Man 2: Them foreigners is lucky.

Man 1: Them yanks is flashy. That's where them money is. It's in dollars.

Man 2: Light, Paddy? Match?

Man 1: Lights both cigarette.

For a while they meditate, enjoying their smoke with long puffs.

Man 1: Wall Street, that's where the money is.

Man 2: Wall Street, you say?

Man 1: Yes, they keep them dollars in Wall Street.

Man 2: Where's that... what you call it... this Wall Street? That's right, them Wall Street where they keep them dollars?

Man 1: That's the place, alright.

Man 2: Them Yanks have it?

Man 1: Sure, sure. Them Yanks got it easy.

Man 2: Not like here though.

Man 1: It's a place, like.

Man 2: What?

Man 1: It's a place, like. Same as anywhere.

Man 2: Not a bad place. Not too bad.

Man 1: Too many foreigners. Wogs, blacks, Greeks, café owners.

Man 2: It's them Jews what are letting them in.

Man 1: There's no room for them all. Where are they going to put them? There's no room anymore. It's all full up.

Man 2: No vacancies, like.

Man 1: It's all them guvnors fault. Taking on them foreign labour.

Man 2: Labour exchange is full up. It's them foreigners.

Man 1: It's them blacks, I tell you.

Man 2: They stand in the queue and wait. Takes their time, they do.

Man 1: With them hats on, new ones. In my opinion, it's the government. That's the way I see it. I told the major. I told him straight.

Man 2: You told the major?

Man 1: I told him straight.

Man 2: What did the major say about it?

Man 1: He says it's in God's hands. All sinners will be saved.

Man 2: Amen. He's a good guvnor, the major.

Man 1: One of the best. A dedicated man. One of God's chosen ones.

Man 2: He understands. I was in last night. Good kip. Had a dream, though. A sort of dream, like

Man 1: I was up East way, last night. Shoreditch.

Man 2: Shoreditch? Last night?

Man 1: Yes, Shoreditch.

Man 2: I was up Shoreditch last year.

Man 1: Yes, I was up Shoreditch way.

Man 2: It's me foot that plays up on me. Them bones is stiff. Them bandages, they're wearing out. My foot is swollen, I told the major. The right one, not this one, though. It's only this one that plays up on me. It'll be the death of me. I told the major. He sent me to them hospital. Out-patients, they calls it. All them blokes in white, doctors and all, standing there. I sits down on the bench. I gets a card, like. With my name on. The porter in uniform is by the door. They gives me this card and I goes to the bench and sits there for bloody ages, like. It's not the right bench, they tell me. I moves onto the other side and sits there for bloody ages. All them nurses running about, like. At last I comes up to the guvnor, them doctor who runs the joint. I says it's my leg that's swollen. He says he can't touch it. He tells me to go back and tell the major I must have a bath. That's what he says. I must bath my foot first. He says there are other people in the cubicles. Other people must go in the cubicles. That's what he says.

Man 1: A bath, he said?

Man 2: Yes, he says a hot bath.

Man 1: He's a right one then, what di you do?

Man 2: I walks out on him. It's all swollen. It's the right one. The other one's alright, though. No trouble from them other one. No trouble at all. I takes my time though.

Man 1: It's the only way to do it. No good rushing about. It gets you nowhere fast.

Scene Six

Dirty basement dive in Soho, well after midnight. Bimbo, and Sally-Anne are talking earnestly together. There is music coming from a jukebox. (There are one or two other youngsters about. Bimbo and Sally-Anne have cups of tea on the table in front of them. Sally-Anne is chewing gum. Bimbo is excessively talkative due to being blocked on pills. He is pouring out his heart.

Sally-Anne: It gets you down living on skippers, don't it?

Bimbo: Of course it does. I try to forget. I try to escape.

Sally-Anne: Try getting a job then.

Bimbo: How? Tell me. If I was to go to work on Monday,

I'd have no fares, nothing to come back to and no home. While I'm out at work, nobody'll be worrying if I'll be in for dinner. You eat in a café. There's nobody there. If I'd get affection, I'd get frightened because I'd play up on it. The same as with my mother. I wouldn't take so many liberties if I had the chance again. I'd be willing to stay in and watch the telly once in a while. Honest I would, I'm easily contented. I want to talk a lot. There's a helluva lot of talking I want to do. I've spent so many nights blocked, carrying on with small talk. It's getting me down, you know what?

Sally-Anne: I know exactly how you feel. It gets you down after awhile. What you need is friendship. Proper, like. Not this hanging about with Gingo. It's all escape, really, trying to cover up all the time.

Bimbo: The other night I got really blocked. I took forty pills. I didn't want to take them. I swear I sort of wanted to shoot away because I might make a fool of myself. It'd be all wrong because it's not really me. I've got a duel sort of complex when I'm blocked.

Sally-Anne: *(She sips her tea)* Have a sip of your tea, it's getting cold.

Bimbo: *(after having a few sips)* You know what I'd like to go up a school and talk to al the kids. I'd let them curse and swear, with no teachers in the class. I'd let all the smart guys shout, who want to do the shouting out, because I was one of them, you know. You can easily quieten them without using any psychology. I wouldn't hit them either. I'd give them hard facts in their own language. I'd let them have it in pornography. I'd tell them everything about life and it's dangers. What do you think brings all the kids together in these clubs? Loneliness and boredom, I'm not capable of lifting myself out of it. I need some help. What does it matter anyway? (He puts his head in his hands and looks away).

Sally-Anne: It does matter, Bimbo. It matters a lot.

Bimbo: Want a fag?

Sally-Anne: Yeh, Alright.

Bimbo: *(he takes one out and hands one to Sally-Anne, lighting them both).* It's funny, but I'd like to go back to school now, starting at primary school. When I was at school I didn't have a conscience, like. I didn't care what happened. They could hit me on the hand and I wouldn't mind. They used to give me ten slaps with the leather strap on the hand. I'd live on the hate of it all day. That's the way I used to be. If I went back to school, I think I could find myself now. I don't mean any real big discovery, but something I could be suited for. If someone had to come to me and say, this is a gem, a hit of a tune I've composed. The music is there, now you put lyrics to it. I bet you I'd do it better than most, because I know the words, I know the people. I've tried it several times. That's what I'd like to do. I'd like to be a songwriter but nobody gives you a chance, I want a break of decency, not of wealth, a decent break. Someone says to me, you deserve this.

Sally-Anne: You've only got to play up to people, you know that. It's the only way to do it.

Bimbo: That's what I mean; I hate this put on business. I've seen through it all. I really hate it. I've seen through these wealthy people with their airs and graces. They still put it on with money. They have what they want, right? Why can't they be themselves? They go round copying Lord so-and-so's ways and such a person's dress. It bothers me something terrible, like. The people who are well off and show it, like a Yank with a loud tie, that's who I don't like. It stands out a mile that they aren't what they think they are. The people that get ahead are the undeserving ones. I know a lot of wealthy people come from poor backgrounds. I think it's ridiculous telling someone you come from a poor background. That's a complex. They're trying to boost themselves up. Why can't I stick people? I put up with a lot of people when I'm blocked up but there are very few people I can stick for long. Women or men.

Gingo: *(Stimbles in, shaking and all on edge. He rushes to Bimbo and Sally-Anne. The pills he has taken are wearing off and he is "coming down")*. Bimbo, come with me, I want you...

Bimbo: Why, what's up?

Gingo: I want you to come with me.

Bimbo: I don't feel like moving. I'm stoned good and proper.

Sally-Anne: *(to Gingo)* What's hit you? You're stoned up to the eyeballs, aren't you?

Gingo: Bimbo, I said I want you to come with me. Listen to me when I talk to you, do you hear?

Bimbo: What do you want?

Gingo: Hell, what must I do, beg you or something? I need your help. It's this geezer, this tramp. I'm going to kill him. I swear it. I want you to come with me. Don't let me down. You're my mate, aren't you? Or are you?

Bimbo: Of course, I'm your mate. I don't follow you. You're all on edge. Now tell me calmly, what's happened?

Gingo: You're stalling time. I want to get my hands on him. The miserable git. Look, I'm going, are you coming?

Bimbo: Sure, I'm coming. but where? What's happened? Gingo? I've never seen you like this.

Gingo: *(sobbing)* He killed my brother. He killed Tom stone dead.

Let me get at him. He laughed. He's starkers, I tell you. He's off his rocker.

Bimbo: Who is? Gongo, come to!

Sally-Anne: I'm frightened. What's he saying?

Gingo: He was only a nipper. He did nobody any harm, Tom did. You saw him laugh to himself. He killed my little brother. I'm going to kill him. You've got to come, Bimbo. I need your help. I need it badly. Don't let me down, Bimbo. Whatever you do, don't let me down. I want you to stand by me.

Bimbo: Alright, Gingo. I'm with you. I won't let you down.

We'll get him. Who is it you want? We'll smash him up.

Gingo: It's that geezer, I tell you. That tramp we was having a laugh with, it's him.

Bimbo: You mean... you mean that sick old man?

Gingo: That's who I mean. That's what I'm trying to tell you all the time.

Bimbo and Sally-Anne look at each other in a horrified stupor. There is frenzied R & B music coming from the jukebox.

REALITY FREAKS vs SPACE CADETS

*"There is a difference between what
a person does and what happens by itself."*

Theatre of Change

International Times No. 44, November 1968:

There is a feeling of change in the air. A new vitality is creeping back into that old bag of bones called the theatre. Adrenalin is surging once more into those tired worn out veins and nice things are starting to happen.

Now that the Lord Chamberlain's powers of stage censorship have gone, we can celebrate the body as well as the mind. The excitement of live theatre is the physical process of other human beings made of flesh and blood, not just walkie-talkie models.

The theatre is a communal act-taking place at a given time between groups of people. All too often this communal act is dead, decadent and bourgeois, reflecting the society from which it emanates. But we want to change that society, and the theatre is as good a place as any to wage battle. I'm not for one moment suggesting burning down all those museums we call theatres; we need a few of those proscenium-arched structures to stage revivals.

But, what of now? We must go back to the living theatre of man, the human family; we must search out the human condition at its core, and this means going out into the streets, or in exploring in communication laboratories, whether they be warehouses, attics or disused railway goods depots, because this is where the theatre is at now.

Being part of a communal act means working, and often living as a group in order to understand our collective myths as well as our individual destiny. We must learn to think with our bodies and to feel with our minds in affirmation and celebration of love, life, peace and energy. Ideally all work is play.

The liberative artist lives in the mode of music instead of language. His entire activity is dancing, rhythm for its own sake; and in this way he becomes a vortex, which draws others into its pattern. He perceives life-rhythms and patterns, those hidden structures and currents that are free from sequential time, life-careers and stories: and like a flash of lightning gives us a personal or collective revelation. That is what the theatre is all about.

In Michael McClure's much awaited play *'The Beard'*, (late night show at the Royal Court) we get such a revelation. In a display of dazzling sexual fireworks he explodes in our faces with great humour and sensuality, the myth of two of America's favourite folk-heroes, Jean Harlow and Billy the Kid.

They confront each other in eternity; she, the bitch goddess, he, the virile all-American male. We are in no-man's territory of sexual desire, where destiny is to do what you want. McClure builds up his image sin repetitive, rhythmic patterns, using a simple word structure to convey the power of the flesh. Billie Dixon, as Harlow soars to the heights of hysterical vanity and protective aggressiveness, and then purrs, licking her wounds like a sullen kitten.

She is well matched by Richard Bright's performance as Billy the Kid. A whining, sleek animal who stalks his prey benignly in the knowledge that he will lick the pussy in the end. Rip Torn has directed this powerful piece of sexual theatre with a deep awareness of the inner rhythms inherent in the work. Let's hope the fuzz will not attempt to protect us from ourselves by closing down this play. Theatre is a communal act among consenting adults.

That includes homosexuals, whose relationships are explored in three current plays. Homosexuality can be seen as a protest against the repressive order of procreative sexuality.

Colin Spencer in his play, *'Splitting Image'* (Duke of York Theatre) beats that problem by allowing one of his characters, a young homosexual, to actually give birth to a baby. We then see the two fathers playing mother to their baby.

By imposing a heterosexual relationship onto a homosexual one, Spencer tries to make us aware that there is nothing queer about two males living together as husband and wife. It is well written and luckily, doesn't take itself too seriously. There are some very funny moments, and it culminates with talk of hundreds of 'homosexual mothers' popping up all over England, a field day for homosexuality.

'Fortune and Men's Eyes' by John Herbert, (Comedy Theatre) is set in a prison for young offenders. A newcomer arrives in his cell and has just enough time to say 'I'm not queer' before he is seduced by the bragging butch who wants to be his old man, but then Queenie, an outrageously bitchy male whore, tricks the boy into screwing her.

By this time he is thoroughly bent and he ends up trying to make it with Mona, a gentle, somewhat masochistic queen. It is both funny and moving, though at times it drifts into the terrain of the gay novelette. Al Mancini gives a memorable performance as Queenie.

This play was the opening production at the *Open Space Theatre*.

Paddy Chayevsky's *'The Latent Heterosexual'* (Aldwych Theatre) is another interesting piece of theatre. A gay, junkie poet who has made his fortune from one book, after spending twenty-five years writing 'Swiftian satire' and 'the lyric poetry of Blake', gets himself formed into a corporation to evade heavy taxation. He loses both his gay and junk habit in the sanctity of his corporate identity. Stripped of his senses, he gains an 'inner sense of numbers' from his soaring profit balance sheets. He goes mad and is transformed into a sacrificial offering to the god Mammon.

These plays deal with sexual themes in a way, which is new in the theatre, and three of them began their life in non-commercial or experimental theatres. It is from the best of these communication laboratories that the new theatrical experience will emerge; from dedicated groups working together like Julian Beck's *'Living Theatre'* and Grotowski's *'Polish Laboratory Theatre'*. It will not happen overnight but the awareness that this is the best way of working is there.

J. Henry Moore and his *Human Family* are pursuing their ideal in a simple, direct way on the Continent. Peter Brook has already begun his work in conjunction with Jean Louis Barrault, a new company called *'The Wherehouse'* has been formed by Beth Porter, a former member of New York's *'Café La Mama'* troupe. There is also the *'Cartoon Archetypal Slogan Theatre'* (CAST), a guerilla street-group, Charles Marowitz's *'Open Space Theatre'*, the *'People Show'*, *'Inter-Action'*, and a host of others.

And then, of course, there is Jim Haynes' *'Arts Laboratory'*, an oasis of varied activities that change from day to day. I've known there to be some thirteen different events in one evening. During the last twelve months, over forty theatrical events have been put on; a magnificent achievement considering that the place isn't self-sufficient and doesn't receive any subsidies.

What is now needed is more open stage structures to house these groups. At present the Roundhouse offers the greatest potential, and it was good to see it used so effectively by John Arden in his latest work, *'The Hero Rises Up'*. Others are also becoming aware of the importance of this large, circular structure, such as Tony Richardson, who is going to mount a new production of *'Hamlet'* there, with Nicol Williamson playing the prince.

The *Arts Council* is well aware of these activities and is meeting in the near future to discuss ways of helping some of these groups financially. They will be severely tested, because no strings must be attached to the handing out of the purse. For today the role of the theatre is to challenge the accepted values of our society, not to confirm them.

Next year, in July, the *International Theatre Club* is sponsoring a three-week festival of avant-garde work by local and foreign companies, to be called *'Experimental London'*. By then a few more groups will have been formed. No doubt, most of these ventures will eventually fold up because of poor resources, mediocre ideas, and the lack of the will to work in harmony as a living unit.

Theatre is a communal act, whether it be holy or rough, and it must help change our society if it is to be of relevance in this day and age. If you want a revolution in theatre, form a group and go out and make one. For the time is NOW.

The Great Penis Question

International Times No. 52, March 1969:

What is it like being a woman? Are you forced to play a passive and submissive role in HIStory of MANkind? Jane Arden delves into these questions in the hope of finding women's identity, in her new play Vagina Rex and the Gas Oven, now at the Arts Lab.

Women are in a prison of their own making; they are the continual affirmation of men's potency. Even psychoanalysis is male-oriented with its jargon implying 'penis-envy' and 'castration complex'. In order that woman can be herself, man will have to take back his own masochistic qualities.

In weaving womb-like images, using song and creative light projects, we see a regressive fantasy of woman in search of her being, only to find the strangled foetal womb. The symbol of the gas oven is the total destruction of woman as fashioned in man's image.

It is a difficult subject to tackle and the production does not quite evoke the clarity of vision that's needed. The most successful moments are the organic fantasies where the group becomes amoebae and nude babies crawling out of a womb.

At these moments the piece opens up new exciting areas, taking on a mystical quality that is almost holy. Other moments are like unfinished shapes. Sheila Allen as woman, the resigned sufferer, the ventriloquist's dummy, the seductress stripper, personify both beauty and intelligence. Jack Bond has directed the play with imagination and perception.

Another interesting play is NARCOLEPSY, which was on at *The Little Theatre* in Garrick Yard. It was written by Momoko Hosokawa, a Japanese writer who died aged twenty-eight in a plane crash. It is a passionate demonic tragedy about a prostitute and her male prostitute son, an oriental variation on the Oedipus legend.

While the son lies on the ground writhing in a deep sleep, his mother recalls the nights spent with drunken sailors to earn money to keep her and her son, the horror of finding out that he also sells his body, her jealousy towards a girl who threatened to come between them, and his boyfriend that she has chased away.

With an obsessive intensity she is drawn to possess her son's naked body and it reaches a climax with her going down to him giving him a maternal orgasm.

Theatricks

International Times No. 48, January 1969:

It was to Sweden that I had to look for some lively and magical moments in the theater. Two companies, one from Gothenburg and the other from Lund, paid short visits to London over the festive season, brightening up our would-be theatre scene. After seeing them one wonders why so little emanates from here.

Theater Fem, a group which has extended from the *Gothenburg Students' Theater*, presented an evocative piece called *'CIRKUS'*, conceived by Hakan Strangberg, at the *Open Space Theatre*. It was by far the most ingenious of the work done at the open space. Using loud and varied musical sounds, creating an aura of excitement and chaos, they subtly caught some of the images and pathos and laughter that remain with us from childhood, suddenly I was thrust back into that fantastic world of clowns and tightrope walkers, brass bands and cruel self-conscious laughter which is the circus. The amusing part of it all is that so little actually happens.

A mad violent clown shouts in gibberish at the audience and then throws himself around covered in a red cloth to some music from Tchaikovsky. Then two white-faced clowns come on and just stare at the spectators in stern silence until the theatre is utterly still. A tightrope act turns into a violent bout of rage with the mad clown kicking and knocking about the ringmaster, until he is subdued into a bundle of fear and bruises.

Not even the spectators are safe from this clown as he roams around looking for victims among us. He might turn viciously on an unsuspecting woman who has laughed at him, poking her in the breast or snatching her handbag, displaying the contents, at one moment he is tied up on a cross, pathetically crying for help and just when all is lost, Donovan's *'Mellow Yellow'* is played with all the other performers dancing about. It is a magnificent moment.

Out of this confusion and mayhem we glimpse at man, the clown laughing adversity in the face. At the height of the human comedy there is tragedy, violence and despair awaiting us. The circus becomes the image of man's passing show. It ends with the clown in a mad rage chasing the ringmaster round the theatre, with the other performers trying to calm him down, But all is just a game and the pageant rolls on in celebration to life. The audience has been liberated and they all came forward to dance in the acting area is if they were in a good party. It was done with great simplicity, appealing to the child in us all.

The other offering, from the *'Lilla Teaten'*, Lund, was Tuli Kupferberg's 'morality play' *FUCKNAM*, which was done at the Arts Lab. Anyone who really digs *The Fugs'* horny humour had plenty here to laugh about. His Yankee soldiers in Vietnam are grotesquely caricatured with huge pricks adorned in the stars and stripes. Their bombing raids turn into beery masturbation ecstasies. Television commercialises violence and war. Napalm has become popular and everybody is using it. The Saigon brothels are doing a roaring trade.

There is a hilarious scene with an American officer and his coarse wife having a meal. They spew out loud vulgarities and end up eating their own child. He makes his point that war is a substitute for a sexually repressed society. Technical effects, such as projection, were haphazard and gave a rough edge to the proceedings.

Many in the packed audience were so busy trying to show that they weren't shocked by the nudity and open sexual play that I feel they must have missed the point. For in the discussions that followed the play, people were interested to explain that it didn't shock them. Are we becoming immune in our 'coolness'?

Sex and the Theatre

International Times, 1968:

We live in a sexually-repressed society, despite all the talk of permissiveness. Who is permitting what, and to whom? Permissiveness is a hangover from Victorian times, an extension of the notions of morality.

A sexually free and liberated society begins with the idea of the awareness of each individual's unique and separate needs and desires. We have different relationships with different human beings on different levels. As long as these relationships do not harm anybody else, they should be socially acceptable. Male and female are polarities in a vast and unexplored territory.

With the abolition of censorship, I forecast that the theatre will begin to explore this tabooed area of human relations with a vengeance. Up to now, sex in the theatre has been treated as a source for dirty jokes, double entendres over cocktails in the drawing room, or for opening and closing doors in bedroom farces. You could write plays about sex as long as they weren't too serious and were the stuff of comedy and human folly. It's the old story about the fat lady who slips on a banana skin; if its funny then it is acceptable.

Sex, treated seriously, became over-earnest and we had the social problem play with long speeches abstractedly intellectulising an essentially emotional experience. Only in the last decade has the ban on homosexuality been lifted in this country's theatres. The plays on the subject that followed served the purpose of making homosexuality more acceptable to the host community. They were people you felt sorry for, who couldn't help what they were. It reeked of permissiveness. Nudity and erotic behavior were hinted at or talked about, but that was as far as it went.

If you could have said that England was a nation of small shopkeepers, with equal validity you could say that we had a theatre of stock characters. Up to the mid-fifties there were the working class stock types - the butler, the maid or the gardener - comic relief, the lot of them. Fortunately, with the turn of time, these figures of fun have disappeared and we are now left with the sexual stereotypes. These are to name a few, the mistress, the prostitute, the queer, the femme fatale or dumb blonde, and the antiseptic lover boy. If you churn them all up together, imagine the farcical or light comedy situations that would arise.

Today we have a new comic stock type - the drag queen. Thanks to the inimitable Danny La Rue, the door is now open for every self-respecting drag queen to come on and do her thing. Transvestism as part of the human comedy, an all-time high in camp theatre. A sop to the idea of permissiveness.

Even the language of sex was forbidden fruit, you could now read sexual epithets in novels, but they were not to be spoken on stage. Another Victorian hang up about being seen and not heard. Now some of these words were being spoken as expletives on stage rather than used their sexual meaning. They are never verbs or nouns only descriptive adjectives. In the revival of *'Look Back In Anger'*, Jimmy Porter calls his wife Allison, 'a fucking cow'. In *'Hair'*, one of the tribe shouts out about this 'fucking world'. Until we hear the word 'fuck', and all those other 'naughty' words, spoken in their sexual context, the theatre, like our society, will still be permissive, and that does not mean liberated!

As for nudity, it has been left to the strip-clubs to free the human form and only the female body at that. The naked body in motion, at a private club, has been permitted for just a decade. The onanistic image of the lone stripper doing her set thing in three obvious stages has made the stripper the stereotype for conveying nudity, catering for the whims of tired businessmen, is another aspect of 'permissiveness' that must be liberated.

Inhibition and repression, on a societal and individual level, have imposed a form of self-censorship on playwrights, resulting in a quantative as well as a qualitive restriction of sexuality. To hail pornography and obscenity as modes of art is to play the game of permissiveness. What is known as pornography is the subterranean level of that which has been repressed. The practice of permissiveness, instead of conscious and radical revaluation of values in our society, leads instead to the gimmicks of dress and undress and other forms of release.

Sexuality is by nature 'polymorphous-perverse'. What are tabooed as perversions are often expression of rebellion against the repressive order of procreative sexuality, and the institutions which guarantee this order. Fantasy, as artistic imaginations, links the perversions with images of integral freedom and gratification. In our repressive society, pleasure for its own sake appears as *fleur du mal*.

Theatre, like the other performing arts, has to be liberated from the bondage of concepts and ideas that belong to the last century. If the theatre is to be revelatory and visionary in its outlook, it must be aware that sexual impulses and erotic energy transcend to relationships between individuals and their environment. Artistic work, where it is genuine, grows out of a non-repressive instinctual constellation and envisages non-repressive aims.

Hair Roots

International Times October 1968:

Lee Harris talks to Tom O'Horgan, director of HAIR.

Lee Harris: Tell us how HAIR came about or how you became involved with it.

Tom O'Horgan: The writers of the show approached me about two years ago, saying that they had written this musical and were going to produce it. At that time I was just leaving on one of the *La Mama* tours on to London and the Edinburgh Festival.

After I came back from that particular tour, *HAIR* was about to be produced at the *Joseph Papa Theatre*, which is off Broadway. I went to see it and it was a successful production. The policies of that particular theatre are somewhat gentler than the writers of HAIR wanted it to be; at the time they spoke of a Broadway production and it seemed pure fantasy at that moment. There isn't much of a history of shows moving from off-Broadway to Broadway, to begin with; anyway from there it moved to a discotheque called the *Cheetah* and it didn't have too great a success because they didn't prepare for the *Cheetah*, they just moved it there. So it closed and I thought that's the end of that. Then I was approached by a complete different source. One of the producers who I'd worked with before asked me to do this show they were doing for Broadway. I said what is it, and they said *HAIR*, so it just seemed as if I was fated to be involved in it.

Usually the notion is to clean a show up for Broadway and make it more Disney-like, but in this case we got back to where the nitty-gritty of the thing was, the real ideas, and tried to go with it that way. It was kind of a love affair as far as I was concerned. I thought it was significant myself to do something to jar that institution called Broadway into some sort of mouth-to-mouth resuscitation.

LH: Is there no way of smashing the commercial set-up that is Broadway?

TO'H: Well I think there is, I think we have to find new types of theatres. That's what it's about. The kind of thing Jim Haynes is doing at the Arts Lab. The things *La Mama* are doing; it has opened a whole new view. 'Off-off-Broadway' just said; 'screw that, we are going to make a kind of theatre that is for artists and people who are really interested in theatre.' Equity say we are putting a lot of professional actors out of work but in reality it has created more theatre, more living, interesting professional theatre than the other establishment routes. Ellen Stewart of *Café La Mama* produces about fifty or sixty new plays a year. The important thing is to be able to produce and give new people the chance to see their work being done. The crap that is put on in the name of professional sense is astounding.

LH: Where would one trace back the germs of the ideas now going on?

TO'H: What's happening in the theatre today is indicative if what's happening in all forms of life, all social revolutions. We've just had it with the old two-faced ideas, the theatre cannot exist as it has in the past. We've just got to pass that over and go onto something else, to find out where the theatre really exists.

A lot of people were so dissatisfied with the kind of double language and so forth that they banded together writing new plays and having new ideas, with new kinds of acting involved.

LH: The visionary aspect of drugs like acid, have they played any part in the ideas and freedom in the writing and images now being presented?

TO'H: I think a lot of expanded vision has come from LSD; many writers have utilized this fruitfully to loosen themselves up. Many writers today are using many different stimuli; just the stimulus of the period we're in is a turn-on for people, the license to say what they really feel is encouraged by the activity of all the anti-establishment movements. The time has now freed people, we're saying things that are closer to what we feel, and hopeful we can get to the real root of the thing.

LH: You use a lot of dance and music in your work.

TO'H: I really believe in the total experience of the theatre; I've just begun to get into it. I think that dance and song and the playing of instruments are part of the basic stream the theatre came out of, the ritual that was, when early man came home and tried without language to explain what his day was like to his family. He did it by singing, dancing and miming, any way he could, and that became a kind of theatre. That's what the essence of it about, trying to communicate something in some way. The beautiful part about now is that everyone is open to every form of communication. We've certainly worked in mysterious ways trying to further that idea. I think the theatre in general is a kind of laboratory of communication.

LH: Tell us about the new sexual ground covered in the theatre.

TO'H: I think the uni-sexual notion is really what's finally being started for the first time in the theatre. I mean more equality of the sexes, and sexual practices in general are not subject to the morals and taboos of yesterday. The whole notion today is what you do is your thing and that's that. It need not infringe upon me as long as in some way it does not hurt me. *HAIR* is a very good example of that kind of relationship, we bar nothing on the stage as far as the inference of sexual behavior is conceived. Yet it is possibly the most naïve child-like piece you'll probably ever see. That famed nude scene is possibly the most innocent and is certainly one of the most tasteful things in the play. The whole question of nudity is crazy, for if you condemn it you will have to condemn all the renaissance art because it was all done for the very same reasons, because we are in love with each other and we love the sight of another human being. I mean, I would hate to throw out all the Blake paintings because you're afraid of a human form.

LH: What do you think of happenings?

TO'H: Well I think that as a pure idea, it has passed. I now like to write very freely with a writer, he brings his material and we work on it and he looks at it and goes away and writes some more, and we come back and do things with it; we give him ideas and he gives us ideas and it becomes a more cooperative venture. I think that's where the reality of the theatre has always been.

LH: The whole notion of going to the theatre seems to be working.

TO'H: We really want an environmental situation - when you arrive the play has already begun. I would love to have people when they buy tickets to be part of the play. It should start then, somehow. Going to the theatre should be a total life experience. The beginnings and ending are so formalized in our minds now. It starts at eight-thirty - bang, the show begins.

LH: You are using English actors in *HAIR*. Does this pose any difficulties?

TO'H: Well it's a completely different quality. They are English people playing Americans. Generally speaking the English youth is somewhat gentler than the New York kid. That works well for this play because it's a play about love.

LH: The hippie's credo is fast changing, and the heightened period of the past summer is over. Will this make *HAIR* somewhat dated?

TO'H: Well who knows, maybe next summer will be even more so? I don't think it's going to get less, a lot of people are worried about where they are because it's not going to remain the same!

Notes on Love Play

International Times No. 56, May 1969:

What to do that is self-justifying when the great social world is unavailable? Heighten experience and get out of one's self. The process of putting *'Love Play'* down on paper was an odd and accidental experience; it was like trying to re-live a dream. The ideas changed so fast that I couldn't keep up with them. How did it all start and when? It is difficult to say.

It was during my first acid experience that I saw the shape emerging for the first time. My setting was in a dive with the deadbeats living a never-ending turn. The comings and goings, the endless search, for what? I asked this of myself but could not find an answer. All I could get was a mood, a feeling.

From Marcuse's *'Eros & Civilisation'*, a theoretical concept emerged. It was an entirely new experience. It was a journey inwards, delving into images and symbols that I was unable to decipher at the time.

I became bogged down and submerged in the weird mood and cadence of my dream-like figures. Sometimes I wondered what others might think of me after seeing it. Were these emerging figures a projection of me and my environment? Do I see people reacting like my characters? I just did not know, I saw my scenes like strange apparitions, twisting and writhing, as if they were never said before. Does that make sense? It is not an intellectual play: there are no rational actions. It was a spiritual experience, which could not be analysed so easily. How little others will understand who look for meaning where none was intended.

To me it was more than a play. It is the culmination of a cycle and the beginning of a new one. I lived through an era in order to wipe my slate clean, to re-authenticate myself. Where better to start than the dives and hellholes of society? Living with people committed to the underworld, peddlers of flesh and weavers of dreams. There were cathartic experiences that opened the gates of regression. I saw neither males nor females, wantons of the flesh, nor virgins, naivety nor worldliness. These were slippery roles that played every game, intertwining from one to the other. The play is emotional revelation; piecing the sore wounds that we try to hide. It is about people at that moment where time seems to stand still. We see them in all their vulnerability for a penetrating flash. It is incestuous in a way that the family is. It is a game of revelation, played by people who know the games played at that moment when desire transforms them into their secret and private selves.

Structurally, I wanted to transcend the everyday reality and go beyond naturalism - beyond sequential time. I was looking for another reality - a dream reality. My characters are twilight people living in the area where madness meets the social reality of our lives. In this domain there are no life careers, only life rhythms, no exposition only explosion, no story, only pattern. Time and space are dismembered. It is a response from the beyond, but the voice must be there in order to hear the echo. There is internal pressure under the surface tension

My sounds and moods are those of the disintegrated language of 'high', which is the mode of music, dance and painting. I have tried to integrate these in a total conception of theatre. I have been influenced by the language of pop music, the movements of modern dance and the abstract in art.

Love Play

A lyrical fantasy.

Love Play was written with the assistance of an Arts Council bursary and was produced at the Arts Laboratory on Drury Lane London on the 13th-27th May, 1969.

'Poppy's Monologue, An extract from Love Play

THE FLOWER POPPY

Poppy slowly comes forward, as they cheer her on and give her confidence. The long monologue is said to the audience. As she starts it, the others slowly walk off, telling her to go on with it.

>**ALL:** Give it to them, Poppy. Let them have it. Give them the works. Do your own thing, baby. You're on your own now.
>
>**POPPY:** I am the flower, poppy, and I do my own thing. A jaded flower, some may say, but I say otherwise. Why? Wouldn't you? I've been around and I've seen a bit, quite a bit. Wouldn't you have done the same, if you could? Come on, out with it. Let's all be open here because that's what it's all about. It's about you and me.
>
>   I mean, all of us. We drop our drawers and we do our own thing. Well, at any rate, that's what most of us do. I could go on pretending, but what for? Playing your game and your game and your game, and can I play games. After all, I'm a born actress. A rare breed, nowadays, right from the cradle, that seedbed of love and destruction. Mind you, I love your games. I've been playing them long enough. But I want to come clean and play it straight, for a change, and see what I'm all about. I know what you're thinking. She's washing her dirty linen in public. God, you straight people get very uptight, I was forgetting. Well relax

and cool it, it's not the end of the world. I'm not going to frighten the children, if there are any here. I was one myself, once. Oh so many years ago. What was I on about? Oh yes, myself, my favourite topic. Narcissus, I am yours, do what you like with me. Ravish my senses and plunder my memory. Look into my here and now, and tell me what you see? A multiplicity of selves, to keep myself intact, for years I was a queen, dragging away in motley succession of wigs and dresses, trying to find myself, in an embrace with myself. Identifying with other queens, princesses and dowager duchess, at nocturnal vigils in unseemly quarters of the city. Glorifying in a parody of what I would like to be. But often the wig did not suit the pose. Dauntlessly, I would wander forth into the night and indulge in fools' play. Fooling the men of the species that want to be fooled. For the right price I could be all things to all men who so desired it, I learnt to cover up my shy glances by painting a bold face. I hid behind a multitude of clichés that I'd picked up in order to cover myself. I was a word acrobat, par excellence. I even fooled myself sometimes, and had to check myself, lest I get lost in the paraphernalia of it all. It was a gift I had acquired. The exception to the rule, that ladies are born, not made. I was a self-made lady, a woman of the world. A product of a highly-developed society but it wasn't always like this, far from it. Once in the days of Hades, where Orpheus romped with Eurydice in the Elysian Fields with the ever-watchful glance of Cerberus guarding over them, then surely I was born. Trapped in a shell not of my own making, I was forced to live out the fantasies of my doting sires. It was then the battle began. What was I? True, outwardly I was a boy and grew up as such with genitals and all. But in my emotional and mental make-up, I blossomed into a girl. A coy and rather shy one, with physical manifestation, I had butterfly hands that flickered and flustered gently about me. I sat with my knees together. But I was a boy, and oh brother, what a boy. Can you imagine what it was like being a girl with the body of a boy? Forget it, its way outside your norm of experience. Don't trouble your imagination because it will only threaten you and make you feel insecure. I can assure you, that is not my motive in telling you all this. I don't believe in shock tactics. Why, if I wanted to, I could give you a clinical investigation into the intricacies of my anatomy, but what for? To give you men a cheap thrill or unnerve the ladies present? You straight people know how to get your vicarious kicks without little me adding to them. There's a whole list of socially-accepted perversions for you to indulge in. You can fondle cars or kick balls about; the ladies can paint their faces and clothe their bodies in silky sheens. So as I say to you fellow fetishists, don't let me bother you. Wait a minute, wait a minute! I sense a vibration in the air. Someone present is feeling flushed and hot by all this vulgar parading of personal fantasies and private parts. They fear the opening of Poppy's box of secrets. Gorgeous! Delicious! Just what I wanted, a secret reaction, an onanistic tingle! Hail, fellow masturbator, wherever you are! We share a common desire. The wank is the secret of our desire. It opens our fantasy portals where all is profane. The past reveries are conjured up in whichever order we choose. We are magicians, by profession, sallying forth with repressions and taboos. The unattainable is at the mercy of our personal seductive whims. Even the virginate is not sacred. Bear with me; artist of desire, all is not lost. Your clarion call found an echo in me. Let us ride our wanking chariots. Now that I've made you feel at home, you can join us. You see how benevolent I am? But let me not digress or become bloated by my seeming lack of humility. I am, after all is said and done, a freak. I grew into a sturdy male despite it all. By the time I had reached twenty, my facial hairs were bristling and down below I was built like a donkey. But it was of no avail to me. It was a cumbersome object that I was none to proud of. A reminder of the boyhood I never knew. I worked at various jobs that no self-respecting lady would be seen dead doing. I was a steward in the Merchant Navy, and a waiter at a seaside hotel. I even worked for British Railways, and on the London to Scotland express. Always playing a role, like those Victorian music-hall artistes. Masquerading was my business, my furtive way of life. I had perfected the art of transvestism to a T. If any of you are trying to suppress your mocking laughter, let me assure you that it is a high art. Not unlike all great art, it is an exacting discipline that takes its toll. Needless to say, I was laughed at, scorned and shunned. I learnt to live by night. Not for me the bright glare of daylight. My days gave way to nights and I became a nocturnal hunter and the prey, a victim of my own circumstances. The end was inevitable, the slow transition to the body female. For a time I was a hermaphrodite. With treatment I developed firm, pointed breasts that any women would be proud of. I would spend hours in front of the mirror, toying with them. Wouldn't you have done the same? But it was not enough. I wanted to be castrated. I became obsessed by it. The hollow penis, take me... take me, somebody! But no one came. I wanted to worship at the altar of phallus, to be taken as other women are. I wanted it off, to be rid of it once and for all. So I had my phallectomy. I went through with it, thinking that I would now be complete, an integral whole, an organic miracle of our time. But it was not to be so, for there was no orgasm, no satisfaction. Like being in a sea that's never calm, that holds no peace. Adrift in the mainstream of life, playing your game and your game and can I play games. Don't pity me, whatever you do, because I am the flower poppy, and I do my own thing. Why? Wouldn't you? I've been around and I've seen a bit, quite a bit. Wouldn't you have done the same, if you could?

If you could, wouldn't you have done the same?

Moving Statics

International Times No. 52, March 1969:

The abstract kinetic art of the Dutch mime Will Spoor. This half-hour film is a brilliant fusion of the art of abstract mime and creative film techniques, presenting a visually exciting conception of the body as a musical instrument.

Will Spoor sees mime as the art of not moving, a form that has a meaning in itself. Technique, to him, is articulation and the body is a supple or rigid object stripped down to its essentials.

The film knowingly moves into the images and ideas of Spoor and his group, expressing their actions with great fluidity by superimposing, animating and speeding their body movements.

This creates a visual dimension that is dynamic and never less than fascinating. The process of creating body images and forms in an abstract kinetic shape is exploding with dedicated intensity.

Spoor's visual talent and sense of perception has been beautifully caught here. It is always interesting observing an artist at work, striving to show people something they don't know about yet.

Through this film, Will Spoor pays homage to the genius of his mentor, Etienne Decroux. *Moving Statics* is a beautifully made film by Arthur and Corinne Cantrill that deserves to get as wide a viewing as possible. Will Spoor's work is already known to those who saw him give many performances at the Arts Lab.

The Fletcher File

The original press release read:

> On Sunday 5th February 1967, at the Roundhouse, Chalk Farm, 'Columbus Arts Productions' presents "The Fletcher file", adapted by Lee Harris from John Taylor's dossier.

Alice and Roy Fletcher are now serving their sixth year of a life sentence for murder. John Taylor, a former prisoner, met Roy Fletcher in H.M. Prison, Wormwood Scrubs and has spent three years collecting information and new evidence to prove the innocence of the Fletchers. Transcripts of the Brief and Appeal, together with fresh evidence and detailed arguments establishing the Fletchers' innocence were sent to the Home Secretary on the 26th. October 1966. So far the Home Office have responded with silence. Similar documents were sent to the *European Commission of Human Rights* in Strasbourg together with an application that the case may be referred to the European Court.

John Taylor's dossier has been edited and adapted by Lee Harris, who has just been awarded an Arts Council Bursary on the recommendation of the drama panel. The event is staged by American J. Henry Moore, a young director who has worked as assistant to Jim Haynes at the *Traverse Theatre* Edinburgh.

This is 'Theatre of Action' rather than 'Theatre of Fact', in that it is not a post-mortem nor a moral judgement, but an explication and an incitement to act. *'The Fletcher File'* is a three-act play - in two acts. The third act must be enacted by the audience.

The Fletcher File: An approach to the theatre of information, by Lee Harris

Public meetings can be entertaining as well as instructive. The theatre can be and often is instructive and entertaining. The documentary programme on television, at its best, is an entertaining dispensation of information.

In preparing *The Fletcher File* I have been conscious of all three approaches in presenting facts as well as encompassing the background to the facts. In searching through John Taylor's dossier, I became aware not only of a grave miscarriage of justice, but also of the social setting that breeds crime, human misery and corruption. The events that heralded this tragedy are symptomatic of a deprived area in the big industrial city - racial prejudice, violence, prostitution and semi-illiteracy.

Surely this is an area the theatre can now explore in an informative manner, without the restrictions which television by necessity must impose. This is the way committed individuals can present facts that the power elite wishes to hide. For in opening these wounds we throw the onus back on to the authorities to put their house in order. Are your courts just? What about the police and their methods? What is being done about housing, immigration and education in our seemingly affluent society? These questions need urgent answers. A lot of people must pull their fingers out and stop being complacent. This is why there will be a "Theatre of Action".

Arts Lab Split

International Times, 1969:

The notice read:

> "They (Human Family) will stay at least until the day after Christmas. During this period, Jack will make the schedule and policy decisions. Anything projected for this period should be mentioned now as time and space will be minimally available throughout the entire building, which will probably be open around the clock.
>
> The overall policy envisioned in the last meeting is hopelessly horse-before-cart and we have vetoed all decisions. We feel that the financial problem is more a question of wise spending and fund raising than one of increased centralised control".

As a result of this notice, a group of Lab people have broken away to form another scene. The following four statements are meant to help clarify what is happening.

Jim Haynes

Basically from our early days we have had two factions - i.e. one group believed that our function was to serve art and artists; while the other considered our prime role to serve the people of the underground community.

A case can be made for both roles, and to a certain extent I have from the beginning attempted both. But in the past few months, pressures from both quarters indicated that one faction had to dominate; that attempting to serve both sides equally meant doing both a disservice.

The interval struggle came to a head only recently. Firstly, there appeared a statement in IT/43 (Arts Lab What's Happening) that 'Jim Haynes is looking for a flat or room in Chelsea' which was a suprise to me because (a) I cannot afford to rent a flat or room and (b) I am happy living in my 'cell' in the back of the lab.

Then at a routine staff meeting, a wave of new regulations were introduced, which would move the lab towards a more laboratory situation. This forced the issue. Now to make a long complex story very short, those members of the staff who wanted to create a laboratory situation have resigned, and hopefully they will find another building soon and will be able to do their thing. Let me say that I have the utmost respect for them and appreciation for everything they have done to help make the Lab a success, and that I will do everything I can to help make any of their ventures a success. Both concepts are badly needed. Ironically, London and all of us will benefit...

Here at the Lab now one finds a renewed sense of direction and a determination to make the Lab a greater contribution to the scene.

Some new developments (which we hope to have in operation by the time you are reading this) include: a restaurant in the back gallery open from noon until the wee hours; a notice board in the back gallery open to everyone to use; a market place in the front gallery open for goods and things; singing, dancing, happenings, films, theatre, *Third Ear Band*, *Wherehouse Theatre Company* etc, etc. Come and do your thing. (P.S We are open again all night on Friday and Saturday).

David Curtis

I have left the Arts Lab and would like to state some of my reasons. The initial Arts Lab as conceived by Jack and Jim, before they had even seen the Drury Lane building, had no place for anything as specific as cinema in it. They envisaged films alright but integrated like they were at UFO - Where I was arranging screenings at the time.

When I saw the basement at 182 I immediately suggested turning it into a cinema and starting shows there, even before we had the lease. I limited myself then to getting a cinema scene going, probably for no more profound reason than that; to think wider was beyond me. Recently I have emphasised the 'cinema' angle because that was the only way that I could guarantee, with OUR administration, that the film-makers would get their full 60% of the box office. (I am part of our admin, by the way.)

The function of the Lab cinema has been to give access to a screen to ALL independent film makers (I have never refused to show a film) and to build up an audience to support them. Also I hoped that the Lab would provide an obvious place for exchange of information. It seemed essential to me to stress both open access to facilities and an efficient organisation to back it eg, maintain the machines, schedule the performances and pay for films.

All the crises at the Lab have been about organisation. The policy of access is universally accepted, but should it be based on efficient administration or on some kind of wider social community scene? Jack's whole approach is based on the latter. Jim has just announced that Jack and the Human Family are to be in sole charge of all 'scheduling and policy' decisions in the Lab from Dec 10th. On past experince I do not believe that he can guarantee either the safety of films, or any financial return to anyone outside his family. So I feel obliged to withdraw, and setup regular open and scheduled screenings elsewhere.

I am hoping that any future scene we manage to establish will include workshops with access to a much wider range of media that we ever had at the Lab. It is essential that we emancipate the guys who work in TV and Radio etc, immediately, by showing them how to use their machines from OUTSIDE their mother industry.

Lee Harris

The *Arts Lab* is alive and well - evolving in a freer form. The space in the building is to be given over more to the people who use it.

Titular heads or control freaks have now become aware that this communication laboratory is as much for people as it is for artists.

For when Art becomes more important than people it is time to evaluate its function in relation to the community it serves. This is now being done by breaking down rigid schedules and structures. There will still be particular events in the two theaters and cinema.

At present a Czech experimental theatre group from Brno, called the *Quidam Theatre*, are presenting two plays from the 28th - 30th Nov. *The Warehouse*, a dynamic new theatre company, are giving their first performances from 26th Nov - 8th December. This will be a bill of work in progress, displaying their new theatre techniques, and in December, *The Human Family* will be returning from the continent with their free flow of energy. Real theatre is for open people.

The *Third Ear Band* and many other beautiful things are always around, so come along and use the *Arts Lab* because it is yours.

Will Spoor, David Jeffrey, Martin Shaan

During the past twelve months the main achievements of the Lab theatre has been the total number of the productions - probably in the vicinity of eighty and a number of performances, which must be nearer one thousand.

They have been music, poetry readings, theatre and mixed-media events, some of which have some to us from outside as complete units, some of which have been born in the Lab. Obviously, standards have varied, but apart from occasional lapses we have avoided the ordinary and some things have been unique and worthwhile. Several companies have based themselves on us and a few productions have toured Britain and the continent.

Problems and possible solutions: Because of pressure of numbers of productions, and consequent demands on time and space in the theatre, productions have had to sacrifice complex machinery, lighting etc., and developments in this direction. Any kind of environmental control has had to be minimal.

For some productions this has been unimportant, for others it has meant an unsatisfactory compromise. More important is that some schemes have been totally impossible and consequently abandoned. We wanted a fully flexible theatre but this has prevented it.

The technical department, though nominally in charge of the entire building, also had to run both theatres. Financial problems had a lot to do with this but it has impeded development in several directions, notably that of setting up an electronics workshop useful to people wanting to involve electronics in their ideas and work. Instead of being able to do this we have had to devote our time and talents to mere maintenance. Also, shows which are bad or mediocre and have to have a free audience virtually dragged in from the gallery space are a waste of everyone's time.

At the recent staff-meeting various suggestions were made concerning the future of the theatre and a plan was adopted incorporating the following improvements:

- All scheduling to be carefully coordinated.
- Productions were to be divided into two categories, the major of which would receive priority in demands on space, time and equipment.
- Those categorised as 'Workshop' would receive a minimal amount of time unless they showed promise.

We felt sure that this would raise the overall standard, reduce the credibility gap apparent in our publicity and that this would be appreciated by our members.

Under the new scheme imposed by Jim Haynes and Jack Moore, none of this will be possible.

Meat Sculptor

International Times No.46, December 1968:

These are edited extracts from a taped conversation, which Michael McClure had with Lee Harris and Bill Levy while he was in England.

McClure's theatre sympathies lie with the 'underground film' and with a vital new Elizabethan theatre for new audiences. Recently, McClure collaborated with George Montana in creating the sound track for Kenneth Anger's next film, and one of his more recent books is in collaboration with filmmaker and artist Bruce Conner. While in England McClure and Rip Torn, The Beard's director, discussed doing a film of the great American naturalist James Audubon with McClure in the starring role.

I have been living in San Francisco now for 14 years. I was born in Kansas, and then lived in Seattle and Arizona.

The Beard was done first in Fullerton State College in the middle of Orange County (California). They're doing the play right now in Munich without my permission, with Picasso's play. I got a letter from an arts theatre in Tel Aviv that wants to do it, and it may be done in Scandinavia, I'm not sure. They have the rights to do it

The Beard is hard to explain without the poster. I was on an airplane going to Los Angeles; I had a copy of *Ring Magazine*, that is a boxing magazine, and over my head flashed that poster with a picture of Harlow and Billy the Kid as if they were contestants in a boxing match, and the whole poem in beast language. It was just there, and I made my trip to LA and I flew back to SF. On my way from the airport to my house I stopped at a liquor store and looked at the boxing poster to see what the company was that prints boxing posters. It was the Telegraph Press. When I went home, I got to bed and the next morning I got up and phoned Telegraph Press and the guy who runs it and I got to be good friends. He smokes a cigar, and he's very proletarian, he's one of the old Wobblies (early 20th century industrial anarchists). And I say I want to make a poem poster, like your boxing poster. So he says, 'Sure, sure kid, come on down'.

He said, 'we make lots of polo posters'. I said, 'No, poem poster'. He says, "That's all right, come on down, we'll do it'. So we went down and I took him this thing. And he looked at it and marked it up on a piece of paper. I asked him if he would do it and he said,

'Well, no'. I said, 'Why not?" He says, 'You young people don't know anything about Harlow, look at that, her neck's ugly in that picture'. I said, "You're right"

I went home and I spent three more days finding the right picture of Harlow. I took it down. He was chewing on a cigarette when I handed it to him. He said, 'Yeah, right. Bring it back in three days.' When I brought it back he wasn't there, there's like his assistant. I looked at the poster; it looked great, so I said - 'Right, great, print it'. I get home and I get a call from the guy telling me I got to okay the poster. I said 'That's okay. Print it'. He said, 'No you've got to come down here and okay it,' so I said 'All right,' so I go down there and he's sitting with the proof of the poster.

He says, 'Love lion, lioness. Right?' He says, 'Rose Silver Silver. Right?' 'Right! GAHR THY ROOH GRAHEER, two E's one R, right? GRAHHR whah gahhr den dreem ezz hrohh hrohhr, right?' We get down the bottom, he says, 'Grahhhr with three h's?' I say, 'Right.' He says 'Grahhr with two h's?' I say 'Right'. We go half way down the last part, the line with the grahhrs, and he turns to me and says, and 'What is this shit anyway?' I says, 'Well, it's a poem and I got a book with a hundred poems written in this language'. So he says, 'Oh, all right'.

So after that we used him for a lot of printing, and he kind of dug it, practically all he printed was boxing posters and racing magazines, and he had the whole inside of his shop lined with boxing posters... Oh... and the poster for the Rolling Stones, and The Beard poster. Everything else were his boxing posters, and he put it right up on his walls with the boxing posters.

Everybody would come in with their business, and he was always trying to work deals with me... like I should do another edition because he met this guy from Alaska who wanted to buy 50,000 to sell as souvenirs, and things like that, and I said, 'No, no'.

So then I took the poster home and the I realized I was going to put it in a liquor store window, and I realized that when you put posters in liquor store windows you give them complimentary tickets. So I went back down and I had the complimentary tickets printed, which were also in beast language, just like the boxing tickets, and then I went around to the liquor stores and I said, 'Can I put this in your window?' and they said 'Yeah'.

So I put them in the liquor store windows then gave them complimentary tickets. And then I took it home and put one on my wall, behind my head where I work, and it started projecting 'Billy the Kid' and Jean Harlow's voices to me, and I started writing the play, I'd no intention of doing it, but it began to project the play into my head. Billy the Kid and Jean Harlow came and acted it out inside my head. Then I typed it. Well, it was a funny thing because I've just done something else like it again for the first time. I worked on a novel in a month; because of circumstances I had to spend seven months writing it so I had to carry it in my head.

It's called 'The Adept'. An adept in alchemy is someone who has discovered how to transmute base metals into gold, so that's the title of that one, but I had to carry it in my head, like one time I couldn't type for six weeks on it and I had to start at the exact point where I left off, and when I was writing 'The Beard', I'd type, but it would take me about seven nights to do it, but then I would have to stop when Billy the Kid and Jean Harlow were not in my head anymore.

They were like 'solid', like opium, more than like opium conditions, they were there, you know, you could hear their feet and smell. I could here their words.

When they stopped, I had to stop and I wasn't at all sure about what I had done in the slightest like it was real, and I had to stop there and then I would have to wait 24 hours until the next evening at the same time to see if they would come back, not knowing if they would come back or not, so I would get very worked up during the day concerned whether they were going to be there that night when I was there, and they always were.

But that's the way I've written all my plays, except one. With the play they had to be there, I can't do it unless they're there. They've got to be there in three-dimensional meat speaking, not only speaking but doing it. It has a lot to do with obsession, too.

The first play I wrote was about Billy the Kid in 1959, and I did a tremendous amount of historical research in it. At first I was obsessed with Billy the Kid and Harlow and ended up with Billy the Kid and Jean Harlow obsessed with me. Like theatre is a matter of obsession.

I think they're obsessed with me. Jean Harlow would come and say her first line to me and I'd say I'm not going to get out of bed, and I wouldn't be able to go to sleep until I got up and wrote the poem. Then the next night Billy the Kid would come and would give me the first line and he wouldn't go away until I would get up and write the poem, then I would say ' That's it, I'm not going to do another'.

Billy the Kid was in the time of the ranch wars, in the 1860s and 70s. He's like a meat-athletic visionary who like, on the rim of the

19th century, like looked into this century and enacted it. He invented violence.

It's the falcon and the rat, but most people when they think of the rat think of a strange creature with a scaly tail, whereas a rat is actually a very beautiful creature that dances by candlelight and is extremely intelligent, almost dainty and is meat, just food for falcon.

You know that Keats said that life is 'a vale of soul making', you can say that the universe is the Messiah. Like the falcon and the rat are locked together in the making of each other's spirit. I watched a falcon kill a coot and it was one of the most beautiful things I've ever seen. It was neat and it was perfect.

The day I left San Francisco the police station three blocks from my house was bombed, three public buildings in Oakland were bombed, I don't think this stuff gets in the international newspapers.

Three firemen were shot, two of them were seriously injured and there was the attempted bombing of a highway patrol car. I don't like shooting fireman, I think that's very bad, because one of those fireman that was shot could have saved some old woman. So far the people who have been shot have been children, black and white and firemen.

Violence? It's here. The whole thing is a miss so far, the whole New Left bag, the whole thing is like a total mistake so far, unless it brings along with it some kind of biological awareness. We're not going to make it at this point unless we find leaders who know what the actual situation is.

The situation is not political, the situation is biological, it's absolutely imminent, it's ecological and it's of incredible importance.

The most intelligent people are bullshitting about politics and bullshitting bout political revolutions, and that is not ever going to do it and it is too late for that shit. That shit would have worked in the thirties. The establishment will have to come down to it, but the establishment will not come down sensibly until it comes down into the hands of people who understand what the biological situation is, the imminence of starvation, the imminence of catastrophic pollution, the imminence of super over-population.

We're going to have to have really gigantic measures taken that are going to go far, far beyond politics. The political thing is a game, and I see the political thing everywhere, I see it in the United States and I see it here. People still playing cops and robbers, but it's too late for cops and robbers because the wolf is on the hunt howling at the moon and the snow is eight feet deep and anything else is shit. It's too late for evolution, we don't have enough time. I only know one man in the world today who knows what is going on, who is an ecologist.

The young people are being deluded by a façade that it's in regard to politics. There are going to have to be steps taken that are going to be much more massive than political steps.

It must be clear to thinking people soon and it's like we will have to find real leaders. People who really know, who can really lead, then we'll have to take our step. I think space flight is tremendously important. Man has to have a frontier. It's absolutely necessary for man to have a physical frontier, because a physical frontier is what he matches himself against, so that he can press his body and shape against a resisting substance somewhere, besides others of your own kind. We'll have to go into space and make many types of men, and many types of beings and have many types of frontiers. If technology evolved, it would be a kind of alchemy, it would cease to exist.

I saw a movie of seals playing with schools of fish. They play with them like they're balls, they shape them and make sculpture out of them. A seal will swim into a school of fish and swim around it and shape it, and play with it, he'll use the actual flesh of the fish as a sculpture. He'll make a spear out of it and then he'll swim around it and make a figure eight.

I know kids man, who don't even know how many buffalo there were and don't know what a passenger pigeon is, and have never heard of a Carolina parakeet, and don't realise that the polar bear is becoming extinct. We have to tell them man, that's our shot. We really must tell them. The only thing we can do is set an example, and that is the only thing we can do.

I don't necessarily think that we should increase the general undercurrent stress condition either. It depends on what the function of the increase in stress is. The question is are you waking them up to the beauty, and are you waking them up to understanding, or are you increasing their strain. I almost think that this could be thought of something akin to our responsibility. You set the best example you can set yourself. I would emulate Shelley, if I could. It would be nice to kiss people awake.

I'm inspired by examples, to see anybody be a total individual is always an inspiration whether it be Genet or anyone else. With Artaud, the great thing is, he went through a lot that we don't have to go through because he went through it. It's almost Messianic, we don't have to, he left an example.

When *The Beard* was first printed, I gave one of the original copies to a guy at the liquor store, a kid who worked down there. One day with the change he handed me a joint, so I went back there the next day and laid a copy of *The Beard* on him and I came back in a few days, and he said, 'My girlfriend and I did that play, she's a blonde, she looks just like Jean Harlow'.

I said, 'Did you do the end?' He said, 'Oh Yeah!' So it's being done all over.

LSD and the Mind Alchemyst

Home Grown Volume 1 No.1, June 1977:

Interview with Michael Hollingshead

There was a time in the late fifties and early sixties when dope was something that the 'beats' and 'spades' took. 'Taking acid' had not become the popular pastime of a turned-on youth, for they didn't exist.

It was in this rather drab and dreary period, which suffered from the after effects of the Cold War, that L.S.D. first emerged on the social scene in America. Such writers as Aldous Huxley and Gerald Heard had used it with quite astonishing results, for in those days it was legal, though not easily available. In 1960 a young Englishman, Michael Hollingshead, who happened to be living and working in New York at the time, telephoned Huxley at his home in Los Angeles to enquire about obtaining some mescaline. During the conversation, Huxley mentioned L.S.D. and a caution: "it is much more potent than mescaline." Huxley's information included the name of Dr. Albert Hofmann, the Swiss biochemist working at the Sandoz Pharmaceutical Laboratories in Basel, who discovered L.S.D. 25 - by chance - in 1943. Michael simply asked an English doctor friend to write the order on a New York hospital letterhead, saying he needed the ergot-derivative as a 'control-drug' for a series of bone marrow experiments.

A Loving Spoonful

A small package from Switzerland arrived in his mail one morning containing one gram of L.S.D. - Hofmann's acid and a bill for 285 dollars. It was in a small dark jar marked "Lot no. H-00047" and looked a bit like malted milk powder.

Michael poured some distilled water in a bowl, and then dissolved the acid into it, adding icing sugar into the mixture to make a thick paste. He then transferred his 'divine confection' spoon by spoon into a large mayonnaise jar.

By some alchemic process the stuff measured exactly 5,000 spoonsful. Like all good chefs, he'd tasted the preparation with his fingers and absorbed about the equivalent of five heavy doses before he had finished. What followed, lasting perhaps some 15 hours, was an experience that would change Michael's life, and that of countless others with far-reaching effect.

After that first 'trip', Michael once more phoned Huxley to discuss his visionary experience. Huxley called him back a few days later and suggested that he contact a Dr. Timothy Leary, a Harvard professor, who had recently presented a paper on induced visionary experience. "If there is any one single investigator in America worth seeing, it is Dr. Leary," said Huxley.

In September 1961, Michael met, and subsequently moved into the home of Timothy Leary in Boston. He had been living there a couple of weeks when Maynard Ferguson, a jazz musician and a close friend of Leary's, arrived with his wife, Flo. At that time Leary didn't smoke marijuana, as it was illegal, and took nothing stronger than a few micrograms of psilocybin, and wine and whiskey, which he believed were "indispensable luxuries".

When Ferguson heard that Michael had some acid, he suggested they all have a session together. Leary excused himself, as he had papers to mark, but said they could take it if they so wished. Michael, Maynard and Flo took a spoonful each and settled down by the log fire. After about thirty minutes, Flo sat up suddenly, and with a huge smile on her face, waved at Leary: "You gotta try this Tim, baby. It's f.a.n.t.a.s.t.i.c."

Leary later wrote in his book 'High Priest' about that experience:

"It has been five years since that first L.S.D. trip with Michael Hollingshead. I have never forgotten it. Nor has it been possible for me to return to the life I had been leading before the session. I have never recovered from the shattering ontological confrontation; I have never been able to take myself, my mind and the social world around me, seriously. Since that time five years ago, I have been acutely aware of the fact that I perceive everything within the world around me as a creation of my own consciousness."

Since then, Michael has turned-on and guided many a great man through their first trip. In his book 'The Man Who Turned On The World', he gives a lucid and well-written account of his part in the early days of the psychedelic era, both in this country and America. It is now over fifteen years since those embryonic sessions that helped change the life-style of a whole generation. *Home Grown* asked Michael Hollingshead, who lives in London, to give us some of his thoughts on acid as he views it today.

HG: There are things of which it has been said the truly wise never try to conceptualise. Is L.S.D. one of them?

MH: I think one can talk about L.S.D. in a non-psychological way, because it is something anyone can experience. Anyone, provided he has his heart and head in the right place, has the right to take L.S.D. as much or as little as he wants. It is Man's Fifth Freedom - the freedom to 'turn on' his nervous system and on his own terms. Alas, it is a freedom that is severely curtailed at this time in our history. On the other hand, L.S.D. is something at which, as at holy springs, one does not drink habitually or lightly.

HG: It is dangerous?

MH: L.S.D. is a dangerous three letter word. Say it to the average lawyer, churchman, clubman, and it will produce serious side effects - they grow red in the face, shake, get high blood pressure, and become incoherent. The stuff itself isn't dangerous. Nobody has ever died of it, if that is what you mean. One of the riddles of L.S.D. is that the user never has to increase the dose. There is no slavery to L.S.D. - it is, on the contrary, liberation. There are those who would have you believe that L.S.D. is an escape from life and that it takes away one's sense of values. But if L.S.D. takes away the old life and the old scale of values from under our feet, it sets up another for us, superior and more delicate.

The L.S.D. user has a third-eye view of himself. One of the interesting things about getting 'high' via L.S.D. - getting in touch with your own inner processes, if you like - is that it gives you, albeit only for a 6-8 hour stretch at a time - a chance to see for yourself the many different motives which seem to underly all one does, thinks, feels. This is seeing yourself a little more consciously than before; the psychedelic experience is not so much a kind of being as a kind of knowing, and memory lingers.

This is why people who have taken L.S.D. often change in quite dramatic ways. They have discovered a new kind of truth about themselves, if by truth we mean to 'come to', to awake to an inner self who is palpably more real. It is one thing to live out your simple life or death as a programmed robot, which one does as the result of a most profound ignorance about the nature of man and his potential. But when one is in possession of all the facts, the 'nothing-but-truth' knowledge about oneself, it is impossible to live the shuttered life of the closed mind and eye.

There is really nothing arbitrary in suggesting that people extend themselves a little via a psychedelic experience. It is the last chance we shall have in life. It helps us feel the tender, know the irrational, feel the invisible and so forth. On the other hand, it takes a lot of L.S.D. to gain even a tiny bit of consciousness.

HG: In what way do people change after an acid session?

MH: They become aware of this tension between, on the one hand, the flowing process and, on the other, the fixed structure. Leary has written at length about expansion-contraction, that which gets you high and that which brings you down, and suggested human life is better suited to getting high. I think that the human mind, like human history, is made for change, is part of the natural flowing process of the universe, and if contracted by societal 'man-made' systems we will lose whatever capacity it is in the human mind for growth, creativity and ultimately of course, happiness.

The real gulf today in our thinking is not, as C.P. Snow spoke about in the fifties, between science and art, but between those who are 'high' and those who are 'down'. When one can see through or beyond the imprinted symbols of a received culture it is to perceive a world in which there has been a fundamental change in men's minds.

I remain convinced, despite my failures, that L.S.D. can be good and that it is entirely up to the individual to make it well-disposed. We must first learn to handle it. Man's need to get in touch with the source of this being is something some of us feel is definitely desirable - and knowable. It is also a certain disposition to act; to act in some primordial and metaphysical way, for an alliance of the mind with the soul, a disposition each time we take LS.D. L.S.D. is the need to emerge from oneself - with flying colours.

HG: Can you tell us something about the *Harvard Psychedelic Project*, which you participated in, between 1960-63? How do you think L.S.D. affected the lives of those who took part in those early sessions? Was the d-LSD-25 that you were using then different in any way from today's street acid?

MH: It was an officially-sponsored research project by Harvard University, run under the aegis of the *Social Relations Department*, and headed by Timothy Leary. Our thesis - subsequently proved - was that L.S.D. and similar agents such as mescaline and psilocybin may at times produce rapid personality changes of a long-lasting nature in normal people, even when no psychotherapy is intended.

We ran about 3,000 sessions for graduates and faculty, and about another 1,000 for artists, musicians, writers, poets, actors; and for prisoners in a maximum security prison at Concord, Massachusetts, and the great majority of these, something like 96% reported major life changes of a positive kind.

As for members of the research team, they were all third-year graduate students in behaviorism, that is, with the exception of Leary, Richard Alpert and myself. We were faculty. On average, I think, each member of the project took L.S.D. in excess of one hundred times, some of us about three hundred times.

It is difficult to say why there should be so many beneficial claims for L.S.D. Some people have likened the L.S.D. induced rapid personality change to the naturally occurring mystical or religious conversation experiences described by such thinkers as William James, Gerald Heard and Aldous Huxley.

There is certainly a lot of evidence around to observe a positive correlation between people who have L.S.D. mystical experiences and those claiming lasting benefits. People at Harvard were reporting for instance, that the L.S.D. experience gave them better understanding of themselves and others, and a high proportion claimed improved personal relationships, more tolerance of others and their viewpoints, and changes of values in several areas. They claimed they were less dogmatic in their thinking and beliefs, that the L.S.D. experience had made them more 'flexible'.

We found at Harvard that most of the bizarre, psychotic-like behaviors, and so forth, stressed by the media can be eliminated or greatly minimised by replacing the cold, impersonal 'clinical' approach with a supportive, 'natural' and protective environment.

We also found that attitudes and the beliefs of the person giving the L.S.D. is almost as important as the state of mind of the person taking it. These are conditions not normally to be found in clinics; hence the number of reports of 'bad' sessions conducted in such places, for which the public turns for information about the subject.

I don't think that it is possible to conceptualise the mode of action in terms of existing psychological theory. Religious metaphors are much closer as descriptions of what happens during an L.S.D. session.

But it is a fact of life at this present time that the phenomenon

L.S.D. is beset with considerable resistance not encountered since the days of the Red Star Chamber.

L.S.D. is the new heresy, it seems. People go to prison for it - so much for our Western ideas of personal freedom. The fact is that L.S.D. is completely outside out current cultural concepts. Thus, to a person who has not thoroughly experienced the effects of L.S.D. on himself, the literature is understandably confusing and contradictory.

As for what has happened to the other members of the Harvard Psychedelic Project, I can report that they are all alive and healthy and very much involved in the 'flowering processes'. Dr. Timothy Leary is out of jail and working on his Starseed project; Dr. Richard Alpert has become a Hindu monk, changed his name to Baba Ram Dass, and heads the Hanuman Foundation in New York; Dr. Ralph Metzner lives in California and also heads a foundation concerned with various forms of psychic healing; Dr. Gunther Weil, who edited the Psychedelic Reader, helps to run the American Gurdjeff group; Dr. Al Cohen heads the American Mehar Baba group; Dr. George Litwin heads up the Crossett Hill Learning Community in Vermont; Dr. Richard Katz has recently published a book, Preludes to Growth: An Experimental Approach and is now living with a tribe in the Kalahari; Dr. David Kolb is lecturing and writing at M.I.T.; Dr. Rolf Von Ekartberg runs the 'Open Door' group in Philadelphia; and I am being interviewed by 'Home Grown'!

As for your last question, about the L.S.D. we were using. Yes, I believe there is an important, if little-understood difference between what we used at Harvard and what is available on the streets, as it were. D-LSD-25, to give it its full title, is a semi-synthetic substance, that is, it requires ergot for its synthesis. Now large amounts of clandestine ergot are simply not available, so underground manufacturers have had to use a synthetic ergot such as ergotamine to produce the synthesis, and the subjective effects are really very different from those reported at Harvard. The street stuff may even be harmful on account of impurities.

It is a difficult situation and I don't know what one can do about it. It seems unlikely, given the climate of the world at the moment, that any government would release a new batch of ergot-based acid for non-clinical purposes. Though paradoxically, the government that did would force everyone to get smarter. But, like everything else I've said, it is my own private opinion.

HG: Should one take acid?

MH: As the old alchemists said, "You need a bit of light to find the light," and that pretty well sums up why acid.

Demystifying Human Violence

Previously unpublished, 1969:

"A unique gathering to demystify human violence in all its forms, the social systems from which it emanates, and to explore new forms of action" - So went the poster advertising *'The International Congress on the Dialectics of Liberation'* at the Round House in London.

They gathered in their hundreds, the subverts from the Third World, the American New Left, and the Western European student dissent movements. Young revolutionaries, tired of old ways of protest; ready for guerrilla operations to corrupt their social institutions. To guide them were their spiritual and cultural heroes.

Men like Allen Ginsberg, the idol of the then flourishing Hippie cult; Stokely Carmichael, the young Black Power firebrand; Herbert Marcuse, the professor whose ideological works have a far reaching influence today; John Gerassi, author of a book on Che Guevara and guerrilla tactics in South America; R. D. Laing, an existential psychoanalyst and guru to many young people; and many others whose works have inspired new modes of thought and action.

The results of that conference, which took place in London last year, and was virtually ignored by the Establishment press, can be seen in the "spontaneous" student revolts now sweeping the Western World.

This 'In' gathering of the young subverts was a time for reflection and a time for exchanging tactics and forms of action. The finer moments of the Congress took place in the private seminars, where ideas were expressed in face-to-face confrontations.

There the activists exchanged his personal experiences without feeling castrated by the social co-ordinates of the academics. There one heard of the individuals and groups working all over the world to bring about social change.

It was the end of an era; the death knell of peaceful protest marches. The *Campaign for Nuclear Disarmament* had fizzled out, leaving disillusionment with pacifist ideas in its wake. Che Guevara's maxim suddenly seemed relevant; "If you want a revolution - go out and make one."

And then there was the Hippie slogan of "Do your own thing." Though the aims of various groups differed, a growing disillusionment with the operating social systems and the sense of the powerlessness of individuals in shaping their own destinies brought about a form of unity in clandestine form. Gone were the days of the burning monks in Vietnam, gone were the Danilo Dolci marches through Sicily and gone were the peaceful Civil Rights movement, the teach-ins and the sit-ins.

Black Power advocate, Stokely Carmichael, a slim aesthetic figure, stoked the fires of motion. Instead of demystifying human violence, the crowd cheered frenziedly at every mention of violence. Calls for non-violent action were booed - racism was once again affirmed. Carmichael didn't think much of Flower Power; however, he did venture a way in which the Hippies could help his cause:

> "Come inside the Ghetto, if you all believe in that love power and so on, and when the cops are shooting at us, stand in-between us and throw your flowers at them."

Somewhere in this call for action the "Beautiful People" petered out.

Professor Herbert Marcuse, the arch-prophet of the concept of a free society, put it this way:

> "I am very happy to see so many flowers here, but flowers have no power in themselves; the power is with those that look after them and use them to fight tyranny."

A rumor circulated that Marcuse had in some way failed to give ideological guidance to the students of the West Berlin Commune during a recent visit to their city. A marijuana 'Smoke-in' was organised and took place during his lecture. The venue was decked with Maoist slogans hanging from the walls, beseeching the students to "Pass the joint" and to "Pass the liberation". Marcuse took this is in his stride, and when an American student got up and handed him a 'joint' he simply took it, had a puff and went on speaking:

> "Today we are in a novel situation," he said, "we must be liberated from affluence. We have been too modest in attacking society. Total eruption is needed. Time has to be arrested and a new time has begun."

Ironically, he spoke of the time of the *Paris Commune* in the last century, where the Parisians threw stones at the clocks in order to arrest time. However, he was wary of the old type of revolution as it replaced one system of domination for another. He called for:

> "The emergence of a new type of man with the consciousness and biological drive capable of breaking through the veil of affluence. The convergence of technique and art; work and play as forces of transformation. Then the creative imagination would become a productive force and a form of reality based on the sensitivity and sensibility of man would emerge, society as a work of art - aesthetic reality. These are not snobistic or romantic ideas, men can be truly free in such a universe."

He likened the phrase "planned obsolescence" to what was happening in the United States and said there was a need for an enemy in a Capitalist state. A Welfare state is a Warfare state. The process of materialism must be sabotaged.

"The intelligentsia has a decisive preparatory function as the catalyst of change," he explained:

> "All education today is more than teaching and learning; it is therapy, political theory and practice. Social, sexual and political change are uniting, causing a trans-valuation of values."

He gave his definition of the intelligentsia, as "one who can break through the lies and hypocrisy of mass communication."

The students and hippies have formed their own underground presses that flourish in every university and major city throughout the Western world. In the United States alone, they claim a readership of over half a million, and are linked by the *Liberation News Service*, which has recently installed 24 Telex machines across the country.

In Europe a communication network has been formed called the *International Freedom News Service*, with the aim of linking people separated geographically but united, and developing international consciousness.

The Service has three main functions:

1. To provide "hard news" about demonstrations and other

events obscured, skipped, or misinterpreted in the Establishment media.

2. To provide reinforcement and encouragement for people working within a national context.

3. To be an obvious medium for organising common action on an International level - for those who want to do so.

Another recent phenomenon is the mushrooming of the "Anti-University" also known as the "Free University". Though their tactics differ in the various national contexts, they aim for a broad cultural revolt.

One thing is certain; this social upheaval is not part of the Cold War strategy between East and West. For the students have no time either for the rigid, doctrinaire, Communist state.

Marcuse, Laing et al, prophets of this new dialectic of liberation involving mind and body, may well look back and remember the anarchic but apt Maoist slogan that hung from the walls of the Congress. It said: "The revolutionary work of the Congress IS the Congress.

Quo Vadis Israel?

International Times, 1968:

Dan Omer, a young Israeli poet, is the enfant terrible of Hebrew literature. He has published four books of poetry, a novel, and has translated Ginsberg, Corso, Ferlinghetti and Gunther Grass into Hebrew. He now edits his second literary magazine. *'Yellow Pages'* and is also one of the editors of the London-based *'Israel Imperial News'*. He is a founder member of the *'Israel Anti-Annexation Movement'*.

This article is extracts of a recorded conversation with Lee Harris in Jerusalem.

Quo Vadis Israel? I asked myself this question after the *'Six Day War'*. What now? We've conquered all this land - What now? My answers were influenced by two turns of events. Firstly, at a certain point, public figures started talking about our 'historical rights'. Secondly - and this hit me sharply and shocked me - I was told of ugly incidents taking place in the occupied West Bank. This actually made me aware of the rising chauvinism and fascism in my country.

During the preparations for the *Six Day War* there was a feeling of apprehension and fear in the air, perpetrated by the hysterical broadcasts and newspaper reports. I was also caught up in this mass of fear. During the war, I had the feelings of any soldier fighting in a war. I fought in the battle for Jerusalem. My feelings were to stay alive and not to be a killer and I succeeded in this.

After the war there was a feeling of incredulity that we had actually conquered so much territory in six days. I read in the papers the names of my friends who were killed in the war and I started weighing the consequences as to the value of such a war. It took a while for me to realize that all my life I had been living in another planet, so to speak, where the events taking place in the rest of the world were distant. For example, Vietnam, the race question in America, the young revolutions in South America, the situations in the Iron Curtain countries. I always knew that there were two wars going on - one military, the other an unarmed struggle.

After the war, I realized sharply that the Middle East was one of these battlefields, actually occurring on my doorstep. I was suddenly in a great dilemma, which I think most of the people in the new world must have felt. A kind of ultra-electric movement had sprung up from the soul of Che Guevara to the wounded body of Rudi Dutschke, through Paris, Rome and Prague, all the places where the young generation started to sing the *Internationale* with power, about destroying the base of the old world. Every day after the war I've witnessed the rise of fascism growing out of the victims of fascism, this is what sent me into this camp.

The New Ghetto

People in Israel are saying that I and friends of mine who think likewise, are still thinking like Jews from the ghettoes, but this is not true. I think the ghetto mentality still exists in Israel, in the frontiers that are the new walls of the new ghetto. Zionism arose out of Russia and its pogroms, and needed an Austro-Hungarian prophet named Herzi to put these yearnings into a political theory; they were influenced by revolutionary movements in Russia at the turn of the century and they were a type of socialist who came to Palestine and bought land from rich Arabs, who resided in Damascus, Cairo and Constantinople.

The Arab peasants, who were eking out a living on those impoverished lands, had to move on. At this point, I feel, the Arab-Jewish conflict started in the Middle East. This Zionist socialism became a kind of colonial movement. After securing land, they started bringing in Jews from the Arab countries, those Jews came to toil the lands and work as labourers. In 1948 the State of Israel was established and the great Aliyah movement began. First the Jews from the Displaced Persons camps came from Europe, later from the Eastern European countries. Then they started paying the Arab governments to allow their Jews to come, they put them into settlements and development areas around the towns.

A Culture of Soldiers' Sweat

Most of those in Israel today are Sabras; of Israel-born. In certain ways the Sabras are so anti-ghetto that they have formed a new-style ghetto mentality, out of a culture built on soldiers' sweat. It is in their Khaki literature, paintings, and their monuments to the heroes and martyrs. From the age of fourteen they receive a sub-military education.

An important part of this culture of soldiers' sweat is the Kibbutzim. In one of the battles of Jerusalem during the Six Day War, I served with a couple of boys from the Kibbutzim; under the fire of the Arab Legion they were so proud that they weren't afraid of the bullets, they just attacked like human robots. I felt sick at that time.

I fear people who aren't afraid of bullets because I think they are people without human instincts. I understand how this comes about and how they are brought up. In the Kibbutzim they put the children into a kind of environmental chicken-run with a collective mother, practically from the day they are born. Lately, they even have a collective father when they begin to study. The parents see their children for an hour a day, and half a day during the weekends. The parents are busy building the country, so the children are brought up together as a group, becoming an egotistical unit, which a stranger would find difficult to penetrate. I've felt this personally in the Kibbutzim I have been to.

Before they do military service, their teachers tell them to be officers. They climb over bodies to become officers. An interesting phenomenon is that some Kibbutzniks have committed suicide while in the army. They are those that usually can't make officership. It reminds me of ancient Sparts, where the weakest children were thrown from a cliff. They just don't understand that life is building again. So important a part do they play in the Israel economy that they have become a strong determining factor in the establishment, which must be smashed to save Israel.

The Golden Age

In the Twelfth Century in Spain, it was the golden age of two cultures; the Jewish and Moslem. They were like twin sisters living together peacefully.

A month after the occupation of East Jerusalem, I had a conversation with an Arabic poet. We translated a poem by Yahuda Ha-Levi, the thirteenth century Hebrew poet, into Arabic and found that the rhythms and meters were similar in both languages. It opened for us a common language, even after a month of the occupation. Christianity killed the golden age of the Hebrew-Arab culture, as it has killed all other cultures in its wake.

Hebrew literature has a problem that someone who knows Arabic might understand. In Arabic there is a literary language and a spoken one. We've got a level of beautiful written words that are as exquisite as they are hollow. I hate this kind of writing. Today if you're reading Hebrew literature, you need an encyclopedia as well as a dictionary.

Even Nobel Prize winner S.Y. Agnon's works, which are steeped in the mysticism of the *Cabbala*, are hard to read in Hebrew. They say my novel is obscene for using cheap language and four-letter words. I think I must be the Columbus of Hebrew literature because nobody has used these words before in writing, although they are used in everyday language.

Building the Third Temple

I'm aware of the first temple of Israel, and the second temple; maybe they are building the third temple. When is the fourth one coming; and what is going to happen in the meantime?

I was born in this country I want my children to be born here, and my grandchildren, and their children, etc. Or should we conquer until we reach Iraq with its oil? I don't believe in such victories, because I've read my history books. This is how I think and feel about the new Israeli chauvinism.

Peace seems to be utopian. I think there will be a lot of blood shed before it can come. I think the first step towards peace is the recognition of the right of all her people to live here. It is true that during the last seventy years of Zionism, we've caused the Arabs a good deal of anguish; we've thrown them out of their land and towns.

This is all part of history, but I don't think any history books ever saved the world. We are now in 1968, and they have to recognise us and we have to recognise them. In Gunnar Jarring's travels from Jerusalem to Cairo and Amman, we are forgetting an important factor; the Palestinians, who Egypt and Jordan have also been using in the last twenty years for political capital, and still go on using them.

The Palestinians are a nation, who should have human rights, but even the United Nations doesn't seem to care about this. I think Israel should give the occupied West Bank and the Gaza Strip to the Palestinians and let them build a country. I think Israel will have to support this country financially; even as the Germans supported Israel financially for the blood they shed.

When the Flowers Wilted in the Winter

Previously unpublished, June 1971:

Johnny arrived at the door of my bedsitter in Bayswater and knocked. I opened it and let him in. He was dressed in a brown tweedy suit and wore a tie. He showed me his hands, which were bruised when he fell last night. It was difficult trying to follow his description of this haphazard rambling tale. Like so much of Johnny's garrulous gab it was spiked with the odd injection of catastrophic dismay. Things sort of happened to him all the time, he was always being mislaid or jettisoned into strange situations like the one he was telling me now.

"Jesus, I had a terrible fall. I crashed through this pile of rubble on the way to Maggie's place. You know where Maggie lives. Don't you?"

I never quite listen and put on a detached air of not wanting to get involved in his messy extravagances. He always seems to catch me using the word 'excesses' when speaking to him. It is a word I don't normally use and he makes me feel rather straight using it.

"Why don't you wash your hands?" I said glancing casually at them as he held them out to show me his bruises.

"They're not dirty, they're sore," he stated in a pained way.

Nevertheless, he went to the basin and washed them. I passed him a towel to dry them and then threw it in the blue polythene laundry bag. I looked at him preening his tousled hair in the mirror above the mantelpiece. He was like a schoolboy on the first day of term, excitedly jabbering away.

"I told them all about you and that you're a writer and you know all about drugs. I said that you should get a job there. Can you paint? I told them I could paint and I volunteered to do some painting today. I'm going to get some bread off them. I'll take you out for lunch."

"Come on I'm ready," I said, "let's get going."

"Wait a minute I forgot about the painting. I promised I'd bring it in and show it to them. You don't really want it, do you?"

"I do want it," I replied. "You gave it to me as a Christmas present, remember?"

"Well I just want to show it to them, say it was something I knocked up last week."

"Why tell them that. The truth is more interesting. Tell them that you painted it when you were an inmate at Grendon Underwood. It sounds much more exciting to say that it was created in a psychiatric prison. That's what they'd like to hear."

He took the picture off the wall and held it in his arms and pondered for a moment over what I'd said, before we left the room.

The painting was rather interesting. I suppose it would be called art therapy, a psychological study with heavy symbolic overtones. In the centre was a barren rocky island surrounded by a vacuous sea. Out of the brown rock of the island, a large steel prison door hung open, displaying a hospital corridor with its black and white checked floor ebbing away in the distance. Above the island is the mainland with its trees and mountains. There, looming on the mountains, half sunk, was a glorious sun painted in bright orange. It was mounted on a white painted wooden frame.

It was midday with its milling rushed lunch-hour crowds, as we came up the escalator at Tottenham Court Road tube station. We walked towards the exit that leads through a long grey passageway that runs underneath the enigmatic monument to planned obsolescence Centre Point, and comes out beyond the one-way traffic diversion. I purposefully chose this way out so that Johnny could hear the busker who regularly plays his music halfway down this draughty, dimly lit passageway.

I have often walked along here entranced by the peaceful, gentle sounds from his guitar. This longhaired youth with his shaggy vagabond appearance seems oblivious to the traffic noise from above and the scurrying tight-lipped passers-by, as he sings songs that stir me into dreams of sadness. I feel a benevolent melancholia come over me as I calmly walk by and up the exit stairs. At other times I'm moved to feelings of life-enhancing joy. I feel at times that he is not singing to us, but for himself because that is how he feels at that moment. There is something very private about him that I do not wish to disturb as I go by.

A couple of months ago as I was walking passed him, a middle-aged woman in a neat coat, bespectacled with greying hair, looked at him with an air of disdain and then at me for a response, as I was the nearest person to her. I just smiled and walked on. She gave him a long hard stare and hurried along mumbling as she caught up with me going up the stairs.

"Why doesn't he work like the rest of us? And look how dirty he is."

The same two clichés, I thought. I turned to her with a smile.

"He's a busker and he sings for a living," I said. "Didn't you listen to that beautiful song he sang as you walked by? Amidst all this hurrying he brought a bit of peace. I look forward to walking through here just to hear him."

She paused in her step and said, "I never thought of it that way."

I bid her "Good afternoon" as I walked on feeling quite pleased with myself.

With Johnny it was different. I wanted him to be affected by the encircling sadness in the singer and the song, a haunting ballad called 'St James Infirmary'. I wanted this moving rendition to calm his inner turbulence. Instead of just listening to the minstrel as we passed by, he stood there right in front of him with a big smile on his face, his hands behind his back holding the painting. He then conducted the busker with outstretched arms swaying in the air, the painting abandoned for the moment. The busker sang on looking straight through him as if he was not there.

It was just like Johnny, I thought. I should have known it. He couldn't walk passed like the rest of us, he had to take on the busker and turn it into a road show. Now he was stopping passersby, imploring them with open arms to fling their coins into the guitar case on the ground. His beseeching manner only made them walk indignantly away from his effrontery. How indiscreet, their shocked, closed faces seemed to say. How intrusive. I was quietly despairing at the spectacle. Then in a grand gesture, he dug his hand deep in his trouser pocket and ostentatiously, in my mind, flung a couple of coins in the guitar case before bowing out. It was all done with natural generosity but what a performance.

We clambered up the steps to street level, Johnny feeling a warm glow inside.

"All you had to do was to listen to him," I muttered almost inaudibly.

You could see that Johnny was getting excited as we walked through the narrow streets that lead towards Drury Lane.

"I'll tell them I just knocked this up last night."

"Why tell them that."

"I told them I was a painter and wrote poems."

"You told them quite a few things, didn't you?"

"I'm going to try and get some money off them. I want to get myself a room. All my clothes are at Maggie's place."

"I thought you were staying there?"

"No, she kicked me out. I had a fight with her father. Didn't I tell you about it?"

"Then where did you sleep last night?"

"In Colville Terrace, I told you some friends of mine, junkies, put me up."

"Jesus, Johnny I just don't understand you. You always get yourself into these situations, complicating the simplest things. Your life is always so messy."

"No man, it's not like that."

He suddenly stopped at a street corner, by the sidewall of a fish and chip shop. Seeing that nobody noticed him, he moved quickly over to a small brown suitcase on a doorstep beside the wall and rummaged through it. The contents with its assortment of brushes and colour slides were obviously the tools of trade of a painter. Indeed, the sidewall was still wet and half-finished as the man was most probably on his lunch break.

Without further ado, Johnny picked up the case and was off, hiding it behind his painting. I thought it a petty thing to do and told him so. I felt sorry for the poor guy. Then the picture fitted. Johnny had told them that he would come over with his brushes and do some painting. He didn't want to come empty-handed, so it seemed. He must have thought it a lucky find. Trying to justify himself in some strange way, he reminded me that he was a thief of long standing.

We arrived at this old building, a former Education Institute, now transformed into a centre for a number of social service agencies. From the name boards at the entrance I could see that the *Child Poverty Action Group* were upstairs. In the basement was the New Horizon Youth Centre. Johnny led the way as we walked down the stairs and into a large room with its white walls covered with drawings and sketches. The mood was calm and easy and there were a few lounge chairs and a large round table with chairs all the way round. Near the entrance was a reception area behind a wooden counter, with the customary desk, typewriter and telephone and in the far corner was a blackboard with the scrawled words 'Clay to win'.

I noticed one or two faces sitting around the table, having seen them in Piccadilly Circus many times hanging about endlessly as junkies do. They all looked up as Johnny, nodding his head at them, banged his painting and the tool case down on the counter. Behind it was a young woman with close-cropped fair hair and a quiet, reserved manner. It was like going back to school. There was an air about the place of a well-run classroom. Young people sat and waited in an orderly manner, blankly staring ahead or delving in a book. Johnny was aware that some of them were glancing over trying to get a glimpse of his work of art. In fact it did shine out from the other more amateurish etchings displayed on the walls.

I was introduced as the friend he told her about yesterday, the one that was a playwright who believed in art for art's sake and didn't write for money. I felt duly embarrassed by all these half-truths and generalisations and vaguely protested. But Johnny has to romanticise, I think it has something to do with him being Irish, the gushes of oozing charm, the verbal dexterities, the nonchalant throwaway manner, all tumbling out of him in an abundance of profusion.

Into the room walked a fellow acquaintance of his and they huddled in a corner murmuring in husky voices. I wasn't interested in what they were saying but I guessed it was the usual banter when two junkies meet, a sizing up of the score, who has what and how many. Johnny's friend had a gaunt pallid face, with a dark beard and intense eyes that darted about the room testily. After a few minutes Johnny came over and charmingly asked the receptionist if he could roll a joint for his friend and himself. She stiffened somewhat and said she'd rather he didn't do it in here. He accepted this and, with the other fellow, disappeared into a cubicle at the end of the room.

The receptionist, who was a volunteer, leaned over and confided in me.

"I know they have gone in the fixing room to have a smoke but what can I do?"

How odd I thought, a fixing room. She discreetly turned a blind eye and entered our names in the day register. Next to Johnny's name she put down the letter A in capitals and said it was for addict.

Speaking to her was pleasant. She had come over here from Australia after completing her university course. She seemed to enjoy working at the centre and learning all about addiction. She went through a bad period a couple of weeks ago when two of the addicts who were regulars, died suddenly from overdoses. It shook her badly and she had to take a few days off to recover. She met

Johnny yesterday for the first time. Marjorie, another volunteer worker, had gone to Tooting Bec hospital to visit an addict they had obtained a treatment place for, and had met Johnny there, who was being booted out after seven weeks in the clinic. It was she who had suggested that he came here.

I told her that I'd first met Johnny over seven years ago when he was just seventeen, that I had lost contact with him over the years thinking him dead by now. What amazed me was how little he had changed. How could so many years of early manhood go by with a person changing so little? She listened intently and smiled as I talked.

There were shuffling sounds from the cubicle and I went over to have a look. Just then the door opened and Johnny stumbled out grabbing hold of the wall. His friend was holding him up. He was swooning and swaying gently. I gathered from his state that he had just had a fix. His friend maneuvered him over to an easy chair and plopped him down. His eyes were dazed and dreamy. The volunteer worker glanced over cautiously.

Johnny was trying to tell her that the centre could have his painting to hang on the wall. He mumbled something incoherently, leaned back in the comfy chair and dropped off into a dreamy sleep, snoring occasionally.

She came over and whispered to me. "Normally we don't allow anyone to sleep in here. I'll leave him for a while. I don't think it will matter."

She then walked behind the counter, which detached her from us.

I sat in one of the easy chairs opposite Johnny watching him sleeping; his head slumped back and I wondered how I had let him talk me into coming here in the first place. I said I would accompany him if he came to call for me, half expecting him not to turn up. Last night he'd rung the bell around nine-thirty just as I was settling down to a discussion on Women's Liberation on *Radio Four*. I went down the stairs, opened the door curiously and there he was smiling up at me. He had a tall quiet bloke with him. He positively gushed from the moment he saw me. I couldn't remember a word he said as he entered, but it was all bombast and euphoria. My only reaction to his overpowering presence was to withdraw into a detached politeness.

On the landing he leaned over and gave me an affectionate peck on the cheek. I found myself pulling away slightly and ushered them into the room. Johnny lounged casually on the bed and gave forth.

His friend sat timidly on the edge of the bed and I sat in a chair on the other side of him. Neither of us, even if we wanted to, could have got a word in. It was obviously a benefit performance on my behalf.

Where to begin? Yesterday he had been kicked out of Tooting Bec. No, he's not fixing. I look at him in amazement. Well, he admits he's taken some pills to keep him going and he has a few sleepers to knock him out later. I knew he was on something by the way he was speeding.

He must have been very stoned because he kept interjecting the phrase 'you know' every few minutes. He had entangled himself in the plethora of images floating out of his mind. It seemed to me that he was trying hard to impress me or ingratiate himself in my eyes. Might be he was living up to an image of himself as he thought I saw him. I don't know.

I heard the story of how he had fucked the Irish nursing sister. He relished the one where he made the good-looking young addict in the ward succumb to his charms, only to abuse him afterwards by telling him that he should bath more often. I think the incident was flung out to shock. I was to think it rather bold and daring, another act of bravado by our unstoppable Johnny. There was his good fortune at being taken on by the youth centre. Out came the coloured snaps of Maggie and Alexis, his two year old son. He smiled silently for a moment as I looked at the photos before speeding on.

Although he had only come out of the treatment centre the day before, he had already had a fight with Maggie's father. He loved describing his fighting escapades and was quite proud of his quick temper. To be honest, I don't remember seeing him ever really lose his temper or hit anyone, though I believe him capable of it.

It all sounded like an absurd farce starring Johnny Collett in the role he originally created for himself of the indomitable clown who takes on the whole world single-handed. I told him as a tragedian Bette Davis has nothing on him. But then he was off in a flurry of good-byes, 'See you tomorrow' and 'Don't forget', taking his quiet friend who hardly opened his mouth, with him. He had brought him along simply because he had transported him on his motorbike.

After they had left the room I noticed that Johnny had left something behind on the bed. On closer scrutiny I saw it was a plastic pack containing a syringe and needles. He was lying. Of course he's fixing again and this is his works.

It must have fallen out of his pocket when he got up off the bed. The poor boy can't even lie with impunity. I ran out to the street and handed him his needy possession, catching him before he sped off as pillion passenger on the bike.

There he sits opposite me in a deep drugged sleep, his agile tongue silenced as his mind, no doubt, weaves dream patterns for him.

Johnny, Johnny what has happened to you? What is to become of you, sliding from one situation to another like a nimble sprat cavorting in a mountain stream, deep and fast you go, careering along in so many directions, filling up time but petrified of the great unknown.

I remember one time, a good few years back, picking up a paperback cover with his stoned doodling on its inside front and back. He had drawn in the centre a surreal bust balanced on a tombstone.

The inscription read:

R.I.P.

J.P. Collett

2nd May 1965

By His Own Hand

The whole inside page was covered with labelled drawings, like a school exercise book. There was a broken brick, and just to make sure, he'd written the word 'BRICK' on it in capital letters. At the side were the words 'HALF OUNCE' and an arrow pointing at the brick. I think he was having a private joke, toying with the idea of having a half ounce piece of hash, as he had also drawn a few spiffs. Above were the words in caps, A BROKEN LIFE.

More doom to come. A drawing of a bottle broken at the neck with a label hanging from it proclaiming, 'DOOMED! HA! HA!' Above it was written 'ALL CUT UP DOLL'. Below an arrow and the words 'NAKED EDGE'

There was a razor blade with the words 'SHAVE YOUR SOUL.' At the bottom of the page he had drawn a broken crucifix, a cracked egg, a pair of burning candles, and some mountains labeled 'ALPS.'

And just in case we didn't get the message, he'd written 'STILL A CHANCE. I MIGHT DIE BEFORE THE DAY IS OVER', scrawled on one side. The page was splattered with tiny red specks of blood. I think Johnny likes his symbols, especially the destructive ones.

I turned the page over to look at the cover of the book and was amused by the irony of it. It was titled 'Kiss the Dark Angel.' The blurb read 'In the wild, wanton days that were left to him, he indulged every sensual whim.'

While Johnny slept I passed the time chatting quietly to a sullen-looking fellow in his early twenties who was a registered addict. He had been injecting heroin and latterly physeptone for five years and was hoping to go on another cure. His hairline had receded giving him a long face. He wanted answers to unanswerable questions. How can I verify the human condition? How do you live up to the image of a dead father? How do you mend a broken marriage? Where is love? And what is it? When innocence has gone will I find peace? Are we all in states of addiction? Why is society against me? Am I my own worst enemy? Must there always be hang-ups and fuck-ups?

Yes and no, yin and yang.

Weighed down by melancholic knowledge, nodding my head somberly, I was as non-committal as an aged guru throwing back his pupil's questions. We somehow struck a happy balance without being too personal. The voluntary worker had sidled over and listened intently to our conversation without actually disturbing us.

Johnny snorted and stirred. He opened his eyes wide, blinking a few times.

"Where am I?" he said.

"You know where you are," I parried.

"Have I been asleep?"

"That's right."

"I must have dozed off. What time is it? Have I been asleep long?"

I looked at my watch and at the clock above the door.

"It's half past two."

"How long have I been asleep?"

"Nearly one hour."

"That long?"

"Yes you were out, stone cold."

"What have I got to do? Oh yes, I've got to find a place to stay and get some money."

He was trying to lift himself up, holding his back as if he was in pain, grimacing as he got up and balanced on his two feet.

In next to no time he had the voluntary worker on her toes. He reminded her that she had told him yesterday that if he came back today he would receive some money and a place to stay. She denied ever having said that, accusing him of misinterpreting her. She had invited him to help paint the kitchen in the adjacent room. In his defense he brashly opened the tool case on the counter and flung out a couple of paintbrushes.

"Look, this is my working gear, the tools of my trade. You can have them for the centre. How much can you give me for the lot, case and all?"

She was flabbergasted and did not know how to answer him. She was already in a defensive position.

"I didn't actually say I'd give you money. What I said, if I remember right, was that if you came here early, no later than mid-morning, I would type out a letter for you to take to the labour exchange and they'd send you to social security, who would have registered your claim for benefit as a disabled person."

At the mention of the word 'disabled', Johnny felt dizzy and swayed slightly, leaning his arm on the counter.

"You can't expect me to go through all that red tape crap. Can't you see I'm not well, I've only been out of the hospital for two days. How can I go through this rigmarole?"

She admonished him gently but firmly.

"I told you yesterday to come early as it usually takes a whole day to get a supplementary allowance. I'm afraid it might be too late now, but if you still want to go, I can give you a note to take with you."

At that moment he let out a groan and winced. His body was racked with pain, anybody could see that. He held out his bruised hands, claiming that they still stung from the fall he suffered yesterday. He carried his burden well, a promising self-styled martyr.

Her heart bled. She felt pity and pain for his dilemma. Perplexed by him she was caught off guard.

"Can you give me some money for this painting? How much do you think it is worth?"

He held it up so that she could view his masterpiece in its true light.

She thought for a moment.

"Well let's see. I'm not authorised to give away money, but if you go to the youth director's office on the floor above, he may be able to give you a few pounds to see you through."

He relaxed for a moment.

"If you want the painting you can have it to put on the wall."

He turned around, fixed his eye on a spot above the mantelpiece, walked over and taking the calendar off its hook, hung his work of art there, the pride of the centre.

He summarily forgot about his pains and winked at me. He had also conveniently forgotten that he had given it to me as a present. At first he even tried to sell it to me, but decided otherwise. I suppose it is now on permanent loan.

He expects others to be as generous as he is. Having taken the painting away from me, he knelt down beside me and asked me to lend him ten shillings, which I curtly refused.

If I had not witnessed and experienced this bravura performance, I don't think I would have believed it. What striking up of attitude, what posturing, a budding ham actor in the making, or on the make.

Johnny braced himself in preparation for the interview with the youth director, a young fellow by the name of John Snow. As he walked I notice that he had developed a limp. He paused for a few deep breaths, squirmed in utter agony and took the steps up, one by one. I watched him as he disappeared from sight.

How long can he carry on like this I thought? Who is he kidding if not himself? Who else can he kid but himself? A couple of years back when he had started to fix heroin on a regular basis, I tried to make him see what he was doing to himself.

"Johnny you cunt, you little stupid fool, you don't seem to understand your predicament. There you go acting as a loon and fucking yourself up. I ask you if you're depressed and you say 'Yeah' just like that. You bandy about strings of little white lies but they don't dazzle me, not for a moment. Don't try and kid me with this hip crap because I don't play your game anymore. You were offhand and couldn't face me straight. You were irritable, nervy and hung up. The only time you turned around was when you thought the fuzz was about. They give you the horrors, do they? Why did you act so strange? Did you think I was your conscience that you can fling off at times like this when you need to cut out from the scene, but don't know when or how? Well let me tell you something. I am going to be around waiting and watching."

And here I am on time.

Johnny entered my dream world then. The dream took place in the Jewish youth club where I taught an evening drama group twice a week. We were producing a play I wrote which was loosely based on my early association with Johnny.

The club was filled with laughter, noisy banter and a youthful zest. Johnny's ominous figure loomed large over the proceedings, an outsider, helpless but vibrant with his distraught nervous energy.

His was a different kind of manic zest, a dissipation of his abundant gifts in unacceptable social behavior. The youth club members represented the socially-accepted element at peace in their social environment, fitting into the meritocratic grooves being laid out for them.

Then Johnny said something that shook their complacent fun. I think he spluttered a few anti-Semitic jibes that were provocative and he was taken aside by the more able-bodied male members of the club. Johnny, the prodder of societal attitudes and stances did not stand down and kept up his barrage of discordant utterances. I looked on fretting at this unavoidable situation, not wanting to take sides. Johnny was taken outside and beaten up for his racist remarks. I protested vehemently trying to get them to understand that he meant no harm, but they didn't want to listen. I was in a state of mixed loyalties when I awoke from the puzzling dream. Was this the battle between conformism and the anti-social and where do I stand?

How little we change and yet how many changes we go through, learning and unlearning, opening up and shutting off, appearing and being. All is paradoxical.

Johnny came back into the room looking somewhat shaken. He was dithering about at the counter, fidgeting awkwardly with the tool case. Distractedly, he dropped a paintbrush on the floor and stooped to pick it up. His movements were strained and unsure. A tall, flat-chested girl with a Scots accent cracked a wry joke, nudging him with her elbow for a response but his mind was elsewhere. He glanced over towards me without actually noticing me. It was as if, briefly, he had lost his bearing, floundered in his world.

I made a decided effort to get up and stretch my legs. I didn't want to stay there any longer. I wanted out,to go home and be on my own.

"I'm splitting, I'm going, I've had enough."

"No don't go. I'll be getting a few quid off them, and I'll take you for lunch."

"I don't feel hungry, anyway it's going on for half past three."

"What difference does time make?"

"No difference. I just don't feel like hanging round here all day."

"I won't be long. They're trying to fix me up. Just wait a few more minutes please."

I gave him a resigned look to counteract his flaccid smile.

"Alright, a few minutes"

My feelings toward him were manifold. I felt a gnawing frustration at being kept waiting while he sorted out his hang-ups. Why was I here in the first place and how do I fit into this setting? Quietly and calmly sitting here observing my surroundings, I might easily be mistaken for an addict. Having already assumed that most of them were, there is no reason why they shouldn't have already assumed that I was one. I even started to feel uncomfortable about being there for so long and projected this onto Johnny. I felt exasperated and irrationally resented him for it. What right did he have to yank me out of my chosen seclusion and put me among these people? I don't want to know anymore. I cared deeply at one time, believing that the ashes of others held embers of me.

I felt cold and detached, shut off in my own isolation. There was a strained distance between Johnny and me; a cleaving gulf. I viewed him as a stranger locked in his own hold, a fellow traveller whose world intermingled with mine. I wanted to console him with a knowing smile. I am also human. I too feel lost at times, raw with exposure. What did Johnny say to me when I visited him that Sunday night at St Charles Hospital?

"You feel you've been through it all, you've been hurt so many times that nothing touches you anymore." And yet I felt hurt for him and touched by him.

"Oh Jesus, I forgot to phone Maggie." He put his head in his hands. "All my clothes are at her place."

"Such a terrible calamity."

"No but you don't understand, I had a fight with her father and she won't let me in now."

"I don't know how you cope with all your hang-ups."

"I think I'd better phone her to see if I can go back tonight and get a change of gear."

He turned round to the voluntary worker, "Can I use your phone? I've got to call my wife." She hesitated for a second. "I'm not really supposed to...." Then relenting, "Alright, go on then, but do be quick."

"Hello Maggie. Maggie can you hear me?" he bellowed into the mouthpiece of the phone. "Listen Maggie, I'm at this place here," he cupped his hands over the mouthpiece, "the one I told you about. Maggie, are you listening?"

He pulled the receiver away from his ear and feigned a wince. She was obviously abusing him.

"Maggie, Maggie will you let me explain?" There was a stunned silence. "She banged the phone down on me. Would you believe it?"

He placed the receiver down and turned to us asking "Would you ring my wife and tell her I want my clothes?"

"Why, what did she say?" enquired the voluntary worker discreetly.

"She said I had enough clothes with me. Tell her you're my Probation Officer."

"Oh no, I couldn't do that. I don't think it's right of me interfering in your personal squabbles with your wife."

I had quietly stolen away, preoccupying myself by glancing through the pages of the day register, which lay at the far end of the counter. There it is, my name, stuck halfway down the list of about ten for the day, Tuesday 23rd of March 1971, neatly written at the top of the page. Seven names with the letter 'A' next to them, ordinary solid Anglo-Saxon names like James Smith, Ian Taylor, Carol Cox and John Collett.

Casually glancing up from my ruminations, I looked up over the half-dozen faces in the room but didn't see Johnny. The voluntary worker was tidying some papers on the desk. There, in its place of prominence above the mantlepiece was the painting of the island with its corridor to infinity and that bright orange sun. It stood out among the others, pinned on all the walls, child-like scenes with pretty colours, boyhood memories of comic book heroes and the inevitable rough self-portrait sketches. Johnny was top of the class in my estimation.

A squandered talent, a wastrel, the world is full of wasted talents, I thought. The French poet Paul Valery once said "Talent without genius isn't much, but genius without talent isn't anything at all."

I remember bumping into Johnny along the Portobello Road on a Saturday afternoon just before Christmas. A few weeks previously he had been discharged from the model prison Grendon Underwood, after serving a year sentence for theft. I had not seen him for over three years and presumed him dead until Billy Bible informed me that he was still alive and kicking, but living in a cell. There he was amongst the thronging crowds of tourists intermingling with the local colour of West Indian immigrants, cockney street traders and exotic longhaired hippie drop-outs. He was just as I imagined him, only a little older. One of the first things he did was to take out a piece of paper from his breast pocket and proudly tell me that he'd just done a psychological test in which he had made forty words out of a key word in five minutes. With a sense of profound accomplishment he brandished the list of words before me and then pocketed it. The only word that caught my eye was 'test'.

I pondered the incident later. So he is bright in his way. He knows it and I know it. But he was playing similar games when I first met him. The only difference is that he is no longer seventeen.

"Talent doesn't have to be developed, only discovered," he proclaimed at that time.

"No one becomes a brilliant writer or artist overnight. It takes a lot of hard work." "I don't want to develop it. I just want to wander," his voice trails off. "You see, discover it without looking for it. I hope to discover myself in the process."

"But you're not going about it in the right way. You're escaping from yourself."

"You're getting too serious. I don't like getting too serious, it frightens me."

And what of me, one more nurtured talent inexorably lost in the debris of yesteryear? I look at myself as I juggle with the mundane mechanics of my everyday existence, stifled and thwarted by the crunch of change. What can I do but grind on with my chin resolutely stuck out and my shoulder heaving a cumbersome wheel, creaking as it revolves round yet another cycle. Over the hill I go to new pastures, barren and not yet toiled, broken in spirit, lethargic in rebellion, tired out by the same means that do not justify their end.

To soar into the sky once more, to be ebullient with glorious, fulfilling life pulsating through my veins, to feel the ecstatic obsessive zeal towards a goal and to find meaning and purpose in the humdrum. I have seen the light through the tunnel of darkness.

I need a response, a personal as well as public one, to feel that I am part and parcel of my surroundings. I need this in order to feel alive. All I seem to get is negativity and exhaustion, so I withdraw into my shell of petty endeavours. Feeling restless and ill at ease at the ebb and flow of my psychic patterns, I moved self-consciously towards the counter once more. Standing there without purpose or reason, I felt translucent as if my person was there for all to see and mock. I leaned over the counter almost too casually, venturing a question to the voluntary worker.

"Excuse me do you know where Johnny has gone?"

She looked up. "More than likely he is in there," she nodded towards the cubicle.

"Thanks" I said.

I opened the door to the small, windowless cell-like compartment, to find Johnny sitting down beside a wooden table, his bare left arm outstretched tautly before him. His head was bowed down in earnest concentration as he hypnotically sought out a vein to prey on. His works were on the table, a disposable syringe, two glass ampoules of a colorless liquid substance, and his necktie. His jacket hung loosely over his other shoulder. I watched him as he scanned his forearm with gentle patience, his fist clenched tightly so that the blue of his veins showed through the white of his skin. Puncture marks blemished the cleft at his elbow joint.

He picked up one of the ampoules, lifted it to the light and then flicked his finger at its fragile tip until it snapped off. He stuck the needle into the ampoule and slowly drew the liquid into the syringe, making sure he had not left a drop. Then he took the tie and wound it tightly round the top part of his arm, using his teeth to grip one end and making a tourniquet. He flexed the arm bending it inward and then outward again, clenching and unclenching the fist, not taking his eyes off this precise motion.

When he felt ready, the hypodermic syringe poised in his free hand, he plunged the needle deeply into the soft flesh. He didn't connect and hit vein, he tried over and over again, the needle sinking into the flesh, not connecting and pulling out, the cold contact of the needle a self-inflicted mild punishment to be well compensated by warmth and flow.

In again and out, self-caressing, a loving touch, tenderly he probed the skin with the steel needle, letting it gently slip in. It was a bit of love play, a form of masturbation and tactile stimulation. At last he connected, flushing the syringe, drawing blood into its chamber he knew he had hit a high. With a heaving sigh he squirted the red-flowing liquid into his body. Closing his eyes, his mouth half-open, saliva glistening on his teeth, his body filled with a light beautiful glow. The corruption and fear of adult life disappeared and he became a child again, a man that is a boy that is a child.

The needle still hung in his arm, limp and drained of its substance. He scratched the pleasant tickle of his flesh, his body quivering with delight. Hooked on the needle, I once knew a guy who injected himself with water just for the thrill of fixing. Junkie John stuck his needle with tender care into the soft flesh of other boy's bums, the phantom skin-popper they called him. Scots Tony, so thin and delicate, demanded a reverent silence as he fixed himself onto a transcendental plane.

Gentle Brian, who cowered in utter disdain when anyone used the word 'fuck', locked himself in the bathroom for his furtive fix. It was on record that it once took him eight hours. I've known some flashy fixers who did it in public places to shock and gain attention, messy ones who squirted blood all over the place and dead ones who overdosed. It is strange to suddenly think back to those distant days of nineteen sixty-seven.

We were building human pyramids as monuments in our efforts to belong to one another under a blanket of love. We conjured dreams and created auras out of our visions of a brave new world. It was the Summer of Love, halcyon days for pipe dreamers. For some it was a fool's paradise, like Anthea who spiked needles into her wrist, or Freaky Fred who would cry, "Why won't they leave me alone?" as if he was followed by an invisible army of spies.

How did it feel to be one of the beautiful people when the flowers wilted in the winter?

So much has happened since, so many changes and so many dying embers. What happened to that brave dream that brought us all together for a brief moment in time? Where have all the flowers gone, a long time in passing? It flooded out into hazy images of sad gentle freaks in labyrinthine enclaves of darkness, drugs and clawing relationships.

When the backlash of outrage and hysteria fell upon us, we huddled into ghettoes of paranoia. A community forced to turn in on itself, wanton with destruction. The casualties of love whimpered in forgotten places. Sunshine Limited, care of the mental hospital, or was it the morgue? Psychedelic Simon played his flute barefoot in the park. "Where are you now, Psyche Si?"

I am pained into the remembrance of things past and half-forgotten. I rarely see any of them nowadays, if they are still floating on this earth's sphere. Distanced by time and circumstance, the floodgates of memory flung open by the swirling currents flowing through me, I just stood there not quite knowing what to do. My body was numbed, my mind lost in the hinterland of other places, other times. My emotions were aroused from their hidden slumber. There is a microcosmic world, plagued by lost armies of the night, which I carry with me, willy-nilly.

"Listen Johnny, I'm going home. I'll see you around in the next few days," I murmured softly, looking down at him lost in communion with himself. I don't think he even heard me, his eyes closed, oblivious to the harsh strains of social reality. I turned back and walked to the counter and bid farewell to the voluntary worker.

"Must you go?"

"Yes I'm afraid so. I want to get home before the rush-hour begins."
"Isn't Johnny going with you?"
"No, I think he is staying on for awhile longer."
"Alright then, goodbye, do pop in again whenever you're in the area."
"Yes I will. Cheerio, it was nice meeting you."

I walked on, passers-by hurrying to and fro, traffic jamming at intersections, perturbed by the rumbling echoes reverberating within me. As in a dream I moved somnambulantly through torrents and gushes of verbosity. Gardens could be nurtured on all this manure. Images formed and floated in to passages and realms so profound they became banal. Grey misted characters escaped me, only to haunt me like ghosts. I saw a boy treading in mud and grime. He walked on, his feet heavy, his movements laboured.

Efforts were made to lift the heavy feet. Not that they were weighted with lead, but they were bogged down with mud. It was so easy to stumble and fall. He pressed on tired and despairing, often wanting to sit down, but then he would get dirty and have to wash.

He knew well that rivers were few and far between. So sitting was out. What was in? He was in, in the mud and grime. He wiped a tear that had trickled down his cheek, lifted his feet once more and with much effort moved on.

How did he get there in the first place I wondered sadly, as I boarded the crowded Central Line tube train at Tottenham Court Road station?

Standing in the tunnelling, speeding tube train, caught in its incessant rhythmic momentum, the grating of sound roaring through me, I felt invisible like a spirit in the sky. The fall into the night of darkness of the soul, not knowing who or where I am or what social role I will play. Seeing dawns breaking through the mists that shroud my being into nothingness, to resume once more the fabric of my life out of the culmination of the I AM. Having come this far through the dissipation and debris that floats in the murky past of distant days gone by, I feel suddenly free to wander forth and create life out of the hewn mists that lie ahead.

The sky was grey and overcast. The air chilled as I surfaced at Lancaster Gate tube station from my subterranean journey. I saw the Bayswater Road, with its interminable onslaught of speeding traffic, fuming with exhaust and petrol, as a ravine, its raging rapids swelling and surging. I anchored in Hyde Park an island of lush green grass laid out as far as the eye can see. The bleak barren trees, their bows shorn of plumage by the winter months, were awaiting the birth of spring. Suddenly the sun shone briefly, shimmering in a pale silver sky. I looked up at that brave energiser audaciously peeking out at me as if we shared this gentle caprice. I found myself smiling, my eyes impishly beckoning the glimmering god of light and warmth. 'Come fill my body with your radiant glow, light my flickering fire kindled in the wake of spring.'

I watched a couple of pigeons flutter to the ground in front of me, strutting about, their heads held high, plumed chests proudly borne. Plucky little creatures weathering the seasons of change, but they have wings to float on high.

The park was near deserted, a lone figure sauntering slowly by as I made my way home. Almost casually my mind drifted back to Johnny and the havoc that binds him, a self-inflicted pain to satisfy an insatiable habit. He once showed me a raw abscess full of pus on his forearm from fixing barbiturates, which clog the veins. His puffed up and blood specked wrist was abandoned for the now swollen ankles, a crucifying sufferance, Holy Jesus who made martyrs of men in pain. He was in such an agonised state that they moved him to St. Charles Hospital to protect him from himself.

I entered my room contented by its cozy familiarity. Settling back in my easy chair I rolled myself a joint, and lit it. How strange to think that I've come to dislike my forays through the embattled thoroughfares of life. But it wasn't always like this, far from it I pondered, exhaling a long column of smoke, which dissolved into thin air. There was a time, along time, when I sought out the hungry world with a vengeance, haunted by an obsessive vision whose aura wrapped itself around me like a cosmic cape.

Tangier Journal

30/9/1969

It is strange; here I am in Tangier, withdrawn and numb, like so many others here who have retreated into themselves.

Before I left I was aware of a certain isolation drawing in on me. I was cutting myself off from so many and so much. I was living a settled existence and seemed to be sure of the future. I had a quiet confidence borne out of a measure of certainty. Now I just don't know - everything seems a blank and the future is as unknown as tomorrow. I've known this state before. It is a sort of biding time in between full moments. In other words I feel an emptiness, which has to be filled with my own energies. I have given of myself and now I must replenish the loss.

How does one fill a void? Here you sit and smoke in communal isolation, listening to entrancing sounds or idly sitting in a cafe in the 'succo chicco' in the casbah watching the endless coming and going of tourists, shoe-shine boys and sundry characters like the perfume man who leaves a trail of smoky sweet scents behind him. I sometimes go miles out into the barren coast by the rocks and sea, dreaming of anything that drifts into my mind from a random choice taken from memory. I sit down at the table in my apartment in solitude, too weary to talk because words are meaningless and communication is a real effort. Yet the quiet is important in helping me face the past without too many pangs of hope or regret for things that are now over. What will come in the months ahead or let alone in the years to come is as open as the eternal sky. Come to think of it, this is actually the first time this year that I've sat back like this and quietly thought out what has happened to me.

After the 'failure' of my labour of love and my attempt at total theatre *'Love Play'*, which did not live up to its possible potential, I flung myself into Paul's postcard board as a street trader in the West End and ended up in a state of depression. Then there was a sort of reprieve in the gratification gained by making money. New problems set in, changes towards more secure things like earning a living, running a business and making a home. I seemed to be losing myself and didn't know where I was going. I stopped seriously thinking of doing some writing; somehow I didn't need it anymore. But I know that I do want to go on writing and I shall in good time.

I have had a very good year so far, productive in many fields that I need to graze in, how to handle my artistic side and to project myself as an artist, how to pursue a relationship in a balanced way without too many controls, and how to earn money in order to be independent. All three are important to me.

1/10/1969

I am playing solitaire with myself, and learning to win. I am slowly finding myself away from the need and interdependence of relationships and back to the self as it falls back on itself. I am looking at me in the calm quiet of the night, with time on my hands and nothing in my mind. It is just me in an apartment in Tangier, feeling nothing in particular. I feel like a washed up shell on a beach in the serene dawn, glowing slightly as the day breaks.

Resting in the timeless, wrestling with the tide of time, trying not to see too much or interpret too deeply the fathomless void that stretches out into infinity. I go by having immersed myself in the warm waters of love, creating whirlpools of confusion that have landed me on craggy rocks. It is now midday and the sky is clear blue with a gentle sun and a slight breeze. I woke up a little while ago but I'm not quite ready for the intrusive company of others, so I take out my notebook and just jot it down, sipping my orange juice. Every day I want to get out into the open away from the noise of the city, away from people and the necessity of verbalising. I am learning to commune with myself and with nature, slowly finding a quiet peace. I now see I needed a form of retreat even if it doesn't yield up any answers, at the least it will give me the time to clear my head of many things.

2/10/1969

I am now out of this world into a paradise of grand heights looking down at the distant sea, blue and still, the rocky ridges jutting out all about me. The wind is strong but held back by a gentle feeling of warmth. Behind me like a silent film is the city of tangier. I am on top of a beautiful hill looking down on all below me listening to the strains of Arabian music, trying to escape an earthbound feeling of cities, culture and civilisation, wanting to lose myself away from the smells and street sounds of a city.

I have the need for this solitude, this monastic touch for the simple things in life. My pleasures are breaking crisp fresh bread and sipping mint tea, smelling the scents of the earth and feeling the wind against my body. Today I stood on top of this plateau and matched myself against the beauty all around me. I opened my arms and galloped about in my boots, like a colt in a field. I could feel my body brushing the wind in its openness. I sat beside a low wall among the neat white tombstones and let the afternoon sun caress me with its sensual warmth. My eyes closed and patterns loomed ahead. My mind wandered pleasantly in a haze of memories. I left London a week ago slightly perplexed and a little lost.

I don't seem to have the desire to go out and meet people, to socialise. This evening I came back to the apartment before seven and spent the rest of the night idly playing cards, eating, listening to the radio, and just lazing about. Tomorrow will come and I will, no doubt, do something, maybe go for a walk, something simple like that.

Phil, the broke and lost young Canadian I let stay in my apartment, is easy to be with. He is just here, never obvious, always contained in his own world. He is an ideal companion for me, so I'm never really alone though we may sit for hours without uttering a word. There are very few people who I know that I could share this experience with.

I feel strange sitting here listening to the radio, with Phil nearby singing to himself. I feel peaceful and do not want to be disturbed. I am into myself, away from the beck and call of the streets, and other people who make me feel unreal because they are so. I have cut myself off, shut off everything that jars and in this way I have found an inner peace.

How long does one retreat? Until I am ready to go forth into a world of desolation - change heralding greater change, and then what, a grand vision of a star in orbit? Here am I, getting to know myself as I sit back trying to see it in a flashing glimmer of insight. The night drifts on, the radio romances so beautifully about love and I sit here dreaming, caught in the flow of this night.

It is strange and kind of funny, about a year ago in Amsterdam I was also going through an emptying phase. At that time it was manic and outgoing and now it is an inner one. The year that followed was a good one with a lot of promise. This time may well bring forth something of great interest. I feel ready for it, as ready as I've ever felt. What now?

It is now nearly midnight. We prepared two meals today and ate them slowly enjoying all the tastes and flavours. Earlier we had garlic sausage, with an egg, tomato and onion, bread and cheese, coffee and biscuits. Not bad. Later we had a Spanish omelette, chips, bread and coffee. A meal can be the highlight of a day.

Writing is also a pleasure, just sitting down and letting it ooze out, nothing in particular, just thoughts and more thoughts, nothing deep or profound, just a pleasant stream. I can now see how the writer Henry Miller sat there in his easy days letting his fertile mind float by, harnessing the images, collating the thoughts, building patterns and rhythms, listening and abiding to his own pulse. This is something delectable.

We play cards in bouts, silent and leisurely. It keeps the mind on form. The score builds up, as the games become marathons. Once in a while one of us suggests that we go out for a walk, but it seems a real effort, as we're so comfortable in here enmeshed in our cocoon-like mood. I can afford to sit back like this for today is a holiday and so is tomorrow.

3/10/69

I took today as it came waking up around midday. Phil and I just wandered off to the beach and chose a quiet spot away from the noise of others. I lay on the soft sand with my shirt off just dreaming of that everything and nothing, letting feelings touch me and memories gently prod me. It was a vision of a past, flashing moments of loss, my mother and my labour of love. Dreams and creations that grew and are now part of my past, 'Love Play' has been lived, created in its original form and is now part of my past.

The pictures in my mind unfolded and I watched them with a quiet sadness, the curl of the lip into a serene smile. I jolted up and out of myself back to the beach with its whispering shore. I felt the silky sand beneath my bare feet and the wind on my open body. I walked triumphantly towards the waves dipping my feet into the clear coldness and my eyes scanned the sea and the harbour with its picture-postcard view of a ship in dock. I watched the boys playing football and felt good being here. I walked among the crowds on the beach trying to avoid them.

My mind was whirring on, taking in Israel, Kenya, South Africa, the Netherlands and this last year in London. I have travelled extensively these last two years seeing and feeling much. Roaming abroad is often a sad reflective time for me, a distancing of the past. The other day I suddenly realised that more or less half my life is over. I have travelled thus far I said to myself today, and it was a good life, then I wondered why I said it 'was'. I dream of the future too, but an unknown one, as open as ever, but what of the day.

4/10/69

I awoke today around three o'clock in the afternoon, with the odd recurring dream still plaguing me. They are tugging little dream patterns, nothing haunting or foreboding, I think I have now been through that scenario. Before writing this I had a few simple words with Phil who also just woke up. 'Do you want some coffee?' I said, and then we settled down to a wonderful silence. For me, so often a compulsive talker, it has become a joy to be silent and quiet outwardly.

Of course there are sounds from the street below, and no doubt later from the radio. But these sounds are in Arabic and the words do not disturb me. The last few days I've had very little real contact with anybody except Phil and it has been quite pleasant, to my surprise. In a few days time I will open up a little more, as I'm regaining my inner strength. Simplicity in everything I do and say is what I want, and then from here on I can go on to other things. I don't know what I shall do today but I do know it will be something simple.

Integrated is the word that cropped up. I felt integrated once more as a person. For a time I lived in a sense for someone else, all my actions were centered on them. Living closely with someone takes a lot of giving and it is easy to lose a certain amount of autonomy. You develop a need for another person. You always want to know where they are at any given moment so you can feel safe and secure. It wasn't easy for me to wrench myself from my state of enclosure into another's orbit, but I did it and I am not sorry. It is the path I will have to tread. It is an avenue I must develop with certitude, for it is the path that leads to love and closeness with others.

I am learning to relax and rest, to do nothing and not feel guilty about it. I have worked hard this year and never quite gave myself the chance to sit back and see where I was going. Not to say that I now know where I am heading or where I am. I don't. But I am at least emptying so much in order to allow a fresh perspective to the present future.

There is a winter ahead and it may augur well.

5/10/69

I woke up today in a hazy, lazy mood around midday. I rose from my bed after half an hour of meandering thoughts of no consequence, had a shit and then soaked in a hot bath. Phil went down to the shop on the corner to buy some food. I had a glass of orange juice, a mug of coffee and two lemon cookies. I smoked a leisurely fag and had a shave. All of this done in silence as Phil was engrossed in writing a letter home. It is Sunday and I've been here for over a week now. I feel resolute, whatever that means. Time is a great healer. I feel more solid and sure, ready to go out and face other people. I am now gaining the will to do things again and am preparing myself with some trepidation for the onslaught of things to come, loves, challenges and whatever blows my way. I think I am re-authenticating myself once more, making myself whole.

On reflection I had a very pleasant day, looking back well after midnight. I left the apartment with a feeling of nice things to come and a warm approach to people. It was like my first day out after a period of convalescence and I was pleased to be back on the streets walking to the casbah. It was a nice stroll and on the way we decided stop by the Istanbul hotel for a smoke.

There always seems to be some good hash about so we sat on cushions on the rooftop and listened to Bob Dylan and the Credence Clearwater Revival playing *'Proud Mary'*, their latest hit song.

We left and sat at the Cafe Central in the 'succo-chicco'. In no time conversational links knitted us together with some comparative strangers from Spain and the four of us left together in their car to speed down the coast, miles out to a quiet deserted stretch of beach. We parked on a ridge overlooking some rocks and a sandy beach, and climbed down walking in silence along the shore watching the dusk fade from grey into a silky blue.

Suddenly the sky was filled with stars and the sea shone and glistened in reflective glory. The sound of the waves lapping against the sandy beach and crashing onto the rocks is tremendous. It is all sound vibration, searing into the memory of all time. We smoked quietly and drifted back to the car. As we drove back along the dark roads I thought about my brother Mervyn and our sharing and acceptance of one another on the first anniversary of our mother's death in May. The room was so bright that night as we talked about the past and agreed that it is the living that counts. I read out aloud Allen Ginsberg's epic poem 'Kaddish' in memory of his mother Naomi, heroically with passion.

I thought of so many minor incidents, often just an expression that I have photographed and kept somewhere in my subconscious mind only to surface now for no apparent reason. The memories seem to choose themselves, informing the pictures and patterns they present to me. I see various situations thrown up in a certain light and learn to understand them in a different way. Everything falls back into an assumed balance and the events of the past seem to make sense.

In this way the confusion that bugged and mystified me a few weeks ago has now gone and I can comprehend things more clearly. I was afraid I would lose someone I cherished and yet I wanted to free myself from it. In other words I had lost what I wanted. In and through them I had found something I wanted, a companion somewhat different to me that I could share things with. I knew a year back that I now wanted to share some of my experiences with another person, for it gives me pleasure. It is a fairly new for me who has gone so long alone. Eventually the car arrived by the casbah in the old city and we all went to the Royal for another long smoke, striking up pointless little conversations and small talk. Later we bought some food and all came back to my apartment for a meal. We were all strangers meeting fleetingly in our separate small worlds, here in Tangier. The night is still except for the odd crow of a cock. How calm I feel as I sit here stoned in my thoughts.

6/10/69

Another day has slowly trundled by bringing with it a thoughtful weariness. I woke up around two-thirty and spent another odd extra three quarters of an hour lying in bed being resolute with myself; half dreaming of things I must get together. I was firm with myself shaping my mind.

Then Phil and I went for a walk having had a puff from my pipe. We sauntered leisurely through the new town picking up a couple of delicious baguettes filled with tuna fish and egg and munched them sitting on a rail at the 'Grand Succo' near the entrance to the casbah by the Rue de Yusafat.

The street was alive with children playing, aging shopkeepers pottering around in their small shops, and everywhere people walking along to and fro. We shared a slice of cheese pie, freshly baked from a street stall on the corner. Later I bought some toffees and we sucked them as we walked slowly up the hill. I got caught up in the designs of the building, the shape of the structures surrounding me. I felt at home in this street that bears life so vividly. At the top near the entrance to the old city we were suddenly confronted by a mob of hustling youths. It is like being caught in a hive of bees. They bustled about us causing confusion and chaos, offering to guide us to Barbara Hutton's palace. If you look vaguely hip they come out with the stock phrases. 'You want some smoke?' or 'I get you kief or hash, what you want?' I try to ignore them and just walk on. After awhile they see that it is a waste of their time and they slowly move off to target another tourist.

I can see how the American playwright Tennessee Williams imagined that last scene in *'Suddenly Last Summer'*. It is easy to see the incessant hungry hustling as some form of a terrifying ritual full of menace and foreboding. I wonder what I represent to them or am I a symbol of our Civilisation. We eventually land up on some paved pathway overlooking the sea. Whenever I come across the ocean I feel a certain comfort, like seeing an old friend, for I have come to love the sea in all its vicious splendour and savage mystery.

When the sky had darkened and night had set in we made our way slowly back to the apartment. We spent the rest of the night playing our long endless game of cards and in between we talked, smoked and nibbled at tasty snacks. The wind came on strong tonight. Walking through the market earlier I had noticed some bead necklaces and other items of jewellery. I am sure I could make some bread if I bought some and took it back with me. It's a market I dealt with a few months ago when I had a stall at the *Isle of Wight Rock Festival* headlined by Bob Dylan.

Death has struck in our apartment building, so I hear. Last night an Englishman in his thirties was found dead in his bath. They say it was a heart attack.

It is strange how circumstances can happen and so much is gone. To die suddenly abroad, to be the tourist on the next landing, witnessed coming into the building by the man in the food shop by the entrance. How strange, it could be you or me. The next few days I'll just idle about and get my head going towards what I am going to do when I get back home. At least I am having a rest.

7/10/69

The wind is relentless in its vibrating vigour, stirring up the sand on the beach. The sun is warm and the sea is splintered with many small breakers. To shelter from the wind I took refuge in an old abandoned fishing vessel, wiping the gritty sand from my eyes. As I lay there with my eye closed, ears attuned to the humming sound of wind and sea, my mind became still and a seeming nothingness engulfed me. My hair blew in wispy shadows against the mellowed wooden boards matured by the seasons and the elements of nature.

With eyes shut so that nobody could see, I let my mind's eye soar like the restless wind, sand and sea. I saw a smooth white pebble among the soft sand dunes on the beach and without conscious effort I bent down and picked it up, continuing my drifting amble along the silky sand, my body brushing against the steady onslaught of the wind. The white pebble in my hand was warm, soft and almost precious. My fingers toyed with it.

Then my mind's eye transported me to a cemetery on a clear winter's day. It was so peaceful there as I walked past the row upon row of tombstones dating back years and years into a distant time. I walked onwards to a more recently laid grey marble-stoned plot with white and grey pebbles adorning it; to say hello and goodbye to someone I loved so deeply. There it was, the tombstone with the grey marble stonework shining in the noon-day winter sun. I smiled in recognition, having seen it before. The etched letters on the marble were chosen by me. 'Our Dear Miriam' it proclaimed. A mistake the fastidious rabbi said adhering to some ancient rule of wording order.

Hello mum, how are you, wherever you are? I still see you now and again, an expression of fear, anxiety or even a call for love, a longing, a deep longing. Having loved you and I still love you, now that you're gone, having shared in sorrow. There were joyous moments in those last few months when I was with you in Johannesburg. Sitting quietly on a bench in Joubert Park, something simple and not wanting to go home. You were like a little girl. I watched you once so full of life, now so near the end of life, seeing the young children screaming with shrill excitement flying through the air on their swings. You knew this park as a little girl yourself, sharing this with me, your son so pleased to be with you. People hurt you deeply and easily little girl, so vulnerable, sitting here on a bench in Joubert park.

Now you are in West Park cemetery buried not so far from Sam. Dear departed Sam, gone twenty-two years before you, exactly to the day. The third of May. I see the pebbles on the beach and I watch them as I go. Listen to the wind as it blows and blows. Where am I? I am just walking here on a sandy, windy beach; opening my eyes I catch a gentle sun. I am in an old dilapidated fishermen's boat, weathered and gnarled by tide and wind and rain. The sea of sand drifting on the wind has settled on me, covering my notebook and me.

I stood on the mast of this old wreck that was once a fishermen's boat stranded in this sea of sand. The wind was bellowing playfully, knocking me off my guard. I held on to an old rope that was hanging from the mast, in order to steady myself. The wind was determined as it blew me here and there. I stood on the brink anticipating my fall below in to the wavy sand dunes. The swelling sand was rising with the whipping wind, smarting against my face and exposed skin. I was thinking of jumping into the torrential gusts and the spray of the howling wind, when I steadied myself, like a swimmer taking a deep breath before the plunge. And then I couldn't move. It was such a lovely youthful feeling that I just burst out laughing. Here I am swaying in the wind, enjoying the freedom of the moment.

Suddenly I am very young, nine or ten, at a public swimming pool, walking out of the changing room, adjusting my trunks by the buttocks, a skinny lad and conscious of it. 'Here sonny, did you leave your muscles behind?' I did not hear that remark, I was determined not to. I plucked up courage, stuck my scrawny chest out and wandered off with my towel over my shoulder. There were screams of delight, cries of excitement and splashing everywhere. I tingled with tremulous but controlled pleasure. I looked to see if I knew anyone, a face from my street, a boy from my class. There is a splatter of wet feet, a belly dive that sprays my feet, then from behind a push, a sudden jolt and a loss of balance. My head is reeling, feet are kicking, I'm spluttering, can't hold my breath; my arms swaying like a drowning man.

I was panic-stricken but here I am laughing with my arms swaying in the wind, about to jump off this rickety old fishermen's craft. Look here I go. See, it is so easy. Look daddy, watch me. Wheeeee!

Back in the sea of sand blowing and bellowing all about me, swishing along in its current. I am cajoled, jostled and swept along by this mischievous wind. I throw my arms out into the air and I am a mast, my jacket is sail flapping in the wind, my hair is sand-blown and curling all over my face. I am a child playing a game with myself, discovering new and secret treasures among the citadels of the mind. A fancy catches my light stroll. There is a dream twinkling in my bright eyes. I looked at the sea and it confirmed me as a dreamer. 'Eli is a sleepy man' my mother wrote in her last but one letter to my brother Mervyn. I am a dreamer who saw an ocean in a sea of sand.

Little boy crying all alone, my daddy died a while ago and now I am in an orphanage. Climbing down the small hill, steadying a foot on a rock I saw a little 'tok-tokkie' scuttling away in fear. I wiped my crying eyes on the sleeve of my cuff, stopped the pleasant whimpering and stared at the beetle jutting between weeds and rocks on the soft brown earth.

I saw the afternoon sun shining through the Jacaranda trees making my eyes blink. From where I stood I could see the wilderness, that overgrown stretch of mountain rock and scrub. It made me dream and I soon forgot about the tears. I thought about the sky so high. Look and see the sun shining like a trickle of gold dropping from the trees. I remembered that I was unhappy about something but I couldn't quite remember what it was. Maybe in a little while it will come back to me. It seemed so important at the time. There is always another time and another.

On a Sunday my mother would come and visit us. It was something to really look forward to, and then there was black Monday, the beginning of a whole new week with all its attendant problems of homework and early nights in a long dormitory with twenty iron beds and grey blankets. A locker to rest your book and to keep all those special little secrets you don't want anybody else to see, your first postcard from mum on holiday in Durban, a photo of all of us I took from mum's shoebox full of pictures of the family. On quiet afternoons when nobody was around, I'd go to my locker and cherish these items, some of my early sentimental possessions. 'Lights out! no talking! Up at six in the morning, Goodnight all' We all replied 'Goodnight Mr. Klevansky'. Eerie noises of the dark night, dogs howling in the wind. Are they crying? I am feeling cold in this cold room of many beds and frightened little boys. A door bangs down the corridor and the old African night watchman passes by huddled in a blanket carrying his knobkerrie. Spooky moving shadows play on the wall opposite. Someone is snoring in his sleep a few beds away, tired after a long day. It is a gloomy place to expect a boy to grow up in.

'Eli! Eli!' everywhere they are calling out my name and when I look no one is there in particular, just people walking along the seafront. Who was calling me, who called out my name? Was it my mother afraid of letting me go? 'Eli don't go, listen to your mother'. But Eli went, he had to someday. 'You will come back', they all said at the clothing factory where I worked as a young apprentice, 'you will be back in three months' but that three months turned into years and many more years, until it didn't matter whether I came back anymore, only to say goodbye again, to go back to my own wilderness of desires and wild dreams, far from the distant cries from the orphanage.

Sabbaths came and Sabbaths passed. Even holy days came in all their pomp and traditions, rejoicing in the blessings of the Torah. I took long walks along the tree-lined driveway with Bella Bortz on a Friday night, me in my new secondhand suit, and she in a pretty summer dress. Too shy to hold hands as we walk up and down the drive smiling at each other, and exchanging pleasant niceties. Feeling nearly a man at ten years old, going on for eleven, will soon be twelve, as mum says. I am waiting for Sunday. Good old Sunday afternoons. Three o'clock at the big gate waiting for the bus to come from the city centre. No, it's not this one, maybe the next. It must be this one. Ah there she is. 'Mummy, mummy what did you bring us? Why are you so late, we were waiting for you.' Little Mervyn was also there, with spindly legs and freckled face. We walked up the long driveway to the lawn by the tennis courts to sit in the sun and have a picnic. My little sister Theresa is only five and stays with the infants and young ones. Sunday afternoons don't last long and when they are over and gone, the evenings are full of yearnings, tugging at the heart for warm laughter, kisses and hugs. The smell of my mother's talcum powder still lingers in my nose.

Most dark nights hold worlds of yearning, midnight lamps burning in back bedrooms in quiet suburbia, stealing the midnight wax while others snore. A flush of a toilet and a sleepy child wanders back to bed. An hour passes in dead silence. Once there were footsteps near the back path, steady and slow. A cat cries out, love-locked on a garage roof, like a newly born child. It fills the silence for a moment and then disappears into the darkness of the night. I sit staring into space, measuring the blank wall in front of me, peeling off its faded creamery with my eyes. I hear a shuffle of feet in slippers in the hallway. Has she seen the light from my room? It is too late to do anything so I sit back and wait. The door is opened and there she stands in her long white nightie, blinking in the bright light.

'What, are you mad? Go to sleep you silly fool. You won't be able to get up in the morning. Do you know what time it is?'

My mother had a technique, developed over the years, of making everything seem more dramatic than it really is. Moments like this demanded big gestures of clasping hands or throwing them into the air in utter exasperation. It was meant to make me feel guilty. Caught in the act again, the midnight dreamer. There is a wisp in the air, a fragrance in the blue of night. I am walking along a quiet road in the early evening, feeling weary after a long day in the hot sun, jostling with passersby on busy thoroughfares, sensing rest in the relaxed ambience of an open garden square, where children are playing before going to bed.

It is a languid droll time for me seeing eternal moments in the haze of youth. I am looking for that boy I knew because he was me some time ago. I watch myself as I grow, feeling my way around the days that become months and years. I see me standing still, seeing myself caught in a wardrobe mirror, my physical presence emanating a glow of life. My blue eyes are sparkling with pleasure, my smooth face is bronzed by the sun, my hair is blonde and free and my body has become of sexual age, caught in the mirror a picture of youth, a snapshot of a young man of seventeen.

I woke up from a dream, a haunting one, where people were playing games while they danced. It was in a large hall, a venue for wedding receptions, academic conferences, and practice classes on meditation and yoga. My dream entwined all of them. At one time young girls, their pretty frocks adorned with big bows at the waist, were dancing with learned academics, swirling as they spun around leaving their partners to choose others. At another moment the professors of the arts and sciences, who were sitting at the main table on the platform, got out of their seats and did yoga exercises.

The whole hall was full of twirling dancers and devotees of yoga dressed in togas that reached the ground. It was a good sight. I sat on a side seat watching the proceedings with a quiet interest as it gathered momentum, encompassing the whole hall with sweeping movements.

The ritualised yoga dance spread to my side of the large room and a young girl with long golden locks tied up in bright silken ribbons, picked up the movement and threaded her way passed me. She was my sister Theresa. My brother was there too, observing in his learned way. And there was my mother in the midst of all this trying to feed me with a spoon. Lady cabinet ministers, looking bright and emancipated, were gracefully kicking their legs up into the air. Learned men were proudly setting a good example by practicing their own teaching. I watched it all with a joyous feeling and woke up from the dream with the sun steaming into my open eyes, playing with my senses. Feeling the slow edge of time, when dreams become part of living, for in the dream is the realisation of the living. It is the fulfillment in moments of remembrance, to catch a glimpse of that which has been hidden, gone from me forever and yet always with me in the dream.

20/10/1969

2 am: Flight from Gibraltar to London. Tangier is now gone, a memory, albeit a fresh one. I am sitting back in my seat quietly thinking as the aeroplane drones on towards destination home, and then the walk up familiar Christchurch Avenue with its many trees now in autumnal brown and gold. What of my room that holds so many memories of love, laughter and sorrow? It is the beginning of making a home. Can I stay there another winter? It is too early to say. I feel calm inside and slightly eager to face the coming days with a quiet joy, seeing old faces and meeting new ones, finding out about events that I have missed and hoping for some surprises. Enough said, as I shall endeavour to make my own surprises. And what of love and how, when and in what shape will it come? There is so much to look forward to, so much to do. How lucky I am, in certain ways.

Have I changed much? Not really, just a more relaxed person with longer hair and a cooler outlook, confident in what I know, and steadily building my mosaic of splendid colours and patterns.

The present future looks bright and open for me to create in. There is much to satisfy me in life and many things awaiting me. If I take each day and make it beautiful by doing good deeds and thinking wisely, I can't go wrong.

Gandhi: His to Love and Behold

Oz Magazine No. 35, 1972:

India is no stranger to many of us. We have journeyed there in search of spiritual enlightenment, followed the pot trail in search of exotic stoned pleasures. Some of us are deceived by enterprising Swamis, who leave for the lucrative West spinning multi-colored versions of Nirvana. *'Hare Krishna Hare Rama'* has become the chant of our spiritual bliss and our music has been enriched by the rhythms of the sitar and tabla. In custom and dress we have taken on an Indian appearance and sense of time. Some of us discard our attachment to possessions at her Holy Ones' counsel. Others are cast out from our society like her pariahs or Untouchables. Above all, in our struggle to be free men in a just society, we have been greatly influenced by the teachings of one of her most illustrious sons, the Mahatma Gandhi.

In the desert of this century of senseless wars and violent revolutions, Gandhi's doctrine of non-violence has stood like a green shoot. Its method used by young revolutionaries the world over has opened the way to new frontiers. Revolutionaries take to violence if they are in haste. Non-violence is a slower method. A revolution as profound as Gandhi's, which required not so much a change in the social regime as the transmutation of the human substance, can only be achieved with the passing of time.

In *'Return to the Source'*, a journal of great poetic and spiritual beauty, Lanza Del Vasto journeyed to India to become a disciple of Gandhi and to make pilgrimage to the source of the Ganges. It is some thirty years since he spent over a year living the austere life of an ascetic tramp through India with its many-faceted gods, its rigid castes and languid poverty. An India in the yoke of British Imperialism, unable to expiate the immemorial sin of attachment to ignorance.

Del Vasto, renamed Shantidas (Servant of Peace) by Gandhi, returned to form his own order, *'The Community of the Ark'* in France based on the Gandhian philosophy. He has undertaken fasts with

Danilo Dolci in protest against cases of torture in Algiers. The French edition of his book has already sold over a million copies.

Although he spent only three months with Gandhi, it was through the Mahatma's living example that he abandoned his Western garb for a self-spun loin cloth and scarf, and wandered, often barefoot, among the thronging mass of people, bathing in the Ganges, worshipping in the Holy Shrines. He studied yoga and many other disciplines with the mystics, marvelling at the physical grandeur of the land, weathering its seasons of change.

Through Gandhi he learnt simple truths, like the work of the hands is the apprentiship of honesty. Honesty is a certain equality one establishes between what one takes and what one gives. Even the man who devotes himself to the superior activities of the mind is not dispensed from hard work unless he gives up everything that costs labour in this world. Honesty requires that every problem shall be solved in its own sphere. Money in the hands of someone who has never worked with his hands is a meaningless token. One must first earn the right to give. Desires should be reduced to needs, and then man will find himself free. Beware of being sublime without depth, great without foundation and perfect in the air. Touch and feel through action, the truth that your intelligence has seen. Let every man be self-sufficient. Provided he is content with what he produces himself. That is the principle of *Swadeshi* (self-reliance).

Gandhi believed that the problem is not how to sweeten the lot of the proletarian so as to make it acceptable to him, but how to get rid of the proletariat, just as we got rid of slavery. The worker enslaved in serial production fritters himself away in work, which has no purpose for him, no end, no taste, and no sense. The time he spends there is time lost, time sold. He is selling what a free man does not sell: his life. He is a slave. The machine enslaves, the hand sets free.

Man has become a machine; he functions and no longer lives. His movements have been mechanized and so have his desires, his fears, his loves and his hates. His tastes and his opinions, the education of his children, his productive activity, his sport and entertainment, the application of law, the police, the army and the government all tend towards the inhuman perfection of the machine. When you have turned the state into a machine, you yourself will have to be its fuel. But although techniques are continuing their progress, the Religion of Progress is receding in the West.

The policy of Gandhi is incomprehensible if one does not know that its aim is not political but spiritual victory. 'Ahimsa', the doctrine and practice of non-violence is commonly called "passive resistance". But it is actually a conscious and deliberate restraint of the desire for revenge, which is born of fear. One can be sure of non-violent victory when one has conquered fear in oneself, it is not the enemy you have to fight, Gandhi teaches, but the enemy's error, the error your neighbor commits when he happens to think of himself as your enemy. Make yourself an ally of his, against his mistake.

Injustice is something that demands that one should oppose it wherever it appears. The non-violent person does not always wait to be attacked with weapons. It is often he who takes the first step and goes forward to meet violence. Not only does he bear blows, he provokes them. To flee is not refusing violence, but giving in to it. It is withdrawing from victory without withdrawing from the fight. "If the choice were only between violence and cowardice," said Gandhi, "I should not hesitate to recommend violence."

Nobody was less pedantic than this great teacher of a great doctrine, nobody more wary of abstract statements or claims that cannot be verified. No one was more devoid of dogmatic obstinacy or blind fanaticism than the Mahatma.

When some foreign visitor launched an attack on his English oppressors, he answered them by saying: "Their system is bad. They are the first to suffer from it. Doubly so because they do not know that it is bad and that they are suffering from it. As for them, they are men, like ourselves, a mixture of good and bad with more good than bad. I know only too well how inclined we are by our nature to see only evil in our enemies and to stuff evil into them at any cost. The evil we see in them, more often than not, depends on the mean and hasty way we have of seeing others.

The evil or the good that shows in them always depends on which side of ourselves we turn towards them: if it is the best in ourselves that we present to them, the best in them will be brought out in spite of themselves, for like attracts like. But whatever our enemies may be I cannot be judge and party in the same lawsuit. The certainty of achieving our aim depends entirely upon the purity of our ways."

Therein lies the whole secret.

Ah, But Your Land Is Free

Knockabout Special, 1984:

We looked out to the island from the hill overlooking the bay with its harbor down on one side and the stretches of golden beaches below us. The island stood out in the mindless ocean with the sun glittering in reflective glory on the waters, like a jewel in its setting.

I turned to my companion and remarked, "ah, but your land is beautiful". "Yes it's beautiful, I often come here and just stare at the island", he said and then cupping his hand above his eyes, he beckoned me to come closer and to tell him what shapes I could see on the island. "Look, can you see that large building?" he said, pointing to the right of the distant island. "Well, it is a prison. The island is a prison fortress", I peered out and could see a few houses in the hazy distance.

The island had taken on another sense of reality for me. It seemed difficult to reconcile the idea that a prison existed in such idyllic surroundings. "What crimes have the prisoners on the island committed?" I enquired. "I've been puzzling over that for some time now. I know most of them are kept there because their ideas and action have helped further the aims of certain banned organisations. They have been made non-persons. Not only has their liberty of movement been taken away, but also their writings and words cannot be quoted in the press or on television. It's as if you can lock up the ideas", he said, his last words almost lost on a gust of wind.

There was stillness in the air as I watched a lizard climb on to a rock nearby. In my land this couldn't happen, I thought. But I was eager to find out more about the prisoners on the island. "Tell me," I said, "How did they end up there? They must have gone beyond the bounds of the law - surely?"

He looked at me blankly. "The rule of law," he mumbled, "it always starts with a breach of the peace. Such is the timbre of the times that I marvel at the sheer gall of those that beg to differ with the current orthodoxy, that let forth views that are unsympathetic to the power wielders. In time, they all end up on the island, some for years and years".

"In my country people are free to write and say what ever they like", I blurted out. "Why, we even have a park where you can go on Sundays, stand on a soap-box and say whatever you like".

My companion smiled wryly and shuffled his feet, as if he'd heard it all before. "These days when you wrote something and then showed it to the Censorship Board are over. Now you have to ask permission even before you put a word to processor", he stated. There followed a silence.

"You see, we are an ordered society. It is the task of the Manipulation Board, with its computers and vast data banks, to ensure that the established point of view prevails at all times. Those that further the aims of forbidden causes are soon singled out. They are first noted, their actions and writings observed. Then their homes and businesses are raided and those foolish enough to have lying around books, notes or magazines that could even remotely further the aims of any deviant activity as deemed by the Manipulation Board, are held in custody and are known as detainees".

Hadn't I seen a brief item in the media that had flashed the news that the number of detainees had gone up by seventy-two percent? I wondered what was happening, why such a society had evolved. I turned to my companion who was slowly walking up the slope of the hill, and then looked back at the island. I was puzzled and perplexed.

A butterfly flitted by, untrammeled in the open stillness. I started to wend my way along the path until I reached my friend, who was standing on the lip of the hill staring down at the island prison.

You see, our society is basically docile, he patiently explained. "There is no stronger sanction on which enforceable law ultimately rests than public opinion. The media has been tamed and regulated, the commentators and pundits acquiring an uncanny knack of avoiding issues that they feel may be dubious in nature. There is an endless flow of the banal and trivial, mind-fillers that are easy to digest".

We both stood there watching the sun setting over the horizon, the island fading in the half-light, when my companion turned to me and said, "Ah, but your land is free".

ALCHEMICAL CHANGES

"And the leaves of the tree were for the healing of the nations."

Tales of the Portobello

Previously unpublished, 2008:

It is a great feeling walking down the Portobello Road on a Saturday morning amidst all the bustle of a busy market day. There is a laissez-faire air about the place, a feeling that anything can happen if you leave yourself open to the passing show, and can sense the richness of its character and history.

Starting from Notting Hill Gate, curving past *'The Sun in Splendour'* pub and the terraced cottages that lead down to the antiques section, streams of eager tourists from all over the world pass by the once-cheap lodging house where a young, shabby genteel George Orwell ventured forth to experience being down and out in London in the nineteen-thirties

The Portobello Road is world-famous as a marketplace for its antiques and bric-a-brac, its street stalls and indoor arcades are much sought after by dealers, collectors and buyers alike. Tables are decked up with dolls dressed in white muslin and silk fabrics, board games, art deco mirrors, vintage postcards, and much else worth making an offer for. This part of the market operates only on Saturdays and is very picturesque with its downhill slope almost heaving with the throng of tourists winding their way along. There has been a market here since the Middle Ages, but the antiques section started in 1867 when conquering soldiers returning from the far corners of the British Empire with their booty of foreign plunder came here to turn it into hard cash.

The next section is the fruit and vegetable market, run by generations of costermongers, whose stalls are piled high with displays of fresh apples and pears, potatoes, carrots and onions, yams, mangoes, coconuts, and a varied mix of exotic produce. Some, like the Spencer family, have been here since the 19th century, working the market three times a week in all seasons, drawing in the crowds with their cockney banter. This is the commercial centre of the market, three blocks of clothes and shoe shops, a *Tesco*, *Woolworth*, the *Body Shop*, chain store coffee shops and the grade-two listed building, The *Electric Cinema*, the second purpose-built picture palace in the land, and the first to have electricity. Which was once a bughouse showing B-movie double features. It has recently been bought by *Soho House* who own celebrity hideouts in the West End and New York, and now has a trendy restaurant as well as a private members' club.

The patch from Lancaster Road onward, beneath the Westway flyover that straddles the area like an electro-magnetic ley line, to Oxford Gardens three blocks up is known as the Portobello village. Every city has its quarter where new and avant-garde ideas take hold, and this section boasts a vegetarian takeaway, organic food supplies, and *Alchemy*, the headshop, that was once busted for selling rolling papers, which celebrated its thirty-fifth year of counter-culture in the heart of this village. In the dip of the road around the flyover, but only at weekends, is the thriving ragbag flea market which comes alive with its hundreds of stalls of trestle tables laden with crystals, knick knacks, home-made arts and crafts, and racks of jeans, leather jackets and ethnic clothing.

There was once a free shop here that operated on a give-and-take basis, give what you can, take what you need, and many a local squatted property was decked out here, an early example of recycling.

Like an oasis in a hub of grey concrete and milling crowds is the Portobello Green with its leafy trees and landscaped greenery, its benches occupied by the winos and lager imbibers whose animated bonhomie bind them in a special camaraderie.

The next stretch of the road is narrow and has stalls selling second-hand clothing and cast-offs, the remnants from jumble sales. This is a Friday and Saturday market and the goods are piled high for the thrifty to scavenge and rummage through the bundles of polyester and acrylic leftovers, to find the elusive bargain that they are always looking for but seldom find. There are no shops here, only a walled Spanish convent school on one side.

Turn right into Golborne Road and you are into another small market with more antiques, pine tables, paintings and ethnic food street-stalls catering for local needs. The shops are mainly run by Portuguese and Moroccans, and the atmosphere is less frenetic and more relaxed than the Portobello. The fashion designer Stella McCartney, daughter of Beatle Sir Paul, set up her office and workshop here, in a former rundown Baptist church. At the end of the road stands the towering high-rise apartment block *Trellick Towers*, designed by the architect Erno Goldfinger in the sixties. Take the lift to the thirtieth floor and you can see all of London, a vast panorama as far as the eye can see in any direction. This urban obelisk is a local landmark, much loved and hated over the years.

There are very few places in the world where there is such a rich and diverse cultural mix of humanity living in such close proximity. Locals refer to the part near the Ladbroke Grove tube station as "the Grove" or you can see someone or something in 'the Bella or 'the Lane'. The top end up the hill is known as 'the Gate', with its garden squares and affluent dwellings.

Here in this royal borough of Kensington with its resplendent palaces and embassies, townhouses and mansions of Holland Park and Notting Hill, reside some of the richest and most influential members of our society, the entrepreneur Lakshmi Mittal, steel magnate and the acclaimed richest man in Europe, Sir Richard Branson who once had close contacts with the alternative culture that thrived here and spawned the famous Virgin moniker. It was William Blake who once said "Every whore was a virgin once.' The area has more than a fair share of actors, pop stars, Russian oligarchs, minor royals, and the odd winner of a Nobel Prize for Literature, Sir Harold Pinter.

Down the other end, by 'the Grove' in North Kensington, hooded teenagers roam the vast estates of social housing run by trusts and the local council. The reggae group Aswad sang of 'African children living in a concrete jungle'. This is the 'university of the street ' for those growing up in the hip-hop era of crack, skunk and one-parent families. Here live, side-by-side, wave after wave of immigrants as well as their children who were born and brought up here, where the community bonds that are forged over the years are strong. To the kids that live and play in this urban ghetto, 'the Grove' is their 'hood'.

Not so long ago 'the Grove', with its wide, leafy tree-lined streets and three-story terraced houses with their faded painted fronts and peeled-plaster stucco facades crumbling, was in a state of neglect and decay. The post-second world war settlers were young Irishmen who came here looking for work and filled the cheap bed-sits. They worked hard during the week as painters and decorators, laborers on the roads and building sites, and at the weekends they would ended up drinking and fighting at the *'KPH'*, the *'Elgin'* or the *'Warwick Castle'* public houses. The *Kensington Park Hotel* on the corner of Ladbroke Grove and Lancaster Road is still an Irish drinking hole with its pool tables and tarnished glory of a bygone era, and is affectionately known by locals as 'Keep Paddy Happy'.

Of the many immigrant groups who came and made their home in this neighborhood, the men and women who came from the then British colonies of Jamaica, Trinidad, and some of the other Caribbean islands, to work on the tube trains and buses as drivers and conductors, have made a most lasting cultural impact on the area, in the form of *The Notting Hill Carnival*. This two-day event over the August Bank Holiday is Europe's largest outdoor festival attracting crowds in excess of a million. The surrounding streets are full of heaving masses dancing to the cacophony of penny whistles and loud ear-splitting music blaring from the speakers of the many sound systems. The carnival procession with its South American flavour and the dancers and performers dressed up in their feathered plumes, sequined masks and lavish and outrageous costumes, pass by parading on slow-moving motorized floats or dancing in pulsating rhythms in the streets.

It has not been an easy ride for that first generation of Afro-Caribbeans who came from the islands in the sun, to drab, grey North Kensington and its cold and unwelcoming locals. In the late nineteen-fifties a young black man, Kelso Cochrane became the first fatal victim of racism in recent history, when he was stabbed to death by a frenzied mob of teddy boys in Golborne Road. He is buried in the cemetery just up the Harrow Road nearby, and a community centre was named after him. There is a large and vibrant West Indian community in the neighborhood with strong cultural roots. The Rastafarians and their celebration of the 'holy weed of wisdom' Ganja, brought them in conflict with the forces of law and order, and over a long period of time All Saints Road, a stone's throw from the Portobello Road, became known as 'The Front Line.'

The next wave of newcomers swept in from Morocco and Portugal to fill the vacancies in the *National Health Service*, for cleaners and porters, and settled in the estates that shoot off Golborne road. The street itself has a distinct foreign feel to it, with the two communities providing the delicate gourmet delights of Moroccan couscous, lamb tagines and freshly-minted tea, and the Portuguese serving coffee with milk in a glass with hot croissants, and patisseries in the crowded Lisboa and Porto cafes.

The area was a safe refuge for those who left the Soviet Union and its satellite states, or the perils of Nazi Germany. There is a Serbian church in Lancaster road, and further down there used to be a Jewish school where the fitness centre now stands, and a synagogue in Kensington Park road, which is now a nursery school. Since the enlargement of the European Union, the area has so many bright, educated young newcomers from the former Eastern Bloc nations, young men working as postmen, bus drivers and refuse collectors, and the girls in the coffee shops and restaurants.

On a Sunday morning when the Portobello is slowly stirring awake, a trickle of early visitors wander downward past the shuttered lock-ups and arcades of the antique market, and past the *Electric* restaurant with its affluent clientele and their families tucking into a breakfast of egg Benedict and toast, past the Travel Bookshop and then the 'Blue Door' made famous by the film *'Notting Hill'*, which was shot on location here, and became an international box-office success.

The "Blue Door" has been sold off at auction, and the bookshop in Blenheim Crescent has become a tourist shrine with Japanese, and nowadays, Chinese and Korean pilgrims being digitally photographed, sitting on the ledge of the shop's window with its display of pictorial tomes extolling the pleasures of travelling abroad.

In the movie Hugh Grant plays a bumbling bookshop owner who inadvertently bumps into Julia Roberts, starring as a Hollywood actor working in London, walking incognito along the Portobello Road, when he spills his takeaway coffee over her. The comedy writer Richard Curtis who wrote the film script and has a golden touch for implausible comic situations, lived for sometime with his partner Emma Freud, great-grand-daughter of the scion of psycho-analysis Sigmund Freud, in a hidden cottage with a courtyard garden which nestled behind a shop with a flat above, just off Portobello in Westbourne Park Road.

The flat above was the setting for the budding romance about to unfold and many of the film's exterior shots were taken outside its decorative blue front door. The *Travel Bookshop* was only the model for the film script, its fictional interior shots were filmed on a sound stage in a studio, and the shop's street location was shot around the corner in the Portobello road using a made-up shop-front.

To many lovers of this bohemian quarter with its artists, poets, musicians, and amiable drifters and bar-stool philosophers, the heyday of the Portobello scene was the nineteen-sixties, "the good old days" for those old enough to remember them, or too stoned to remember them. This was the epicenter of the counter-culture of love and peace that burgeoned out of the freewheeling swinging sixties of the earlier part of the decade, when the market was described as the street of self-made millionaires. The fashion for decorative vintage army jackets as worn by the Beatles on the cover of *'Sergeant Pepper's Lonely Hearts Club Band'*, was started from a shop in the heart of Portobello village called *'I Was Lord Kitchener's Valet'* and spread to Carnaby Street to became an emblem of swinging London. Antonioni, the Italian film director, dressed his characters in *'Blow Up'*, one of the quintessential films of that decade, in the brocaded uniforms with gold-braided epaulettes.

The Portobello Road was at the crossroads of Haight-Ashbury in San Francisco, the Damstraat in Amsterdam, the island of Ibiza, and the far outreaches of Goa and Kathmandu, which were the final destinations for those who made it on the overland journey East in search of the ultimate spiritual high, or just a good puff of hand-rolled Nepalese temple balls. The *'Summer of Love'* of 1967 heralded a new era with the legendary beat poet Allen Ginsberg chanting mantras at the *Legalize Pot Rally* in Hyde Park, within walking distance to the market, where five thousand of 'the beautiful people' gathered looking splendid in the multi-colored hippie garb of kaftans, headbands and flowing capes. The Portobello was part of a global village that preached and practiced alternative lifestyle choices.

The village in the late sixties and early seventies was the seedbed of the new underground culture that would permeate beyond its confines and whose influence would be generational.

The first wholefood shop *Ceres* opened selling organically grown vegetables, brown rice, mu tea and vegan cakes and breads, in an environmentally-friendly ambience, to the longhaired, fresh-faced, often bare-footed customers. Since then hundreds of similar shops have opened all over Britain. The shop was started by the Sams family, who are expatriates from America, father Ken and his sons Craig and Greg, who pioneered sugar-free jams, veggie-burgers and organic produce and 'Fairtrade'. Craig Sams, who lived and worked in the Portobello village for thirty years, is the founder of the brand *Green and Black* chocolates, which he has recently sold to *Cadbury-Schweppes* for eighty million pounds.

For many years one of the delights of the Saturday market was the procession of Krishna devotees with their shaven heads and flowing orange robes ecstatically singing 'Hare Krishna, Hare Rama' and dancing in praise of their blissful godhead. At one time everybody seemed to be a devotee or follower of one guru or another, depending how fashionable they were at the time. A leaflet posted on a wall at the time read, 'God is alive and well and will be giving a lecture in Kilburn on Thursday night'.

Many young musicians have served their apprenticeship living and working in 'the Gate' and 'the Grove', and its influence on new musical styles has been important. One of the earliest *Pink Floyd* gigs was in All Saints Church hall, a few hundred yards from the Portobello, with hippies gyrating under stroboscopic lights operated by art students. Van Morrison sang on an early album 'Saw you down by Ladbroke Grove this morning', in a haunting come-down ballad, and Yusuf Islam, then a young Cat Stevens sang *'Walking down the Portobello'*, *Quintessence* with their eastern beats evoked 'We're getting it straight in Notting Hill Gate, we sit and meditate'. *Virgin Records* had its head-office in Vernon Yard, a mews in the antique section, and its first retail outlet was in 'the Gate' with its reclining beanbags to sit on while you listened on the earphones.

Both punk and reggae music have their British roots in the Portobello, and the dub beats of reggae still echo down the road on market days blaring from shops and record stalls, and the aging rockers in the village are in mourning for Joe Strummer of the *Clash*, a long time habitué, and godfather of punk, who is no more with us. Bob Marley was busted in the seventies for a small deal of marijuana found in his sock while being searched by the local police, and locked up in the Harrow Road nick, charged and later fined in the magistrate' court.

The *Mountain Grill* café, latterly called *George's Fish Bar*, closed a few years ago. Situated just before the Westway, by the tube train tracks, that leads to Ladbroke Grove station, it was a legendary haunt for young starving musicians to meet and tuck into the cheap fried English breakfasts on offer all day. *Hawkwind*, *Motorhead*, the *Pink Fairies* and the *Deviants* were regulars and all local outfits. *Hawkwind* immortalized the café by entitling an early album *'In The Hall Of The Mountain Grill'*, with lyrics such as 'twixt clatter and platter.' A generation of fans have come to pay homage at the now-demised premises. George, who ran the business for decades with his family, and has now retired to his homeland of Cyprus, used to say, "It's all lies what they write and say."

The Portobello grapevine is awash with rumours of sudden and accidental tragedies and deaths, some unverifiable, others a sad loss, like the death of the great guitarist and rock icon Jimi Hendrix, who died while choking on his own vomit, in his flat in Powis Square. On a sad Sunday morning Paula Yates, television presenter and former wife of Sir Bob Geldof was found dead from an accidental overdose of drugs in her house in St. Luke's Mews, her young daughter at her side. To some this is the street of broken dreams and the road to ruin, a trap they fall into when yesterday's careless pleasures turn into today's addictions.

Being a market street it attracts many characters that rant to themselves or no-one in particular, and can become menacing and threatening when not taking their medication. There is a young woman caked in layers of dirt who walks the street on a regular basis, carrying her personal belongings in plastic bags, with a far-off look in her dead eyes as she trundles past. This wandering, lonely and loveless figure is a haunting reminder to all those that fleetingly pass her by that 'There by the grace of God, go I.'

Local bard and long-time resident and community activist Michael Horovitz can still be seen in the area pulling his trolley behind him, shopping or handing out information. A veteran of the legendary Beat poetry recital of 1965 at the Royal Albert Hall, he has dedicated his life to writing and presenting poetry, publishing the anthologies, *'New Departures'* and *'Children Of Albion'*, and staging the *'Poetry Olympics'*. At present he is the standard-bearer in the campaign to save the derelict underground men's convenience at the junction of Talbot and Portobello road from turning into yet another coffee house.

The Portobello and its circumference has always been a magnet for creative synchronicities that draws novelists, poets, dreamers and visionaries in close proximity, where life-long friendships are lived out until the grim reaper takes his toll.

The novelists Martin Amis and Michael Moorcock have lived many years in the Ladbroke Grove area, the thinker and Druid, John Michell who wrote the cult sixties classic *'View Over Atlantis'* and put ancient Ley lines in the public domain, is a familiar figure in the street. So is Tony Allen, the doyen of alternative comedy who still performs at the *'Inn on the Green'* under the flyover. The writer and acid-guru Brian Barrit who lived in the Grove for decades, wrote "If you take a map of West London and draw a line linking the tube stations of Ladbroke Grove, Notting Hill and Westbourne Park, it will enclose an area known to the wise as the Portobello Triangle."

One of the most talked about and in historical terms infamous characters who lived there must be Peter Rachman, the bald-headed, stocky refugee from war-torn Poland and the ravages of the concentration camps, who amassed a small fortune as a landlord in the confines of North Kensington in the fifties and early sixties, using strong-arm tactics and intimidation against sitting tenants who were made to leave their properties so he could let the rooms off to the newly-arrived immigrants at exorbitant rents. Questions were raised in the *Houses of Commons* by the Member of Parliament for Paddington Ben Parker, a housing scandal was exposed and Peter Rachman was vilified by the popular press. Rachman was linked through his girlfriend Mandy Rice Davis, who with Christine Keeler were the major players, in the Profumo scandal of 1963, that brought down the Conservative government of Harold MacMillan, and ushered in the permissive society. A new word entered the English lexicon; 'Rachmanism' - 'the exploitation and intimidation of tenants by unscrupulous landlords'.

There has always been a seedy underbelly to the Grove, with crack houses, gambling dens, street dealers, gay clubs and prostitution operating at different times. There were many basement dives and all-night cafes, like the *Eldorada* in Westbourne Park Road, which was the haunt of young black hustlers and was where Christine Keeler met Johnny Edgecombe and Lucky Gordon.

The Profumo scandal erupted when Edgecombe, the boyfriend of Keeler, came to the mews house of Stephen Ward, a society osteopath, where Christine was staying, and fired seven shots from a pistol. The trouble was that he was not her only lover, for she was sleeping with John Profumo, the Minister for War, and the Defense Attaché at the Russian embassy. Profumo had to resign in ignominy for lying to the House, Stephen Ward was found guilty of living off immoral earnings, but committed suicide before sentence was passed. Christine Keeler went to prison for perjury and perverting the course of justice.

One of Rachman's henchmen and strong-arm enforcers was a smooth-talking, charismatic Trinidadian migrant called Michael de Freitas, who converted to the Nation of Islam and became known as Michael Abdul Malik, aka Michael X, a leading exponent of Black Power in the radical sixties. Michael had many friends in the alternative movement including John Lennon and John Michell, and spent a lot of time around the village.

He became friends with Nigel Samuels, the young vulnerable heir to a property fortune, who helped Michael to buy what became '*The Black House*' in Islington. Nigel Samuels once remarked that he and Michael were two of five people who were going to rule the world. When asked who the other three were, he replied, "We haven't decided yet." Michael was charged with blackmail and kidnapping in this country but fled to Trinidad and while there was arrested for the murder of a barber. He escaped and was hunted down in Guyana, brought back to Trinidad and hanged on the orders of the Privy Council, his death warrant signed by the Queen. The words 'MICHAEL X' appeared forty feet off the ground on the railway bridge by the Ladbroke tube station.

The place has a rich and vibrant if somewhat dark social history that in recent times includes the race riots of the fifties, the confrontations outside the Mangrove café on the 'frontline' and at carnival time, between the police and the local Afro-Caribbean community, the unsolved murder in the Grove of six prostitutes who were found naked by canal waterways in Acton and Ealing, the discovery of the gruesome remains of women's bodies hidden under the floorboards of 10 Rillington Place, having been murdered by John Christie, a projectionist at the *Electric Cinema* who was later hanged, and other tales too numerous to mention here.

For many sojourners and wayfarers who have passed the time mingling in the anonymity of the multi-coloured social fabric that is woven into the surroundings, it is a community full of energy and happy memories of shared moments in the busy marketplace, and a nostalgic reminder of friendships and love affairs in bygone days.

Hundreds of years ago, the land around Portobello was a wild and wooded place, where vagrants and vagabonds, gypsies and outlaws held sway. Apart from a few farms on the edges of the woods such as Barley Shotts, near to what is now the heart of Portobello village under the Westway flyover, most of the area remained dangerous with highwaymen waylaying the occasional traveller.

Like many people in London in 1737, the farmer of Barley Shotts was excited about Admiral Vernon's capture from the Spanish of Puerto Bello in Panama, a victory that was seen as a major step to British conquest of North America. In his patriotic zeal he renamed his farm Portobello Farm. The cart-track leading from the farm to the main road to London, which passed through Notting Hill, became known locally as Portobello Farm Lane.

By the early nineteen-hundreds the scene around Portobello Farm Lane was described by Sir William Bull in the *Times*: "Saturday was carnival time in the winter, when the market was thronged like a fair. The people overflowed from the pavement so that the roadway was quite impassable for horse traffic, on the east side were coster's barrows, in the streets were side shows."

Seven Years of Alchemy

Home Grown Magazine Volume 1 No.5, 1979:

On April Fools' Day in 1972, the *Alchemy* stall began trading in the indoor market at 253 Portobello Road. It came about and grew out of the needs of the alternative culture that spawned around Ladbroke Grove. It was a colourful time when nearly everyone you met had either just come back from India, or was about to embark on the overland journey. They had acquired a taste for Oriental and ethnic items such as incense, perfumed oils, balms and henna. Chillums from the East and sipsis from Morocco were the way you smoked dope, besides rolling a three-skinned joint.

To me it has always been a sort of magical stall, reflecting the current of events and people that flow through the Portobello on a Saturday. At the tide of the great gurus you encountered beatific smiles and enlightened spirits, and everyone was into macrobiotics and the like. It was a period when the oriental root ginseng was eagerly sought after by a band of fervent devotees and out of *Alchemy* came the *Emperor Ginseng Company*, which sells ginseng and royal jelly to this day. At the end of our first year we put out the *Alchemical Almanac* and *Handbook of Herbal Highs*, which is now long out of print, and a year later the *Guide to the East*, an account of the overland journey to India, and as the passing show unfolded we brought out the *Brain Storm Comix* series, which featured Bryan Talbot's trilogy of the adventures of Chester P. Hakenbush, the psychedelic alchemist, and out of this experience came the magazine you are now reading, *Home Grown*. In all we have now published over 130,000 copies over the years, which have been read by a great many more people, and have drifted to many a distant shore.

To think it all came out of a Saturday stall in the Portobello, out of the desires and wants, and the changing times of the good folk who passed through there over the years, stopping awhile to have a chat and buy a pipe or packet of skins. It is to all of you *Alchemy* says a big thank you for these seven years. Here's to the wisdom of the weed and the many strange and beautiful people I have met through it.

Stay high!

Komix Kudos: The story behind *Brainstorm Comix*

"My cousin Adam found the first Brainstorm comic. He was a fifteen-year old proto-hippy, I was a fourteen year-old comics fan, but we both loved Brainstorm. Over the next few years I picked up all the Brainstorms (and Mixed Bunch) and loved watching Bryan Talbot learn his craft and grow beyond the underground, as an artist, as a writer and as a storyteller." - Neil Gaiman.

Northern Lightz No 8, 2003:

Wow! I can't believe it. Bryan Talbot's cartoon strip in *Komix Comics* (1977) is to be published again and this time in full colour. In the first few panels there are scenes from my flat in the Portobello Road area of London. And there I am with Bryan (in silhouette) saying. "Let's do it!" I was going to publish Bryan's twenty-page strip *'Out of the Crucible'* featuring the adventures of a longhaired, bespectacled and bearded hippy named Chester P. Hakenbush, the psychedelic alchemist. It was a momentous occasion, now immortalized in the esteemed publication *Northern Lightz* twenty-seven years later.

How did it all start? In 1972 I opened a headshop stall in an indoor market on the famous Portobello Road, called *Alchemy*, selling ethnic items people were bringing back from India, anything associated with the alternative culture at the time. I dispensed balms from the East, exotic herbal highs in large glass jars, perfumed oils, incense. I thought of myself as some sort of 'medicine head', and when I moved into that flat around the corner, my lounge-turned-workroom was full of bags of nervines and excitants, for I was preparing for my *Alchemical Almanac* of herbal highs.

I met Bryan soon after when he came to my stall to buy goods for a headshop he was about to open in his hometown Preston in Lancashire, called *White Rabbit*, and we hit it off right away. He was a twenty-year-old graphic art student influenced by the burgeoning underground comix scene with its mainly American cartoonists like Gilbert Shelton, Robert Crumb, Rick Griffin and many more, who were living legends.

During one of those forays down to London to submit a comic strip to *Cozmic Comics*, published by Felix Dennis of *Oz Magazine* fame, he came to see me in my flat and felt rather dejected, as the strip was not printed. I said, "If you ever do a comic I'll publish it." Bryan had finished college and had been unemployed for a year. He had married his childhood sweetheart Mary and they had two kids to feed and instead of doing something sensible, like getting a job as a dustman, he decided to do the comic for me.

He had already done four pages of *'Out of the Crucible'* while still at college (two of which he redrew). The other sixteen pages took him five months to draw, and then he hitchhiked down to London to present it to me. On the day he came to my flat, some 'bob-a-job' kids I'd let in to clean the place had just robbed me.

I had gone to look for them and felt let down because I'd put my trust in them. When I returned Bryan was waiting for me. My German girlfriend Brigitte had made him some tea. I sat down and Bryan put the pages of artwork on my lap. I felt deeply moved. Something had been taken and there was something given. I felt as if it was drawn especially for me.

From the moment I first set eyes on Chester P. Hakenbush, the psychedelic alchemist in his first inner-space adventure, I identified with his search for ultimate reality. *Brainstorm Comix* was to come into the light. At that stage we had no cover and I had to find advertising to fill it out and pay for the printer.

Two magical events took place on the same day, the 26th November 1975. On that day Brigitte and I were married in a Buddhist temple. A few close friends, of whom Bryan was one, attended the ceremony. When we returned to my flat, many guests had gathered, lounging on cushions and carpets. I got a call from the printer informing me that the first batch of comics would be arriving at nearby Paddington railway station. We rushed off to pick them up and when we got back Bryan took one out and just looked at it in wonderment and awe. I passed a few copies around and soon nearly everyone was reading them.

Publishing the three epic adventures of Chester P. and in so doing, 'discovering' the fresh instinctive talent about to flow out of Bryan Talbot, is one of the labours of love I am most proud of. It was a seminal work, an experiment in visual storytelling styles that encompasses many popular cultural influences. Chester's cerebral journey into inner and outer space takes us along a mystical quest for spiritual unity. Like the alchemical text it is riddled with subtle hidden references and allegorical situations that delight the adept and enlighten the apprentice.

In all I published six *Brainstorm Comix* which, in retrospect, are seen as a landmark in comic history, at least in British underground comics. I went on to publish and edit *Home Grown*, Europe's first dope magazine, and I still run *Alchemy*, which is situated just a few doors from the original place. This year it is celebrating thirty years of counter-culture.

Of course Bryan has gone on to do great works like the *'Luther Arkwright Adventures'*, *'Tale of One Bad Rat'* and *'Heart of Empire'*. Today he has an international reputation and is much-loved and respected for his unique graphic storytelling. This year I was at Bryan's fiftieth birthday. My, how time flies.

In the last frame of *Komix Comics*, there is a man with a bow-tie chewing on a cigar, selling *Kung Fu* and other magazines. It is a thinly-veiled skit of Felix Dennis, who published *Cozmic Comics* all those years ago. Today Felix is one of the hundred richest people in the UK, with a worldwide publishing empire. Just this month I received a copy of one of his books, signed:

"To Lee, keeping the faith, Felix".

Thoroughly Ripped with Gilbert Shelton

Home Grown Magazine Vol 1. No. 9, 1981:

> *Underground comix are a modern art form with a large cult following. Like a hall of mirrors, they distort and exaggerate reality, turning the sublime into the ridiculous, the serious into absurdity, tickling the rib and poking an outrageous finger at social convention and humbug. The golden age of underground comics spawned artists like Gilbert Shelton and Robert Crumb, among others, with their unique and anarchic talents. Lee Harris spoke to Gilbert Shelton, creator of Those Fabulous Furry Freak Brothers, when he was in London, and is proud to present him here, in his own words.*

I first smoked marijuana in Mexico in 1959, while I was going to the University of Texas. On weekends we'd drive down to Mexico, it's only two hundred miles. It was just another form of entertainment. I remember we were so paranoiac at first. On the rare occasion when anyone would have marijuana to smoke we would all go into the bathroom and shut the door and put a towel under the crack in the door so that the smoke wouldn't escape and get out of the house and go down to the police station four miles away and cause the police to come and arrest us all. The laws have been changed since then, of course, and now Texas has a fairly liberal marijuana law, more liberal than California even. In those days though, you could get life imprisonment for possession for possession of marijuana, third offence.

At the University of Texas, the Students' Association actually published a humour magazine, which they paid the editor to edit, and in fact that was my education. I attended classes and got a degree, but actually my chief interest was working on the humour magazine. It was not a credit course, it was just for fun. The magazine was called *The Texas Ranger*. We would exchange magazines with other colleges, so the jokes and cartoons were published in more than one magazine. I did some Wonder Warthog comics, that's when I started it. There was a board of censors that had to approve of everything that went into the magazine. If the college magazines kind of mentioned dope, it would have to be a secret reference to get by the board of censors, who of course didn't know anything about marijuana. I remember it was quite a game trying to sneak things by the censors. In fact one entire editorial staff got fired all at once because they sneaked the word "fuck" by the censors by hiding it in an illustration, and after the magazine was printed and distributed to all the students, then the discovery was made. The dreaded word was printed in the magazine, so they were all dismissed.

When I was in the eighth grade, I presented a play at school that I adapted from a Donald Duck comic book, and memorized all the lines and had actors with duck costumes and beaks playing all the parts. That forced me to analyse that comic strip very closely. It was one written by Carl Barks, and it had Donald Duck, and it also had Donald's cousin, Gladstone Gander, the duck with the best luck in the world. We turned this into a fifteen-minute play. I was twelve years old at the time. After that I understood how to draw a comic strip because I had turned a comic strip into a play. I think it pointed out to me that what the comic strip could do I could not do live, and made me appreciate it. One of the things was to have an earthquake by tossing the furniture around, that was the fun part of the play.

I always drew, I can't remember not drawing. I would copy comic strips out of the paper and draw things in my notebooks when I was supposed to be doing my homework, that sort of thing. When drawing with marijuana helps a little bit because mainly it enabled me to sit still a little longer. It doesn't seem to act on that part of the brain that produces patience, and concentration is the result. It takes hours and hours, a long time for me to finish a drawing. I'll put black ink down for awhile and then I'll cover up mistakes and changes with white paint, and then I'll go back and forth, back and forth with black ink and white paint. Maybe a real artist is somebody that can do it effortlessly, although that's the technique, I think. I don't think a good technique is necessary to make a good comic strip. It's the words and the story that are more important than the technique.

When I left college I didn't know what I was going to do. I went and looked up Harvey Kurtzman in New York City and he was very helpful. He printed my comic strips and paid me money. I was paid for the Texas Ranger job, that was a hundred dollars a month, enough to live on when I was a student. I earned as much later when

I was working for *Help* magazine. They didn't publish as often. In fact *Help* finally went out of business forever in 1965. In New York I moved around a lot, you live off other people basically. One time in New York I lived in someone else's apartment in the living room on the sofa for three or four months. That was Terry Gilliam who is an American who now works with *Monty Python*. He was the assistant editor of *Help* magazine. He had a humour magazine at his college too in Los Angeles, *The Occidental College Fang*.

In 1965 I went to California for the first time. At that time I went to Los Angeles, where I established the *Wonder Warthog* comics for Drag Cartoons. Then I moved back to Texas for two years, doing the Warthog comics and mailing them to Los Angeles. Finally that publisher went out of business in 1967, after publishing two issues of Wonder Warthog Quarterly. A sixty-four page comic book. That's what bankrupted him. Drag Cartoons had a tremendous circulation; I think it was two hundred thousand a month. They were very automotive oriented, most of it was done by the publisher himself. Pete Millar, who is a cartoonist. I have an interest in cars and hot-rods that comes from growing up in Texas. I came to have automobiles after I came to live in California for a while.

Back in Texas in 1967, I and two of my friends who happened to be working on *Wonder Warthog Quarterly* with me, opened up a headshop in Austin, Texas. It was the first one in all of Texas. It was right across the street from the State Capitol building. It was first called Underground City Hall and then the name was changed to Oatwillies Campaign Headquarters. I left soon after the store opened. I couldn't stand the pressures of actually working in a headshop, even under the most favourable conditions in Texas. We put our earnings from *Wonder Warthog Quarterly* into that store, a cheque for a thousand dollars. We waited months and months for that cheque. The shop is still open now, thirteen years later, due to the efforts of the current owners, the people who took it over after I left.

I suppose we were trying to imitate the Californian scene like everybody else was. We opened up a rock and roll dance hall, a big old dilapidated building that had been a department store. We had remodeled and turned it into a concert hall, of sorts. I was the sign painter. I painted a big sign for the outside front that said Vulcan Gas Company.

Then I did a series of posters, each week we'd print up some nice posters, and put them up in various store windows all over town, on the model of the Avalon Ballroom and Fillmore West in San Francisco, who were having some really beautiful posters done by Victor Moscoso, Rick Griffin and Wes Wilson. Throughout '67 and '68, I seem to recall I was going to be a poster artist myself.

The Avalon Ballroom lost its license to have concerts because of too much noise. I'd been doing posters for the Avalon Ballroom and invested in a printing press, we were printing the posters as well. When they quit giving the concerts, that's how the Rip Off Press got started. We were going to print rock and roll posters, however the reality of economics made us be in the comic book business. Besides me, there was the cartoonist Jack Jaxon and the guy who ran the printing press whose name was Dave Moriarty.

In early '68, back in Texas, I did a little ten-minute movie in black and white in 16mm called *'The Freak Brothers March on Capitol'*. Anyway, the only copy of that movie was lost. I did a comic strip to advertise the movie. In the comic strip the three Freak Brothers, Phineas, Fat Freddy and Freewheelin' Franklin appear for the first time. It appeared on a single sheet of paper as a handbill.

Now it's part of the *Freak Brothers Comic Book, Number One*. It's the story about the giant magic marijuana seed, like Jack and the Beanstalk. People seemed to like the comic strip so much that I forgot about the movie and just kept doing the comic strips. I did it for magazine and comics. They were traded and exchanged around the underground press.

Fat Freddy's Cat first appeared when the *Freak Brothers* were in a weekly feature in the *Los Angeles Free Press* in 1970. It used to be on the back page every week with the *Freak Brothers* being most of the page and *Fat Freddy's Cat* would be a small strip down at the bottom. Which is like the old-fashioned, traditional form that the comics were in the American newspapers on Sunday. They would be a large strip and a related smaller strip. That *Krazy Kat* started as a small strip underneath a larger one.

It was the cat that lived underneath the house that was occupied by the family. Later Krazy Kat became more important than the original large comic strip, taking up the whole page, and the original one was forgotten.

I've been around cats a lot. Cats just get along better with stoned people. It certainly doesn't bother the cat if human beings just sit there and don't move, that's fine with the cat.

Actually it was someone here in London who first published a separate edition of only the cat strips, a small edition but it sold fairly well. So we published our version of the same thing in San Francisco, from *Rip Off Press*.

I first became aware of Robert Crumb's cartoons in *Help* magazine. The first thing of Crumb's that I remember seeing was *Robert Crumb Visits Harlem*, it's kind of a spoof on a series that was in *Playboy*, called Shel Silverstein visits here and there, Robert Crumb's visit to Harlem wasn't funny like Silverstein's series, but instead it was a cartoony drawing of reality with all the real graffiti on the walls and everything. It was really fantastic and original stuff at the time.

Robert Crumb and his friends in San Francisco did *Zap Comix* that kind of started that side of the movement. There's a publisher in Berkeley called the *Print Mint*, it was doing first a comic newspaper, then a book called *Yellow Dog*. Then *Rip Off Press* started doing comix, and a third one called *Last Gasp*. Those three publishers started in the late sixties or early seventies. The word "Comix" was probably Robert Crumb's doing with *Zap Comix*. For the lack of a better term, that is what it is, comics with an "x", or underground comix, but they're not, and never have been really underground.

The *Fabulous Furry Freak Brothers*, Number One, was printed by *Rip Off Press* in 1970. Up to date we've printed eight or nine hundred thousand, I should think. We keep reprinting them. I think the first print-run was 20,000. It's the famous *Rip Off Press* distribution system that uses the trickle technique. That is, it keeps selling over a long period of time at a slow rate. That's how *Rip Off Press* got started, by groping around in the darkness, with the mailing list left over from the rock and roll business, that is the list of headshops and record stores that sold rock and roll posters.

I never had any capital, except the original two hundred and fifty dollars it took to buy the printing press. I quickly refused to have anything to do with the printing press as it was too dirty to be a printer and an artist in the same lifetime. I had to do dark-room duty for a while. Now, although I'm still an officer for *Rip Off Press*, I mainly do just drawing cartoons and little public relations work, and the less I know about the business, the happier I am. That's the other department. There's Fred Todd, who's the fourth original owner, he's the president now. We are all from Texas. I can't explain why the underground comix came to be centred in San Francisco, except that Robert Crumb lived there for a while and started *Zap Comix*, which was the model for most of the succeeding comix. *Rip Off Press* just grew organically, kind of around the *Freak Brothers* comix. Being self sufficient and independent was one of the most appealing things about the hippie ethic. There's been a number of European translations of the *Freak Brothers*. I think Italy was the first country to translate the Freak Brothers back in '73, then France was next, then the English *Fat Freddy's Cat* book was done, and since then there has been various other translations, German, Danish, ten or twelve altogether. I've seen it in Finnish, Norwegian, but when I see it in Russian then I'll know it really translates.

In the summer of '79 *Universal Studios* in Los Angeles bought the movie rights to the *Freak Brothers*. I sold the rights first to *Rip Off Press*, and *Rip Off Press* in turn sold the movie rights to Universal. That's so I personally wouldn't have to be against fifty lawyers, Universal's law staff. It was a reasonable sum. The screenwriter and director is supposed to be Bill Norton. They're still working on the film or sitting on it or something, I don't really know, I'm not keeping in that close contact. The contact from my side is Dave Sheridan, who's supposed to be technical consultant, whatever that means. I trust Dave to see that it's right when they're doing it.

The *Freak Brothers* is being done now by Dave Sheridan and Paul Mavrides doing artwork and myself doing the writing and I'm doing *Fat Freddy's Cat* by myself. That will appear in various places such as *Knockabout Comix* in London. I never know from one month to the next what I'll be working on. *Rip Off Press*, being a corporation is like a hungry live creature that is eating up everybody's lives now as it grows and grows, you know the way businesses are.

I think it all started with the *Whole Earth Catalog*, which had such a tremendous success ten years ago, and it led directly to other publishing and distribution ventures which greatly strengthened the West Coast publishing thing. It strengthened what was just beginning to grow there.

The Home Grown Years

'The Best of Home Grown' 1994:

> High, Welcome to Home Grown, Europe's first dope magazine. In this premiere issue we present the most authoritative writers on dope-oriented subjects and an array of fine graphic art.

Thus began the editorial to *Home Grown*, No.1, published in June 1977. In that first editorial I stated that *Home Grown* would aim at presenting an enlightened and informative, as well as entertaining, attitude to its subject - views and approaches not expressed by the popular media. It was produced as a celebration of 10 years of alternative culture. The flower children of that *'Summer of Love'* had grown up and most of the culture they spawned had been assimilated into a wider society. Cannabis, which was once something the hippies took, was used and accepted by people in all walks of life. Like many others, I believed that the laws on cannabis were immoral in principle and unworkable in practice. Cannabis has been illegal in Britain since 1928, and by the mid-seventies over 100,000 persons had been convicted of cannabis offences.

Looking back over the years it is hard to believe the furore that first issue caused. It received widespread publicity with reports appearing in many parts of the world. The press had a field day. "DANGER OF THE DRUG MAGAZINE. This bookstall horror is a nasty threat to your children" ran the lurid headline of a Sunday tabloid. "SHOCKING DISCOVERY IN GLASGOW RECORD SHOP" and "POLICE KEEP EYE ON DRUG MAGAZINE" were some of the responses of the provincial press. In a thumbs-down review in an underground paper I was called a 'crypto-fascist' for signing off with the words "Into the New Age".

As the dust settled and the threat of writs from a seed and tobacco company receded, the headline "BAN THIS NEW DRUGS MAG, DEMANDS MP", appeared in the popular press. A long forgotten Labour Member of Parliament, Peter Hardy, had written to the then Home Secretary, Merlyn Rees, asking him to ban the magazine and prosecute us for "inciting people by implication to break the law".

The press reported that the Home Office were "taking a keen interest" in the magazine and had asked to be sent future copies. So the Home Office's 'Dangerous Drugs Branch' became one of our first subscribers.

After all the hue and cry it became increasingly difficult to find distributors and stockists brave enough to take further issues. To top it all, our first distributor went bankrupt owing us money, and making our hard sacrifice seem fruitless, but somehow, by sheer dint of determination, we overcame the various hurdles in our path, and with scant financial resources continued to publish two issues of Home Grown each year, for the next five years, improving and learning as we went along. In the ten issues we published over 150,000 copies of the magazine, reaching many parts of the world. Today copies of *Home Grown* are much-revered collectors' items; a complete set being valued at $200 in an American catalogue of rare drug and counter-culture works.

Being a publisher and erstwhile editor of *Home Grown* as well as advertising manager, street-seller and general dogsbody, was a labour of love. Out of painful and difficult experiences often come rich rewards. One of them was the privilege of meeting and working with an interesting group of writers, illustrators and photographers, whom I shall call the 'Home Grown Generation'.

In the Ladbroke Grove area of West London in the late seventies there existed a high society of writers, poets, visionaries, artists, thinkers, musicians, performing artists and street-hustlers. A creative community of counter-culturists, a veritable bohemia of activity, that thrived through a stagnant cultural climate of collectivism and conformity.

This Ladbroke Grove renaissance took place in the wake of the serious demise of the underground press of the late sixties, which left a lot of nurtured talent high and dry. In the changed atmosphere of repression and censoriousness, a small number of radical publications emerged and flourished for a time, like beacons in a dark landscape.

Notably, there was *'The Fanatic'*, an anarchic journal put out by Richard Adams and Heathcote Williams; *'The Beast'*, the first animal liberation magazine, published and edited by John May, who was an associate editor of *Home Grown*; *The Index of Possibilities*, by the collective from the last days of *'Frendz Magazine'*, which included Michael Marten, John Chesterman, John Trux et al; *'Bananas'*, a literary magazine edited by Emma Tennant; Michael Horowitz's poetry journal *'New Departures'*; and John Michell's *'Radical Traditionalist Papers'*.

It was a very productive time. Andy Leighton revived that old stalwart of the alternative society, *'International Times' (IT)* (continued later by Max Handley, an associate editor of *Home Grown*, with Mike Lessor, Chris Sanders and Lynn Soloman). Tony and Carol Bennet began publishing Gilbert Shelton's underground comics, *'The Fabulous Furry Freak Brothers'*, and the work of Hunt Emerson. In the years preceding *Home Grown*, I published the *Brainstorm Comix* series, which featured the then unknown Bryan Talbot's trilogy, the *'Adventures of Chester P. Hakenbush'*, the psychedelic alchemist. The Sams family, Ken and his sons, Gregory and Craig, put out *'Seed'*, the journal of organic living, Amon Saba Saakana (Sebastian Clarke) published *'Frontline'* on black politics and culture and Georgina Downs published *'Alternative London'*.

In this cauldron of creativity there were community presses run by Mike Braybrook and Colin Bennet, and Tony Allen's *'Corrugated Times'*, writers and artists of calibre like Mick Farren, Ed Barker, Michelle Mortimer (Mikki Rain), and the photographer Ron Reid. There were the typesetters Caroline McKechnie and *Dark Moon's* Helen Lowe and Ann Lewis. There was also the explosion of punk fanzines that emanated from the presses of Joly MacFie's *Better Badges* on the Portobello Road.

I lived and worked in the Grove amidst this creative hub of people, many of who contributed to the magazine. It was a coming together of many interesting characters; What Ram Dass might call "The most exquisite rascals of our age". Some were luminaries of the underground and my culture heroes from the early days of psychedelia, such as Michael Hollingshead, who wrote *'The Man Who Turned On The World'*; George Andrews who co-edited with Simon Vinkenoog *'The Book of Grass'*; and David Soloman, author of *'The Marijuana Papers'* and *'LSD - The Consciousness Expanding Drug'*, published in 1964.

Heathcote Williams, the poet, playwright and polemicist of the free state of Albion, introduced me to David Soloman just two weeks before he was arrested on LSD conspiracy charges in March 1977, in the biggest bust ever mounted in this country, code named *Operation Julie*. The gentle 52-year-old writer, who had cycled to my flat, was made out to be 'Mr. Big' in the show trial that followed and sentenced to ten years imprisonment, and later deported to America. Such was the spirit of the time.

There was Steve Abrams, founder of *SOMA*, and initiator of the full-page advert in *The Times* in July 1967, which called for the decriminalisation of cannabis, and Brian Barritt, author of *'Whisper'*; a former merchant seaman and dope smuggler, who was back in the Grove writing "loon-time scripts as a method of getting high".

We highlighted the plight of prisoners in foreign jails, publishing the moving letters of Danny de Souza, from Ladbroke Grove, who was busted in Turkey in 1975 for importing five kilos of hashish, and sentenced to 30 years in jail, later reduced to eighteen. Danny de Souza served twelve years of his sentence, and I had the pleasure of eventually meeting him in the Grove in 1990.

As time passed new talent appeared and made their mark on Home Grown, like Tim Malyon, broadcaster, photographer and founder member in 1978 of the *Legalise Cannabis Campaign*, which had an office in the area; Don Irving, photographer and writer, an associate editor and art director of the magazine; Harry Shapiro, author of books such as *'Jimi Hendrix: Electric Gypsy'*, whom we first published; Jan Pawlowicz, art teacher who designed some of the issue; and Chris Render, bookseller and photographer, who is co-editor of this anthology.

The list of featured contributors to *Home Grown* over the five years, some commissioned, others reprinted from their published work, is voluminous, and, in retrospect, quite impressive. Besides those already mentioned, we published work by Timothy Leary, George Melly, Patti Smith, Julie Burchill and Tony Parsons, Anthony Henman (Antonil), Simon Vinkenoog, William Levy, Dr Fred Hickling, Alexis Korner, Peter Stafford and Bruce Eisner, Paul Krassner, Simon Gandolfi, Siva Kalki Swami, Laurence Cherniak, Peter Tosh, Mim Scala, Mervyn Harris, Freddie Venn, Dr. Max Arbesfeld, Sean Sprague and many others too numerous to mention here. I proffer my sincere apologies to them and hope they will forgive me.

Taking on the task of publishing the magazine, often sailing close to the wind and against the prevailing tide, was a bracing experience that I can now look back on with warm affection, like rediscovering an old friend. In the winter of 1981 we published the tenth and final issue of *Home Grown*, though we reprinted a limited edition of the first issue at the end of 1982, and decided that the time had come to stop.

The chill winds of Thatcherism were blowing and there was a climactic change. A new ethos of greed and individuality, at the expense of community and caring, rent the social fabric asunder. There were riots by unemployed black youths in the front-line urban wastelands of our inner cities. The issue of ganja smoking was at the barricades of the political scene, inextricably wound up with racial and social tensions. The *War on Drugs* was hotting up.

Danny De Souza writes...

Home Grown Magazine Vol 1. No. 5, 1979:

Dear Mr. Harris,

I've just received *Home Grown*, No. 4, it's like meeting a new friend, something really valuable in this place.

Life here is still, very depressing, I'm back in the tourist block, no showers, no plates, no spoons, seventy-two people in forty-two beds using two toilets, twelve tapes simultaneously playing music from twelve different countries, the man with the biggest muscles gets the water and the calmest corner and the biggest national group gets most of the food.

Mehdi and Hussein, the Palestinians have escaped so now the tourists are getting generally screwed in a dozen trivial ways. For instance, the consuls no longer have access to the shop so we have no way to obtain the few goodies that are still available. Money necessary to repair the block, like window panes, plumbing materials or TV repairs have to be paid from working, so we don't get the special privileges that the workers enjoy. This is despite the fact that according to the Minister of justice, there is no difference between Turkish or foreign prisoners.

The contradiction makes me angry and everybody from the governor down began to tell me barefaced lies to soothe me, which just makes me angrier, now they just avoid me altogether. When anybody important visits the block, they make a point of isolating me in advance because I've got a reputation of asking embarrassing questions.

It's evident that the prison authorities are sick of me but the feeling is pretty mutual, so I'm working hard at arranging a transfer-to anywhere. I've been trying to enlist the help of the consulate who are "looking into the possibility".

At the same time I'm pushing hard on other levels too. A letter to Ecevit, the Turkish P.M., still no answer, and more recently one to the Ambassador.

As you may have guessed, this letter isn't intended to be a display of goodwill.

It's obvious that with a thirty-year sentence there's no point in my pretending to be penitent, and publicity is about the only weapon I have in exposing this absurd tragedy. It's equally obvious that my being the freak with the least serving the longest is a convenient cause spotlighting the need for legalising dope. Thus it would appear we both have a mutual interest in attempting to extricate me from this situation. So I'd like your advice and co-operation. To whom-and about what should I write?

I want to start plugging a new line, one that even Amnesty International can't duck. Regardless of the crime and conditions, imprisoning a person for such a long period in a country with a totally alien culture amounts to punishment of a cruel and unusual nature although, I don't think I really suffer in this respect.

Also I want to start talking about the real explanation of this mess. That I'm just a pawn in a propaganda game being played with the full participation of the UK and the US governments. If the UK wanted, they could have had me transferred to England a long time ago in the same manner that a Swede (Bjorkland) was sent back to Sweden in 1972. The necessary agreement has been in existence for a long time (Hague International Court 1972, Law 260) - but they don't want to because as long as I'm here it deters other people attempting the same feat. The objections to dope have all been scientifically disproved and have ceased to be sensible. Our "leaders" may be cunning and dishonest but they are not stupid, so perhaps we should look for objections, which for political reasons, they cannot admit to. Like, the underlying reason for their opposition is of a racialistic nature. Maybe they are afraid of Westerners being contaminated by a habit enjoyed primarily in the Third World countries because if the worst comes to the worst, it's much easier to justify against people with a totally alien lifestyle.

The news on the radio blasting in my ear is frightening, war between China and Vietnam. My own predicament is definitely trivial in comparison but I've got a sneaking suspicion that the basic issues have an importance that still isn't being fully appreciated. What do you think?

Hanging on to my sanity,

Danny De Souza,
Bayrampasa Cezaevi,
Istanbul, Turkey.

Home Grown Replies...

Home Grown Magazine Vol 1. No. 5, 1979:

Dear Danny,

It was a real pleasure hearing from you. I hope that *Home Grown* will prove to be a friend in deed, as well as a friend in need.

Your letters, which we published in our last issue, have deeply moved many people. The other day while I was at the *Release* offices, I met the person who had come to collect a pair of jeans to deliver to you personally, which had come from a reader of *Home Grown*. For most people it is difficult to know how they can help, after being moved by your tragic plight.

Most people's sensibilities and emotions have already been aroused by the impact of Billy Hayes' story in the movie *'Midnight Express'*. Maybe, in the not too distant future through the communication of certain individuals on an international level, and the formation of pressure groups, the government of this country will feel obliged to bow to compassionate reason and draft some form of legislation to enable UK citizens in prisons abroad to serve their sentences over here. I sense that things are still at an embryonic stage and the process is starting to take shape.

At any given time there are approximately one hundred and fifty Britons languishing in foreign jails on cannabis offences, more often than not in distressing circumstances. *Amnesty International* concern themselves with political prisoners and the *Red Cross* with prisoners of war, and it is only now that the needs of these prisoners are being taken note of on a more serious level.

In this country the newly formed *National Council for the Welfare of Prisoners Abroad* (N.C.W.P.A), an offshoot of *Release*, is still finding its feet. It is through your letters and the difficulties of sending money for medical supplies and other essentials to you, that the organisation came into being. Its task is to make sure that each prisoner, when located, has people writing to him, and that travellers can get goods to them, as things sent by post frequently disappear.

The N.C.W.P.A. explains:

"In many of these prisons the standard of food and medical

care is below that necessary to ensure a minimum level of health. Many prisoners are suffering from malnutrition. Overcrowding is common and the risk of disease and infestation is high.

In many countries prisoners are not provided with such essentials as soap, toothbrushes and shampoo, nor are books and writing materials provided. Legal representation, when available, is inevitably expensive, usually inadequate and rarely effective. All these things together with isolation and cultural alienation regularly lead to mental breakdowns especially among young prisoners."

Someone said to me the other day that there are dozens of Dannys in prisons in many parts of the world, living in conditions that are appalling and sometimes suffering cruel and unusual punishments. I will quote from a letter written by the girlfriend of a man who had returned from a prison term in Afghanistan for a cannabis offence.

"I saw him like this (stripped to the waist) and I asked him what the marks all over his chest and arms were. About three dozen, the size and shape of a halfpence. He replied that the warders in Afghanistan didn't use ashtrays, they used prisoners."

From a person who did three months in Tangiers for possession of a very small amount:

"There were seventy of us in a cell no bigger than the average front room".

And from someone back from Iran after serving the standard three and a half years for trafficking:

"In the summer we could fry an egg in one minute, ten seconds by leaving it on the front door step. In the winter if you threw a cup of tea into the air, it fell as ice. We had two blankets each. Sometimes it was so cold we didn't get out of our blankets to get food."

Another from an ex-prisoner who had served two and a half years in a bleak camp in a remote swampland in the Soviet Union for smuggling one and a half pounds of marijuana through Moscow airport:

> "The guards treated us like scum. It was just like the pictures you see of a German concentration camp, it housed 1,500 prisoners."

There are still four other Britons convicted on cannabis charges in the same camp. In a letter to Bob Nightingale of the N.C.W.P.A./Release, you wrote:

> "All I can tell you about is life in prison but that just happens to be an ingredient of the human rights bandwagon currently being pushed."

You are right. Where are those people in high places who profess to be concerned with human rights? Do their Christian principles extend to human beings who are imprisoned on cannabis charges? Why is the Foreign and Commonwealth Office afraid to act? Now is the time for legislation from the Home Office to enable UK citizens in prison abroad to serve their sentences in this country. This delicate subject is being discussed by officials of various Government departments on a general rather than particular basis. As yet the Government is not prepared to use public funds to alleviate the situation of prisoners abroad, but will forward any funds that come from private sources. So much for concern of human rights.

Maybe expedience rules the day. Cannabis traffickers, however vulnerable and naïve they may be, are not a cause to elicit political capitol out of. You can't win votes on this issue; it is a taboo subject. As far as politicians are concerned, it is something they wish to wash their hands of. However, the subject of drug trafficking was introduced at the recent joint meeting of the European Parliamentarians and members of the "Latin American Parliament", whereby they agreed to the constitution of some sort of committee between the two bodies in the future, to discuss the matter further. Just vague moves that often don't come to fruition.

If the situation is to be changed, it will have to be done on an international basis, and the only way of doing that is to remove cannabis from the *Single Convention Treaty* on Narcotic Drugs. the *International Cannabis Alliance for Reform* (ICAR), headed by the Rev. William B. Deane, is dedicated to doing just that.

Its goals include working together with international reform groups to change conditions of cannabis prisoners around the world;

encouraging and endorsing the concept of prisoner transfer treaties; and educating members of the United Nations about cannabis law reform.

ICAR is working closely with the *Committee of Concerned Parents* in preparing a manual for American drug prisoners abroad that contains

> "not only the technical information, like the responsibilities of the consular services of the State Dept., but also to provide information that will help them to cope with the severe physical and emotional abuse which they will more than likely encounter in foreign jails."

Unfortunately, due to the State Department's continuous policy of non-support of drug offenders and their refusal to supply legitimately-concerned U.S citizens with the names of prisoners, it is extremely difficult to know who is serving what sentence and in which foreign jail.

Ultimately, it is at the U.N that the battle will be fought. Rev. Deane has obtained an application to form a Non-Governmental Organisation (NGO) of marijuana law reform groups to lobby directly for the removal of cannabis from the 1961 Treaty. He has attended two meetings of the Alliance of NGO's in New York and has joined the Working-Party on Prisoner Transfers, which is in the process of writing to the Ministers of Justice of all the worlds governments to find out if they have any transfer sanctions currently in force; if they would be interested in initiating transfer sanctions; and whether or not they would like the help of the Working Party in putting together such sanctions. Thus, the Alliance of NGOs on Crime Prevention and Criminal justice is instrumental in acting as a clearing-house for information and as an initiator for general prisoner transfer treaties. This work has resulted in the present prisoner transfer treaties the U.S has with Canada, Mexico and Bolivia.

I hope all this puts you in the picture as to what is happening in the "outside world". I don't want to raise false hopes, as these moves are in an early stage of development. The point is that something is beginning to happen at last, which may take some time to reach fruition.

As you know Merfyn Turner of *Norman House*, a rehabilitation centre in London, visited Turkey recently to look at prisons and detention centres. His report on conditions there may not be known for some time, but I understand that he found no corruption and brutality as part of official policy, although he doesn't doubt that it exists. As for British prisoners, he believes they should be repatriated as fast as possible and made to do community service in this country.

I have just heard from Jane de Mendelsohn, with whom you correspond, that Alan Parker, the director of *'Midnight Express'* has sent her a cheque for £240, so that you will have £20 a month for the next twelve months. Jane suggested the idea of getting people to "adopt" a prisoner; write to him, send money for essential needs and campaign on his behalf. Not a bad idea. What do you think?

Well Danny, although we haven't met, I feel that we have become friends. I believe that it is an outrage to send a man down for so long for a crime of this nature, and the sooner the British government tries to arrange a transfer for you the better. Those who profess concern for human rights and the dignity of man should not fail in their responsibility to their fellow-citizens in foreign jails. Your voice has not gone unheard. Keep your spirits high, with love and peace,

Lee Harris

At the Magnetic Centre of the New Stoned Age

Home Grown Magazine Volume 1 No. 7, 1980:

It was a bright wintery day, Friday the 8th of February 1980, as I approached that grand building at 142 Prins Hendrickkade, which houses the *Kosmos* meditation centre. I looked out over the stretch of water and the jumble of houseboats that lie just across the street, and felt a feeling of exhilaration, a sense of pleasure at coming back to familiar sight. During a brief sojourn in late 1968, when the place was known as the *Fantasia* I had come here with a friend to enter a large room with crowds of brightly-clad hippies lounging on layers of carpeted rostra. It was a heady and stoned time and Amsterdam was the magnetic centre of a new Stoned Age of the Western World.

Since that time I've been back to the *Kosmos* several times during the seventies, to listen to some good music, to enjoy wholesome food, or to take a leisurely sauna while high from the good dope purchased from the house-dealer. I was last here some six months ago when it was decided that the *Kosmos* was to be the venue for the *1st International Cannabis Alliance for Reform Conference*.

I had arrived in Amsterdam the previous day and had booked in at a hotel managed by a friend of mine called Mr. Natural. As soon as I was settled in my room on the top floor, I was turned on to some excellent Durban Poison by my host, whose agile, darting mind kept me amused and informed about the goings on in this easy, relaxed city. There was an air of excitement and speed about, I was in a new and fresh environment away from my every day cares, looking forward to the next few days, and I was out of my head. Mr. Natural has a way of turning me on, challenging my conceptions and spacing my head out on the finest dope imaginable, and then I was left tired but exhilarated.

In the evening I joined Mr. Natural and his beautiful lady in their large and tranquil room where we sat quietly puffing away at some Afghani, listening to the gentle, harmonious rhythms emitting from the speakers. Mr. Natural was expecting s friend who duly arrived and the atmosphere in the room somewhat speeded up. In walked this blonde, bronzed guy who had just arrived back from the Canary Islands, beaming and full of vitality. It was just what was needed to spark Mr. Natural off, as they were old buddies from way back in sunny South Africa.

He prepared a large chillum of "boom" as the dagga plant is sometimes called, and we lit up and passed the chillum round a good few times until it steadily burnt itself out. The conversation became quite animated and lively, interspersed with laughter. I listened to the old friends raving on about shared exploits in different parts of the globe. The bouncy, sunburnt guy turned out to be a surfer. "The greatest high for me is riding on a fast-flowing wave, just drifting with the surf. It's my all-time high, greater than the best smoke you can lay on me, "he said with his eyes shining from the glow of his high.

Later, I ventured on to the *Melkweg*, one of my favorite haunts to savour the atmosphere on a Thursday around midnight in late winter. The thing that struck me about the place, is that it never changes, being caught in a timeless Bohemia, like the sixties were still with us. We are back in the multimedia environment of rock club, avant-garde cinema, whole food eat house, hippie market-place selling trinkets from the East, upstairs area for impromptu musical or poetic interludes, and a teahouse lounge. Mind you, it looks a bit tatty these days, as if it's seen its hey-day. Nevertheless, the joint seemed to buzz with stoned activity.

A rock group from Germany, looking like California cowboys were belting out a frenzied version of "Panama Red" and the crowd was caught in this mindless pleasure, swaying, twirling and rhythmically pounding to the beat. It could have been London or San Francisco circa sixty-seven to sixty-nine. It was as if nothing had changed except that this was another generation who were too young to have experienced those heady times. This was today and the dealer sitting at his table among the merchants in the market place was offering four kinds of dope, and space cake made with Moroccan. The smoking club has come of age and is now a part of the culture of the city, and long may it live.

The next day I got up around nine and went down to breakfast. Mr. Natural was up and about in his dressing gown, welcoming in some newly arrived guests from Hamburg who had also come for the conference. We all got into a rap over coffee and the joints started to roll. By noon, when the conference was supposed to begin, I was raving on about something or other absolutely zonked out of my mind and still at the hotel. I panicked myself into action and off we went to the *Kosmos*.

As I entered the building a line of people were still registering for the conference. My new friends from Hamburg, who I had met over breakfast, decided not to pay the registration fee and handed me an anarchistic manifesto against legalisation, written in German, and asked me to read it out if I had the chance.

1st International Cannabis Alliance for Reform Conference

I registered in some bewilderment and wandered in among the throng of delegates, recognizing a friend or two. The conference was about to begin. We all entered this large crowded area, spaced out with rostra, for the welcome to Amsterdam, which was delivered by Jurgen Schilling from *'Ons Genoegen'* (Our Pleasure), a Dutch cannabis organisation.

Then followed Simon Vinkenoog, poet extraordinaire, manic collector and archivist of the post-war Avant-garde writers and poets, and a sparkling light of youthful exuberance. I first came across Simon in 1965 at the *Poetry Incarnation*, which took place at the Royal Albert Hall. Some 7,500 people turned up to hear the great poets that grew up around the beat generation.

They were all there: Ferlinghetti, Ginsberg, Corso, Trocchi, et al, and as Harry Fainlight was reading his *Spider* poem, written under the influence of mescaline, this tall blonde figure got up with his arms flaying in the air, yelling in ecstasy, "Love, love, love!" This event with its mayhem and vision was a catalytic communion for what was to follow.

I was to hear Simon reciting some poems at the Drury Lane *Arts Lab* a few years later, and I saw him again in Amsterdam during my first. In the sixties he co-edited with George Andrews *'The Book of Grass'*, and has become a cannabis enthusiast since the early days.

I was to meet him six months before, when the conference was being definitely planned and Simon was the obvious choice for a host. He has long been one of my culture heroes. Simon Vinkenoog is now 51, and the father of four children ranging in age from two to thirty-three years old. He has a new book, a collection of writings and poems called *'Moeder Gras'*. Throughout the conference he would lift the proceedings when they sagged, interjecting here and there, always probing, and bringing with it his own inimitable style and sense of humour.

The conference was beginning in earnest. In the large room followed the introduction to the *International Cannabis Alliance for Reform*, and in an adjacent room, no smoking or shoes, the workshops began with 'Cannabis and the Media'.

After listening to the introduction I wandered downstairs to the lounge where you could watch the proceedings on a video set. It was quite crowded with groups of people sitting about rolling joints and chatting away.

It was here that I met Martin of the *Rusland* coffee shop, one of Amsterdam's famous dope haunts. He asked me if I had a copy of *Home Grown No.2* with me, which I did and there among the Junk Mail was a letter from Chan and the Man extolling the pleasures of the *Rusland*. It said:

> "Of the large number of cafes where it's cool to toke and score, the best by far we found was the Rusland. It is tucked away down a pretty nondescript street devoid of people and activity. It has an antique-like façade, and one has to venture inside to savour the instant change of atmosphere. As it was late afternoon when we arrived we ordered a hearty continental breakfast of beer and space cake. One barely has time to get a pipe together before a chillum and maybe a couple of numbers are passed in your direction and you readily acknowledge. Sitting in the corner is the man with the brown leather satchel - the resident dealer."

"That's my coffee shop!" - he beamed with pleasure and invited me to a party he was throwing on the Sunday night. He took out of his pocket a piece of black hash, and as we were talking he rolled it gently in a circular movement in the palms of his hands until it was a round black ball. He broke a bit off and gave it to me. We made a pipe and smoked it. I wanted to find out more about the coffee shop dealer and this was my chance.

> *"...And the leaves of the tree were for the healing of the nations." Revelations 22*

Lo and behold, the holy herb Ganja has been reborn in the religions of black peoples, the Rastafarian movement of *Jah*, and the *Ethiopian Zionist Coptic Church* with one God for us all. Out of the chaos of the white man's Babylon with its oppression and exploitation, its destruction of other cultures that lie in its wake, a ganja brotherhood is emerging who believe in the radical dualism of the constant struggle between good and evil, the natural and the unnatural, clean and unclean, true believers and false believers. Thus the nature of God is radically different and opposed to the Sky-God worshipped by Christendom the false religion of the corrupt, unclean Christian powers of Rome, Great Britain and the United States. Ganja, the green herb of the bible is good, natural and a true sacrament, whereas wine alcohol is evil and unnatural, distilled by corrupted man, a "dead spirit".

One of the highlights of the conference was listening to the melodic cadences of an emissary from the Third World, Dr. Fred Hickling, who is senior Medical Officer at the Bellevue Mental Hospital in Kingston, Jamaica.

The plight of cannabis prisoners around the world is the cause for real concern. Under the guise of drug control the *Universal Declaration of Human Rights* is violated on a wide scale, with indiscriminate and harsh treatment meted out to those unlucky enough to be caught. ICAR is dedicated to encouraging the concept of prisoner transfer treaties, so that prisoners abroad can serve their sentences out in their own countries. The cannabis prisoner thrust in a foreign jail is a constant reminder of the harsh realities of international prohibition.

I received two letters, dated a week or so before the conference, from cannabis prisoners in foreign jails, they speak more eloquently of their plight than I can, giving us glimpses of what it is like being inside a cell and fighting their own battles for legalisation.

The first was from Geoff Betts, serving a sentence for 16 kilos in Sweden. and the second was from Danny de Souza, a Londoner from Notting Hill Gate, who was busted in Turkey on May the 7th 1975, and charged with importing 5 kilos of hashish. He was sentenced to thirty years, later reduced to 18 years. His poignant, moving letters, often full of despair, which have been published in the last three issues of *Home Grown*, have touched many of our hearts.

Here is the voice of the unheard, a prisoner of conscience pleading that 'regardless of the crime and conditions, imprisoning a person for such a long period in a country with a totally alien culture, amounts to punishment of a cruel and unusual nature'. Danny was in Bayrampasa prison, portrayed in *Midnight Express*, and the jail at

Burhaniye. He has now been moved to the prison in Izmir, and his latest letter finds him in a more relaxed frame of mind.

The 1st Church of Discordia - where the ultimate choice is yours

Amsterdam, the relaxed and high city of Europe proved to be the perfect choice for such an auspicious occasion. The Saturday came with a clear blue sky as I awoke in my room on the top floor of the Wasted Towers, the name conferred on the establishment during the high sessions at breakfast. The talk became speedy and excited, I felt elated again after being drained by the images of the previous day. That Durban pot, like all good grass was a terrific energiser. I felt as bright and as brisk as the day, as I made my way to the conference.

On my way I stopped off at the Headshop in Kloverniersburgwal, and there in the window among the pipes, bongs and other items of paraphernalia, was a potted cannabis plant looking radiant in the bright winter sunshine. So this is what its all about, this hardy plant that can thrive in a shop window, detached from the life that flows through this city.

That evening, after a day of discussions on the medical and legal aspects, we were entertained at the benefit concert for *ICAR* at the *Paradiso*. It was Mr. Natural's favourite place and he waxed eloquently about it, christening it *The First Church of Discordia;* where the ultimate choice is yours.

Hanging on tow with Mr. Natural and his lady leading the way, we managed to squeeze our way through the jostling throng at the entrance. *The Paradiso*, a venue for rock concerts with its large, high-ceilinged hall and balcony, was buzzing with revelry and high spirits. In between the music sessions, on the far side of the hall, poets mounted a pedestal to rant verses in praise of the weed, a troupe of players - attired in gaudy garb performed a bizarre surrealist play, and a bevvy of showgirls sang "I owe a lot, to Iowa pot".

The music was rocking, the place was throbbing, the air was thick with smoke, and everyone seemed nicely stoned, as these balloons with joints wired to them on a leaflet, came floating down from the balcony. I got one and thought it a great way of offering a joint and then Mr. Natural read me the leaflet attached, written in Dutch.

Music has always played an important part in high-culture. At the *Paradiso*, we had *Lee Roberts* explosion of soul music, *Sugar Minnott's* reggae sounds, and *Alexis Korner* and his friends giving us lively renditions of blues and jazz.

It was with the birth of jazz in the honky-tonk joint of the black ghettoes of the South, and with its spread to the large cities, that marijuana, tea, gage, shuzzit, became a popular intoxicant for the growing number of enthusiast of this music that was sweeping the young off their feet.

The previous evening in the final session on 'Cannabis and Culture', Alexis Korner a long time cannabis campaigner and much-loved blues musician in the UK, spoke of his relationship with the weed.

We know very little about the cannabis-culture that exists in the Eastern block of nations, separated from many of the cultural manifestations of Western society. So it was with great interest that I listened to Zbigniew Thielle MD, Chairman of the *Commission on Drug Problems*, at the Polish psychiatric Society in Warsaw, presenting his paper *'Pot and Culture - A new image of the Polish drug scene'*.

Western medicine, caught up in its instantaneous successes with antibiotics, and its armory of chemical and synthetic agents, is too obsessed with curing diseases rather than preventing them, so there is little wonder that cannabis has played such a small part in its therapies.

Most of the scientific research done on cannabis was either to prove or disprove a possible negative effect, rather than explore a potential therapeutic quality. Robert Randall, a glaucoma sufferer, and a member of *NORML's* advisory board, speaking on cannabis as medicine, told us how he became the first legal cannabis smoker in the West.

There are now about sixteen legalisation groups in Europe, North America, Australia, New Zealand and Japan, the newest being *CALUMED* in France, which was formed after the conference and held its own *Cannabis Legalisation Conference* in Paris.

In the session on Cannabis Criminalisation around the World, delegates from these groups gave us some idea of what they were doing to combat the effects of criminalization in their respective countries. One of these speakers was Philippe Antoine from Belgium who represented the *Comite pour la Reforme des Lois sur le Cannabis*. As the European Parliament operates from Belgium, it is interesting to hear what is happening there.

Liberate Cannabis

By the Sunday I was feeling rather shattered, my muscles aching from dancing too much and my senses reeling from the myriad images and sensations that I was experiencing, but somehow I managed to keep alert throughout most of the long wrangles of the plenary session that was to ratify the constitution of *ICAR*. In a letter from Amsterdam, written by Jurgen Schilling two days later. The session was described in a high, tangible way.

By late evening I was feeling high once more as I bid the *Kosmos* a fond farewell and made my way to Martin of the Rusland's place for a party, a final celebration before we all went our separate ways. It was a time to cement new friendships in a party atmosphere. We were no more playing our respective roles of reformer, artist, publisher, dealer or activist. We had come to get high together, to release the flow of energy of the last few days, and to just dig each other's company.

There were the paraphernalia merchants and high-media people; there were poets and ranters, and the chroniclers of the cannabis culture. There were beautiful women glowing radiantly in the soft light and there was an abundance of the most amazing dope about. I was filled with optimism and bright hopes for the future.

I recalled the amazing little book, four by five centimeters, titled *Jeremiad Chants*, an absolute polemic by Bill Levy, an expatriate American long resident in Amsterdam, which he gave me at the plenary session a few hours earlier.

It is rampant with iconoclastic images, an annal out of Discordia, but should we not heed the chants of Jeremiah? BREATH DOES NOT CREATE WIND. IT IS PURSUED BY IT. And THE WORD CANNOT CAUSE LIFE OR DEATH. IT IS CALLED BY IT.

Healing of the Nations

> *"The greatest service which can be rendered to any country is to add a useful plant to its culture."* - Thomas Jefferson

I looked around the lounge. There were people from all over the place gathered together here to change the cannabis laws, a momentous occasion.

During these three days, some three hundred of us from twenty different nations came together to exchange ideas and to talk about our experiences in our particular homelands. It was the public inauguration of ICAR, an alliance of legalisation organisations from most of Western nations, who will lobby the United Nations to remove cannabis from the Single Conventions Treaty - the International treaty that forbids governments from legalizing public production, distribution and sale of cannabis.

In a high plane, it was a coming together of the cannabis cognoscenti from many different cultures, languages and backgrounds, learned in diverse disciplines from medicine, law, penal reform, ethnobotany to poetry, music, anarchy and high culture. They were all there, the law reform campaigners and direct-activists, the home growers and cultivating tipsters, the historians, scientists and other pundits, and the media people who would spread the word far and wide.

Cannabis - the drug, plant, herb, known in many tongues as grass, marijuana, hashish, ganja, bhang, dagga, hemp etc, this ageless weed, plant of the gods - has brought together emissaries from many of the different cultures that co-exist on this planet Earth. An eclectic body of people from a wide spectrum of human activity, encompassing various spiritual beliefs and political ideologies. It was this cultural diffusion that gave the occasion an extra dimension.

Where else would you find a Episcopalian priest from Philadelphia, an Iberian anarchist, a Polish psychiatrist, a scaffolder from Brixton, a Japanese lawyer, a businessman from Chicago, a Rastafarian doctor, and a mystical and high lady just back from the East, all gathered together with others for three days in mutual harmony and respect? We had come to Amsterdam to discuss strategies and means of removing cannabis from the prohibition on its social and medical use. Which was a long and difficult task, by any standards. Anti-cannabis laws violate our basic human rights and perpetuate social lies to the detriment of societies as a whole. All sorts of areas are brought into play if you mention cannabis, from the plight of prisoners in foreign jails to the repression of minorities that don't adhere to the cultural norms of the conglomerate state. Attuned to the times and with growing conviction, a dissident voice is striving to be heard amidst the scientific half-truths and media misrepresentation that masquerades as "informed opinion".

A generation has grown up immersed in the multi-facets of their favorite high.

There are the logically-minded, adepts at drafting constitutions and framing statutes, looking for loopholes in the morass of legal jargon that binds us to outdated laws. They are the scientists and legal beavers that burrow through the mass of conflicting data that has amassed over recent years, steadily seeing through the contradictions that riddle the law and science. In the process they are discovering flaws in the very nature of scientific analysis and legalistic procedures. They will deal with the echelons of power, using their highly-educated minds and skills, which are rooted in Western culture, to play them at their own game.

Then there are the liberators of cannabis; those that want to free the weed. They are the cultivators of plants, the guerilla growers using halide lamps and hydroponics, the botanists and taxonomists of the species of Cannabis *'Indica'*, *'Sativa'* and *'Ruderalis'*. To them the outlawing of one of nature's oldest plants is beyond comprehension, an absurd quirk in the mind of rational men. Their noble task is to see forbidden fruit flowering freely in variable climes. The seeds have already been sown.

There are those who raise the cannabis flag at the barricades, who see it as their right and duty as citizens to defy an unjust law. They are aware that direct action and civil disobedience are often the methods of effecting change in a pluralistic system. The repeated violation of a law obviously diminishes its effectiveness and practicality. If the process of changing an unworkable law is blocked, usually because the body politic is too cumbersome and stultified to read the writing on the wall, direct actions and symbolic gestures have a way of influencing these processes and speeding up the necessary steps towards change. Where would the liberation movements of women, blacks, gays etc. be today without their direct-activists pushing for social acceptance and creating attention with their "street theatre" antics?

There are the mystics and mendicants who see cannabis as a gift from the Gods, a sacrament given to man so that he may commune with nature and live in harmony on this planet. There is no doubt that the whole Oriental spiritual trip that has surged through the consumer paradises of the West was helped along its way by the seminal influence of this conscious-altering substance. It was no coincidence that the conference should take place in a meditation centre, with whole-foods and herbal teas to nourish the body. At one time during a lengthy discourse on a legal issue, this beatific lady, blissfully spaced out, sat on the platform in the lotus position, her arms carving the air with flowing mudras and confounded the gathering by serenely stating that "Cannabis is lingam" (the phallus).

Here was Kali, the mother of creation and destruction, of the darkness, the moon and emotion, balancing the logic, intellect and brightness of Shiva.

Another Time, Another Space

The following evening, feeling utterly exhausted and speeded by the actions of the last few days, I boarded the boat for the night crossing to England. As it steadily droned on through the dark night, staring at the powerful surge and sway of the sea, I had a long-lost memory recall of my first visit to Amsterdam nearly twelve years ago.

It was in the time of flower power and I had come to Amsterdam in search of a roving street theatre group called *'The Human Family'*. I was to meet them at the *Fantasia* In Prins Hendrikkade, now the *Kosmos*, on the evening I arrived. Images flashed back at me of the *Fantasia* that night, it was like setting foot on some strange film set done up in psychedelic colours and patterns; a surreal movie of groups of characters lounging about and smoking dope. It was so long ago that its memory has taken on dream-like qualities. We left the *Fantasia* and had a long walk to the pad we were going to sleep at. It was a large wood-beamed garret at the top of some studios, which once housed a parochial school. Here dossed *'The Human Family'*, some twenty of us in sleeping bags or loused up blankets. We were an international group, Dutch, Italian, French, British, Argentinian, and one Brazilian and American.

I was almost resigned to my hunger when a beggars banquet of rive, fried beans onions and carrots was laid out before us. I squatted in the loose circle and ate quietly. Then I relaxed with the few joints passing by, my mind blown by the heightened intensity of the music seeping through the earphones I had on. It was a great time. The following evening at an informal gathering, Simon Vinkenoog welcomed D. Allen Cohen, a former pupil of Leary and Alpert, who had then become a disciple of Meher Baber, to Amsterdam the magnetic centre. It was a seminal time, the acid-converts were turning away from psychedelics and journeying East in search of gurus, a spiritual upsurge was in the offing.

Then it happened... we were busted by a whole bunch of plain-clothes detectives, and nineteen of us were bundled off to the central police station. We weren't told what crime we'd committed. It looked as if they were doing a clearing up job. Anyways, we were herded into a cell just big enough to house our baggage and us.

We sat on the floor and rolled two three-skinned joints with some dope we'd salvaged, and passed it around. Somehow, all nineteen of us managed to get two drags each. There was a great feeling of solidarity among us.

One by one, we were searched in the corridor, our belts and personal belongings were taken away and we were locked up in cells on our own. After the initial outraged excitement, the angry enjoyment of this experience, the perverse pleasure of an absurd situation, I felt calm and relaxed. The endless banging and prolonged screams from my brothers and sisters had subsided in exhaustion.

Long hours of random thoughts and growing claustrophobia passed by. Then I heard Sandos, one of my Italian friends banging against his cell door and letting out a strange, terrible scream that ended in uncontrollable weeping. There was a deep silence as we all listened. That night I was taken by van to the Hoek of Holland, and locked up in a detention cell ready for deportation, without having committed a crime nor being charged with one. I read the graffiti on the walls of the cell and noted them down.

> *Kicked out 9 July '68. Crime being poor, Shit is cheaper in London anyway. Bunny John.*
>
> *Richard Wright deported for having more hair than bread. Landed in Holland 6 hours ago.*
>
> *Defended a guy who stole soup taking a trip, now off the hook.*
>
> *Police are just mean. Got not soul - just cheese.*
>
> *Told to leave Holland on my birthday.*
>
> *Crime to cops is being a human being.*
>
> *Free acid for fuzz, they need it more than we do.*
>
> *My trip has been a pleasant one, But I still do not know what it is I done wrong - Nick April '68.*
>
> *Forgive them for they know not what they do. Jesus '68.*

I thought of that almost forgotten few days, distanced in time and blurred by memory, as the ship sailed across the dark waters of the English Channel. It is now 1980, and I am returning home after a few days in that same city, in another time, another space. There is a saying that time is longer than rope. May the seeds that were cultivated at the First International Cannabis conference grow and flower and always bear fruit.

Decades of Dope

Home Grown Magazine Volume 1 No. 6, 1980:

High!

Welcome to the sixth *'Home Grown'*, our special turn-of-the-decade issue. As we enter the eighties the cannabis flag seems to be flying high with the mushrooming of legalisation groups in many parts of the world and the coming of The 1st *International Cannabis Alliance for Reform Conference* in Amsterdam in February 1980. "Legalise without commerce, except small scale cash crop for family farmers" suggested Allen Ginsberg, poet and sage of our times, when he passed through London in November 1979. In October a customs officer was shot dead while intercepting a lorry with a large amount of cannabis hidden in its hold; the *Legalise Cannabis Campaign* puts its case on television in an *'Open Door'* program and Cheech and Chong at last hit our screens in the dope movie *'Up In Smoke'*. What a strange sequence, with each in its own way highlighting a facet of what is happening on the cannabis front at this time. As the market place expands the consignments of cannabis get larger, ripe pickings for big business, with its insatiable need for bulk buying. In some spectacular operations using the combined forces of many police authorities and customs, a considerable amount of cannabis has been impounded and we now have the first death of a customs officer in the course of duty.

At Odds With The Law

There are other ways of dealing with a problem that has got out of control. A recent report of a study group, *Cannabis - Options for Control* (Quartermaine House, 1979) put forward four options:

1. Changes in maximum penalties.
2. Decriminalization.
3. A licensing system.
4. Legalization.

I quote from the report:

> "it cannot be said, therefore, that the quite massive deployment of resources by the state to enforce the ban on cannabis has achieved its objectives. On all the available evidence, consumption and illicit supply have increased greatly over the past ten years, and it is an open question whether or not this trend will continue."

So much for the present inept system of control:

> "At the same time enforcement has had a number of undesirable social consequences, the most important being that considerable numbers of young people of good character have found themselves at odds with the law who would not otherwise have done so."

That brings us round to these "Young people of good character... at odds with the law", as the report so succinctly puts it. Under the title *'Stand Up And Be Counted'* the *Legalise Cannabis Campaign* (LCC) presented a balanced, sober argument for changing the law, on a repeated slot on BBC television. With access to the public at large, the case for cannabis has became a legitimate cause for concern, a subject for debate and a reasoned argument. In a remarkably short time cannabis has received a degree of respectability few would have thought possible a decade ago.

Even the *National Association of Probation Officers* supports the aims of the campaign, though no current member of parliament has seen fit to ally him/herself to this shift in public attitudes. Then came Cheech and Chong in *'Up In Smoke'* and the emphasis was shifted to anarchic, outrageous fun. Getting stoned is a funny business, especially on grass, and the cops versus dope smokers charade was treated like something out of the *Fabulous Furry Freak Brothers*.

The posters proclaim that the movie will have you "Rolling in the aisles", and at the box-office the cashier asks if you would like to sit in the 'Smoking' or 'No Smoking' side with a wink of the eye and a knowing smile.

Historical Precursors

Maybe it's a good time to look back and fathom out some of the events of the past decade or so, and to briefly trace the social history of cannabis in this country. Although much has been written about its use during this decade gone by, it is not widely known that in the mid-nineteenth century, *"Opium and cannabis were available over the counter (including the corner grocer's) without any form of restriction,"* (Virginia Berridge, Institute of Historical Research), University of London. 1978). As recently as 1972, in the back of Bradford's oldest chemist shop four packets of Grimault's famous Indian cigarettes, made in 1893 and containing cannabis were found. Note the directions on the packet:

> "In order to obtain the best results it is necessary, contrary to the case with cigarettes of ordinary tobacco, to inhale the fumes little by little so that they pass gradually down the respiratory tract where they come in contact with the larynx and lungs and then return through the nasal orifices. They are more efficacious when smoked in a quiet room with the patient reclining in an easy chair or lying on a couch secure from all draughts."

Through most of this century, due to a complex web of bureaucratic maneuverings, professional self-interests, international pressures, public health concern and panic reaction often on a misinformed basis, the social and medical use of cannabis has been prohibited. The *Misuse of Drugs Act* of 1971, which is operative today, is based on a succession of *Dangerous Drugs Acts*, the prototype of which was the original 1920 Act.

There seems to be every reason to believe that current drug policies, as direct descendants of their historical precursors, are motivated more by political considerations and vested self-interest than by rational assessment of any public health consequences.

The over-reaction and hysteria which greeted the publication of the *Wootton Report* in 1969, which recommended a reduction in penalties for cannabis offences, proved once more that prejudice and fear play a considerable part in determining people's views rather than reason and common sense. Little wonder that the Established Order's position has hardly changed in these last fifty years. John Stuart Mill's view that:

> "The only purpose for which power can rightly be exercised over any member of a civilized community against his will is to prevent harm to others. His own good, either physical or moral, is not a sufficient warrant."

still holds strong today. It is the basis of our democratic system, or it should be.

With the large influx of new Commonwealth immigrants to this country in the late fifties and early sixties cannabis use became associated with these minority groups. Until 1964, the majority of those convicted of cannabis offences were still black. By 1967 as the Psychedelic Revolution reverberated around the world, London witnessed *"The beautiful people"* in colourful regalia at a *'Legalise Pot Rally'* in Hyde Park. In the same month of the summer of love, sponsored by an organisation called SOMA, a full-page advert appeared in *The Times*, listing the names of many illustrious and distinguished persons of the time, stating that *"The laws against cannabis are immoral in principle and unworkable in practice"*.

Later when the *Wootton Report* was debated, the then Home Secretary, James Callaghan, recorded his shock at the appearance of *"That notorious advertisement"* and learning of the existence of *"A lobby in favour of legalizing cannabis"*. Shock and horror are part and parcel of the politician's performance, the tricks of his trade, and his moral indignation served him well. He was duly given credit for adopting the "hard" line on "soft" drugs and his stance suggested "that he was more concerned to show himself a tough Home Secretary than to deal with the case on its merits". (*Observer*, April 1969)

Hash Trail

By 1971, when the *Oz* obscenity trial took place at the Old Bailey, the great surge that was "flower power" was on the wane, destroyed by its own excesses as well as the vindictive forces of an establishment backlash. It was the time of the great gurus and the acid-converts turned onto Eastern deities with enthusiastic relish. Shiva and Kali danced about as the divine light shone and *'Hare Krishna, Hare Rama'* was chanted in ecstatic union with the Godhead. The aroma of patchouli and the heady scents of *Spiritual Sky* and *Fragrance of Love* incense are echoes of those times. The years ahead saw a great exodus to the East, as thousands of young people from many walks of life made the journey, often overland to Afghanistan, Nepal and India, in what was to be known as the "hash trail".

The romance with the mystical orient was a legacy of the hippy movement, inspired by tales of temple balls in Kathmandu, hash dens in Kabul, and the chillum-smoking sadhus of Benares. When the time came for these transformed "pilgrims" to return home, many of them earned their fare by bringing back some of their spoils to share with friends who had never made the trip. Morocco, the Middle East, Thailand were all opened up as a generation of hashish-smokers partook of the delights of these exotic places.

"Hey man, you want some hash?" cried the street-vendors as young westerners ebbed and flowed throughout the cannabis-smoking countries of the world, becoming adepts at the varieties of the hashish experience.

But sometimes the price of this adventure was heavy and many a traveller found himself/herself incarcerated in primitive conditions in prisons serving unduly long sentences. Even at the end of this decade there were about a hundred and fifty Britons still languishing in foreign jails for cannabis offences, including Danny de Souza who is serving thirty years in Turkey.

Back home people were being busted all over the place. I estimate, on current form, that around 100,000 persons, mostly aged between seventeen and thirty, have been found guilty of cannabis offences throughout the seventies, the vast majority for unlawful possession.

Every police force in England and Wales (except the city of London police) has full-time drug squads, with approximately 560 officers assigned to them. As cannabis offences provide by far the greatest number of cases they deal with, it is easy to understand why young people all over the country feel at odds with the law, to say the least.

Grass Roots

"Boring pot smoking is on the way out", stated the *Daily Mail* in 1973. At that time the *Release*-inspired *Cannabis Action Reform Organisation* and the *Campaign for the Legalization of Cannabis* both flourished for a while then disappeared into inactivity due to a number of reasons.

The former, the more professional of the two, floundered mainly because of the climate of the times, which as we've witnessed, was repressive and rather harsh.

The latter was a grass roots movement without a solid base, because people were afraid to identify themselves with the weed openly.

For a few years cannabis smokers went about their business in a quiet subdued manner, with the threat of being busted in the privacy of their homes always there. *"Condemnation doesn't liberate"*, observed

Carl Jung, and the close-knit clandestine communities of cannabists withdrew into themselves and it seemed as if the boozing, tranquilized, tobacco-addicted populace at large had won the day.

In 1977, ten years after the birth of *Release* and that psychedelic 'Summer of Love', events took an interesting turn, inspired by what was happening in America. With the *National Organisation to Reform the Marijuana Laws (NORMAL)* successfully getting many states to decriminalize marijuana , and with the meteoric rise of the glossy dope magazines, like *High Times*, an awareness of the growing social acceptability of pot among the middle cases dawned. Seeds of a new cannabis consciousness were about to be planted over here.

On the same day in July 1977 as a *Release*-organised group of about five hundred lobbied the Houses of Parliament with the help of the elderly Marcus Lipton MP (now deceased), the first issue of *Home Grown* appeared on the streets billed as *"Europe's first dope magazine"*. It was pure coincidence that the two events occurred at that time, but nevertheless an interesting pointer to what was to follow.

In this same year a *"Cannabis Crusader"* Tony Read, arrived back having been given an amnesty from a twelve year prison sentence in Algeria, and staged a one-man smoke-in outside Buckingham Palace and elsewhere, urging others to follow suit. Direct action, in open defiance of an unjust law, naturally led to the ritual of *"Smoke-ins"* in Hyde Park, organised by an amorphous group calling themselves the *'Smokey Bears'*. Sensing that the time was now ripe for an efficient pressure group to emerge, the *Legalise Cannabis Campaign* (LCC) was duly inaugurated at a meeting in a hall situated opposite the Houses of Parliament in June 1978.

Meanwhile research on the effects of cannabis continues unabated:

> "So far there are more than 20 books and almost 3000 papers on the subject, and further papers are appearing at the rate of almost one a day" (*New Scientist*, August 1979).

Also, there are few experiences where the participants themselves know so much about what they are doing, for a generation has grown up with a truly encyclopedic knowledge of the many facets that make up the cannabis mythology.

Subterfuge has taught many a young enthusiast how to grow the plant indoors with artificial lighting; dealing in dope has helped launch the careers of budding entrepreneurs by giving them initial capitol and know-how; and being persecuted for a peaceful and pleasurable pastime has taught people to be more aware, and bonded communities around the country into a camaraderie that few share in our impersonal world.

It is in a positive sense that we move on into the next decade in the hope that we shall show the powers that be the errors of their ways. Into the eighties, stay high.

Interview with Martin of the Rusland

Home Grown Magazine Volume 1 No. 7, 1980:

How long has the Rusland been going? About three and a half years.

When did the coffee shop dealer scene begin? About six years ago, the first one was the *Mellow Yellow*, but it has since burnt down.

Do you think it natural for dealers to operate from coffee shops? Well, you want to get a steady outlet instead of being dependent on the dealer scene around you. If you have to work on the open market it's much nicer to have a shop, then you can simply sell to smokers on a very steady basis. A regular outlet, with a regular quality and a regular turnover, which is most beneficial for the dealer and the consumer, otherwise the consumer has to go on the street to buy, where neither quality nor safety is assured.

If a straight tourist came into your place from the street, would he have any way of knowing what place he had wandered into? Oh yes, in one look, and he'd walk out fast.

What is the position regarding cannabis? In Dutch law up to an ounce is misdemeanor, so if you're not selling it you are officially quite legal. So what we did is this, I had the small plastic bags in which the hash comes printed saying 'Not for commercial purposes'. So if anyone has a bag and the police ask something, they immediately show them the bag and point out that it is for their own use, as it says so on the bag. In Holland it's legal to 30 grams.

Do you supply a service? Yes. From the buyer's point of view, he's assured of quality. It's a little bit pricier than you could get if you had a friendly dealer living near you. But if you want good Moroccan you can be assured it is there. The friendly dealer who works from home does not have any overheads, and he's got to be home when you want him. In a place like this from 11.30 in the morning until 8 at night he is there, always. We usually do three or four kinds of dope. One good blonde one, either a good Lebanese or a Moroccan, one good black, and one good grass, and sometimes it's extended to a fourth kind if something comes in. So I do two blondes instead of one, or two blacks instead of one. The minimum you can buy is ten guilders (£2.50). There are usually joints going round all the time. In summer we have a lot of tourists in here, in winter not many, but all the customers that do come, come back as well. In winter there are more Dutch and less foreigners.

How come you're allowed to work? I'm not. It's just that they can't bust me. If they catch the dealer, who sits in front of the bar, which occasionally happens, he's got about an ounce on him. They have to release him after six hours, he's fine and the lawyer gets paid, and his hours in the nick are paid, so he's sitting comfortably there for six hours. And the next day the shop is simply opened with somebody dealing there again, so they can't stop it, they can occasionally interrupt it, but only for a few hours. It takes at least ten or twelve policemen to bust the place, let's say with all the briefing and after-reports it takes them at least 30 to 40 man-hours. Now for all those hours they have one ounce. Every time they want to get that one-ounce they have to put in 30 to 40 man-hours. Well, they tried that fifteen times, and after a while they got pretty sick of it.

Can't they have you up for intent to supply or conspiracy like in Britain? No, we don't have conspiracy laws here, so they can only bust him for the amount he has on him. He has a quantity on him and simply goes and refills.

How much does the dealer get paid? Does he work on a commission basis? Yes, that's right. Let's say he gets well paid. I do not want to go into details

I see you only deal in cannabis? Oh yes. I keep clear of anything else

In other words you have taken cannabis out of the black market away from the dealing scene, which usually involves other illicit drugs as well. This is about as legal as it can be without it being fully legalised. The selling of hash this way has got nothing to do with any crime anymore. It is run on a perfectly normal, stable basis. People normally work in it over longer periods of time.

How many other coffee shops like yours are there in Amsterdam? About twenty.

In a way, it's like the hash dens of Kathmandu. That's basically the idea. I've been to the East twice.

How do the coffee shops differ from one another? Well, they differ to a great extent, actually. It depends where the people come from who start it. You have relaxed coffee shops, like mine, and you also have really quite criminal underground sort of scenes, really heavy scenes. You have a couple that do coke as well. You also have the ones in the centre who are there simply for the tourists, who have low-quality and are very expensive, but as it's right on the route of tourists they sell plenty anyway.

Besides dope what do you present to you customers at the Rusland? Good food and good music. We play rock and reggae. We have a chessboard and pieces. We have a daily menu, with a meal that changes everyday. We have a lot of people who come only for the dope, buy it and walk out. Also we have people who come in, buy it and sit down. The people who sit there for a number of hours drinking coffee and talking, those are mainly regulars and you have the tourists who are here for a week, and for the whole week they sit in the *Rusland*.

How do the authorities view your activities? Well they haven't been around for a while fortunately, but actually I did expect them during November and December, but to my surprise they didn't show up. That was cleaning up time; they were busting places all around me. My surprise is that they didn't bust me.

Is there any police corruption involved? No, not in the hash business, there was in the smack business, but it doesn't happen in the hash business with regard to coffee shops.

Have any gangsters tried to cash in on your business? No, they can't. There's no way in Amsterdam that you can be forced into certain things like that. 'I'm not paranoid, it is just that everybody is persecuting me', I think that for a dealer it is an occupational hazard.

How do you see yourself in the dope culture? Coffee shops in the dope culture are a stabilizing factor, in my opinion. They don't make it too tough, but they keep you on your toes. They're not really too fanatical about it.

How do people view you in the straight world? Mostly I get along quite well, they can understand what's going on and find it acceptable. There are certain straight businessmen I have to work with, of course, for my coffee shop goods and the tax people and so on, and they all know what the Rusland is. Well that's quite acceptable.

Would you say that Amsterdam is the centre for international dope dealing? I should say that, yes, but I stay clear of that. You can't burn both ends of the stick at the same time. The other is high finance, high-risk thing, very expensive to run, also very profitable if it comes off. In Amsterdam, you can get a ten guilder piece, or for a thousand pounds, only it's not usually the same people working in it. I cannot afford to go into £500 deals and sell 10 guilder pieces in the coffee shop.

Have you ever had a dry period where there was no hash about? I've never had a period where there's nothing about, never, not in the 15 years that I've been smoking in Amsterdam.

Coffee Shop Amsterdam

Home Grown Magazine Volume 1 No. 10, 1981:

It was late July and Amsterdam was in the full swing of its tourist season, bustling with young foreigners in search of a high time in this city of dope dreams. The *Orange Full Moon Affair* was on and the followers of "The God that fled" could be seen wandering around in couples entwined in their bright robes that seemed to dance in the soft wind and glow in the sunshine.

Walking across Dam Square I could hear the street hustlers hissing the word 'Hash' to the dreamy denizens ensconced in small groups around the embankments of the ornate fountain. In the red light district I stood on a canal bridge watching a party of middle-aged tourists being guided past *The Sex Theatre*, 'live' performances since 'Anno 1969', and on down the street where they viewed the seductive sirens who sit motionless in their beguiling lingerie, staring out of their windows like display dummies.

As I walked on, I noticed a gay couple ambling by arm in arm, a member of the mackintosh brigade intensely engaged in the contents of a sex shop window, and then I came across a coffee shop with loud music blaring from its speakers, and on entering saw that the clientele sitting at the bar or at tables were all skinning up joints or leisurely passing them on to their companions.

Amsterdam has a tradition of tolerance that dates way back, and is a haven for radicals, expatriates and outsiders of all kinds. It offers the wayfarer the freedom to partake in a particular activity without necessarily coming into contact or infringing on someone else's space and so caters for separate needs on many levels.

One of the most interesting examples of this tolerance at work is the rise and growth of the dope coffee shops that have opened up in various parts of the city over the last few years, where you can sit in congenial surroundings and buy hash or grass from a house dealer at set prices and know you aren't being ripped off. There are twenty such coffee shops scattered throughout the city, each in turn catering for a particular and regular clientele.

The coffee shop dealers have taken cannabis out of the black market, which involves other illicit drugs like heroin and cocaine, and into a legitimate business setting as is the way with alcohol or tea and coffee consumption, and ply their trade in an orderly and contained environment. It is the principle of de facto decriminalisation put in practice, and the nearest thing to legalisation to be seen in the western world, and could well serve as a working model to other enlightened societies.

It is a beautiful summer evening, and as I stroll about aimlessly dreaming in the moving light reflections glimmering in the water of a canal, a group of newly-arrived young German tourists stop me. "Can I ask you two questions?" begins the spokesman for the four of them in English, "Where is the Milky Way, and where can I buy some hash?"

The *Melkweg* (Milky Way), a multi-media youth centre, was one of the first places to have a house dealer, in the heyday of flower power when Amsterdam was a mecca for the stoned hippie. Last year it celebrated its tenth year and is attracting more foreign visitors than ever before with its mixture of rock music, fringe theatre, cinema, wholefood, and good dope.

The house dealer rents a table in the marketplace, selling nuts and raisins as well as dope, displaying his list of goodies and their price per gram, on the table in front of him; there are four varieties on sale already weighed and packed in small plastic bags costing from ten to twenty-five guilders (£2 or £5 deals). As he opens shop and prepares his table for the evening a queue has already formed and from then on he will be busy supplying these small amounts to a steady and continuous flow of customers. No-one would say how much money he makes and it's a closely-guarded house secret how much he pays the centre to rent the table.

In the marketplace you can buy chillums, hand made jewellery, a book or magazine, or a juicy slice of watermelon and pineapple if you've got the munchies.

In the teahouse upstairs, a large high-ceilinged room, serving herbal teas and chocolate and spice cake, the place is packed with young people from all over the world rolling joints and smoking them, while a singer-guitarist fills the smoke-laden atmosphere with a hauntingly sad song. From the large high windows of the teahouse you can see inside the brightly lit rooms on the first floor of the police station just across the street. It slowly dawns on you that the selling and smoking of cannabis this way has got nothing to do with crime anymore.

"About the necessity to fight as much as possible the international trafficking in opiates like heroin almost every one agrees. Because the police lack the capacity to do so, one cannot afford the luxury of powerful action against the users of cannabis." - H.P. Wooldrik, Public Prosecutor of Amsterdam.

It is this sort of pragmatic approach which has characterized the change in attitudes of the lawmakers in Holland. The law divides forbidden drugs into two categories. List 1 contains assorted substances such as heroin, cocaine, LSD, and amphetamines, and carries stiff sentences, the maximum being twelve years for large amounts. In list 2 there are only two substances, hashish and marijuana, and the maximum sentence for big consignments is four years.

On the 19th August 1976 a user of cannabis was defined as a person with no more than 29 grams in his possession, and the offence was treated as a misdemeanor. If apprehended a ticket is handed out like a traffic offence, but if you don't pay up they can put you in jail for a month or fine you a maximum of £100. So a move was made to liberalise the law and shift the emphasis between hard and soft drugs still further apart.

"You're sitting In this coffee shop, your hand under your chin, feeling a little clammy in a 'Smoke The Russians Out of Afghanistan' tee-shirt. Your tea has long gone cold; you ask yourself if you put sugar in it. You look at the sugar bowl; you see a stoned fly circling it as if it's a fly-heaven. You are not aware of other people, the music blasts in your ears, it is hot, my God it is hot. You dream of a freshly-juiced orange drink, you watch a group of punks leaving - their lunch break is over - and two school-types take their place. The fly is lost in a world of sugar and can't keep still, the last of the smoke? And while all this is going through your head the door opens, and you hear a voice say, 'Stay where you are'... and that is enough.

Suddenly there are eight policemen, you heart starts to pound, you swallow hard, a cold sweat on your forehead, you think, think, you must immediately get rid of your dope, you rummage wildly through your pockets and throw away the plastic bag and by mistake your library card. Bad luck.

They come further in, asking questions here and there, it's quiet, an eerie silence, you are aware that the music has stopped, that you're sitting still. The drug squad has got you in their grip, they've seen that your hands are shaking, that it was you who had thrown the piece away. But what can the police do? There lies this hash and grass on the floor. They search your pockets while they hold your arms above your head against the wall. How long in the nick, a few hours, a day? And all this for a few joints of hash or grass..."

I was at the office of the newly-formed *Cannabis Union*, an amalgam of two organisations, surrounded by index filing cards and reams of broadsheets ready to be mailed out, watching Koos Swart enacting the bust. For after five years without any trouble the coffee shops have experienced a series of raids these last few months.

About twenty shops were raided about thirty-six times in all, and the *Cannabis Union* was coming to the rescue, collating the busts, how much was taken, how many officers took part and how many man-hours were spent on these actions. They showed that during the same period only a couple of places were busted for heroin.

They had maps pinpointing the coffee shops that had been raided and by which police districts, which were on display at most of the coffee shops. Usually very little was found, the dealer taken away for a few hours, and it was business as usual.

I heard at one place that a counter-hand was knocked out, and I saw at another shop they'd ripped open the bar stools, ostensibly looking for hard drugs, and yet at another one they came in, looked around, couldn't find anything and walked out. The house dealer told me he had put his leather satchel with the dope in it on top of one of the speakers and they just didn't see it.

So here was a joint action between the coffee shop owners and the Union of cannabis users, who put out a newsletter called '*Own Grown*', and whose envelopes bear the slogan, 'Don't pay the dealer, Grow your own'.

On joining the Union a member is sent a large foolscap envelope containing seven varieties of seed packets with instructions on how to grow them, recipes, and a list of standard works to read up on. Seeds are perfectly legal and can be distributed freely.

The Union has branches in other cities and towns and its members come from all walks of life. The Amsterdam branch undertook the coffee shop action, and is a unique example of the cooperative growers working with the commercial dealers together for the benefit of the cannabis consumer. It also marks the emergence and recognition of the coffee shops as part of the business community.

The *People's Party for Freedom and Democracy* and the *Labour Party* took up the issue of the raids in the council chambers and in a series of written questions to the mayor, wanted to know who supervised the destruction of the confiscated cannabis, and of informing them of the police districts involved. It was not long before the raids stopped and the coffee shops were left in peace once more.

I was walking through the Zeedijk, the old seedy and run-down red light district with a lean, wiry man aged about thirty with an abundance of nervous energy, speaking rapidly in fluent English, The area is now the territory of the newer immigrants, Surinamese, Turks and Chinese. In the one street there are forty-six places where they sell heroin. He pointed to a building and said, "I was born there, brought up in this street. I know the area very well." He then greeted someone who was waving to him from the top floor window of an old house. "You see that man there, in the old days he was a big dealer importing from the Lebanon. Made a lot of money, runs gaming houses in the street. But he still lives in the same two rooms with his wife."

"I started my coffee shop over five years ago in a businesslike way with plastics bags. Before it was under the table and weighed out to make it efficient." His is a local-boy-makes-good story. He was selling porno magazines in a basement in the red light district when he suddenly got sick of it and threw the whole lot in the canal after an English tourist asked to see even more lurid stuff than he had to offer, and started his coffee shop in the same premises. He now has another one in the Hague.

"My name and everything I started was bad, my name doesn't matter, but the name of my coffee shop matters. With every guilder you make, you make an enemy" he says philosophically. The success of the coffee shops lies in their wise decision to keep cannabis as far remove from heroin and cocaine as they possibly could. "Sometimes you get young policemen eager to try their luck. They come in and wish and hope to find some heroin, they search the place, take the dope off the dealer and walk out, and that's the last you hear of it."

We were now sitting on the wooden bench outside his coffee shop, which over-looks a canal. He took a cigarette from his packet, mixed the tobacco with some resinous double-zero Moroccan, and kneaded it in the palm of his hand for some while before making a short, fat joint.

"It's better to eliminate the street seller and know where it's happening. That way they can control it. The coffee shops have already cornered the market, local and tourist, now that it's taken off the street."

But how do you turn black money into white money? First you start a business, pay rent and rates, hire staff, and then you reach the point where you have to declare your income and pay taxes. Like all businesses you have an accountant and lawyer who deal with these problems, advising you and negotiating with the authorities to assess the amount you will have to pay.

"The market has now reached saturation point. You can only come into it if you have a lot of money to finance the thing. It's more like a machine, it's so busy you can't really speak to the customers." From inside the coffee shop I could hear the incessant pounding beat of the non-stop music as I watched the casual comings and goings, with the pleasant aroma of good coffee and dope wafting by in the late afternoon air.

One coffee shop is the headquarters of the local chapter of the Hell's Angels. Whose leader, Jack, had recently died in a motorway collision while doing a ton on his bike. At a table stood an artist fervently painting a portrait of Jack from a photograph, etching the lines and furrows on his beaming face with great love and intense concentration. The bar assistant was a wee Scotsman whose tee shirt brandished the words Fuck Off. Heavy metal emanated from the sound system as the Angels rapped about Jack's funeral procession, which included a guard of honor of 140 bikers.

I'm sitting in a Space-O-Theek in a quiet street in the old Jewish quarter of the city. It is early on a Saturday evening and the place is calm and relaxed. A couple of neighborhood youths are playing *Space Invaders* near the door. Sitting at the counter besides me is an attractive middle-aged lady sipping a herbal tea, whilst watching the young people coming in to buy their weekend supply of hash or grass from the counter, then going to the rear disco room with its mirrors and coloured lights, to skin up and listen to the rhythmic sounds. It has the appearance of a modern youth club and is a focal point for the neighborhood teenagers. The lady next to me treats it as her 'local', finding it a pleasure to see young people in an alcohol free environment with no need to hang-out on street corners.

The Space-O-Theek is unique in that it doesn't sell coffee, but boasts a variety of 28 herb teas. The young owner, who was brought up in the neighborhood and used to work in a bank, was looking for places where he and his friends could go and have a smoke together, when he saw this empty shop, and now he has been in operation for just over a year and it has become a popular local haunt.

This latest addition to the coffee shops had just opened for the

Summer season, its blue and white décor carefully chosen to appeal to the affluent young tourists who flock to Amsterdam from all over the world to smoke cannabis in a relaxed and easy atmosphere, often far removed from their paranoiac home ground.

Cannabis is now one of Holland's biggest tourist attractions and a large earner of foreign currency. But the coffee shop, teahouse and smoking room have long been an established part of European culture and to frequent them at one time or another was thought to be daring or even outrageous. They were often the haunts of artists, painters, poets and revolutionaries, spending hours plotting the overthrow of the state while puffing cigarettes and drinking coffee.

There is no reason at all why the buying and smoking of cannabis should not become a part of this culture and just blend into the social scene. After all, Amsterdam has a long tradition in exotic herbs and spices from the East. Long may the dope coffee shops reign.

Home Grown Editorial

Home Grown Magazine Volume 1 No. 10, 1981:

Cannabis Connections - an open submission to the Home Office in response to the Report of the Royal Commission on Criminal Procedure.

We feel it is important to draw your attention to the cannabis issue in your deliberations on the *Royal Commission Report on Criminal Procedure.*

We believe that cannabis law enforcement is immoral in principle and unworkable in practice and that its consequences create grave social damage to the fabric of our society. There is a limit to the amount of control or forms of coercion which can be employed in any country where democratic freedom exists.

Archaic Laws

> "Britain is a nation of drab and dreary people bogged down with archaic laws whose restrictions on society create more problems than they solve. One needs a minimum of rules to ensure that antisocial people don't interfere with other people's rights. These are my opinions and I'm sure that many people will disagree with them. But unless there are some pretty radical changes the future looks very grim indeed."

Mr. Michael Gibson, Assistant Chief Constable of Kent made these remarks during an interview (as reported in the press) at his police headquarters in Maidstone in 1980. He went on to say that cannabis should be decriminalised and put the use of "pot" and the police involvement in detecting users in the same category as many motoring offences.

> "It is a petty matter which takes up valuable police resources at a time when efficiency is being stretched to the limits. People should be able to make up their own minds about what is right and wrong. What we need is less Whitehall interference and fewer laws."

Riot Connections

Attempts to enforce the law in relation to cannabis undoubtedly account for a large proportion of contact between the police and the black community, creating friction and the riots that followed.

The Bristol riots of April 1980 arose out of a police raid on a West Indian café where cannabis was used and the drug squad officers were the first target of the crowd that gathered, although they numbered only seven of the forty policemen present. Giving evidence at the trial that followed a drug squad officer told the court that trouble began as they were leaving the café with around three-quarters of a pound of cannabis. There was a large crowd of youths and he heard one man say "He has got the dope." Another officer said that they were chased to the car by a crowd of about seventy. He gained the clear impression that they were trying to retrieve the cannabis.

On the 3rd of November 1980 around fifty officers arrived at All Saints Road in Notting Hill, London and blocked off the street, raiding a pub and betting shop, and stopping and searching the predominantly black people in the street. This in the middle of the afternoon on the pretext of "information received" on a large cannabis deal. The only arrests made during the entire operation were three men for possession of small quantities of cannabis, and one other man for handling a stolen driving license.

At the Scarman inquiry hearings allegations which were current in Brixton at the time of the riots in April of this year surfaced for the first time. In a statement submitted by the MP for Norwood, Mr. John Fraser, he listed among what he believed were causes of the riot "The widespread belief that cannabis is being kept by police for illicit purposes". He suggested that they "recycled" it and took bribes. Lord Scarman said that Mr. Fraser had volunteered to give evidence "surprising reluctantly considering he is an MP."

It is known that the trigger for the rioting in Brixton on April 11th, was the search of a black youth for drugs. It is also worth noting that the raids carried out on fourteen properties in Railton Road on July 15th, most of which suffered extensive damage, were authorised by search warrants issued under the Misuse of Drugs Act. They said that they were acting on a "reliable" tip that petrol bombs were being stored there. As a result of this operation five men were charged with possession of cannabis, and one with obstruction.

Facts and Fictions

The recently-released statistics of the *Misuse of Drugs Act* in 1980 shows the highest number of cannabis offences in any year since the coming into force of the *Misuse of Drugs Act* in 1973. A total of 14,910 persons were found guilty of or cautioned for cannabis offences, 12,410 of them for simple possession.

There were 8,039 drug seizures resulting from raids on private premises; street searches accounted for a further 5,716 seizures, 86% of which were in respect of cannabis.

In 1980 the average age of drug offenders continued to increase; of those found guilty or cautioned, about half were aged 25 or over as compared with about a quarter in 1973. However, because of the large increase in the number of offenders, the numbers in the younger age group were higher in 1980 than in any year since 1975.

The increases occurred in most of the police force areas in England and Wales, although in Scotland the number decreased.

An important factor in the overall increase was a very large increase in the number of offenders found guilty or cautioned for cultivation of cannabis plants. The number recorded about 2,000 was more than twice the number dealt with in 1977/78 and nearly five times as many as that in 1974.

The number of custodial sentences given for offenders involving cannabis (about 1,800) was the largest recorded in any year since 1973.

Out of 10,586 persons who were fined for cannabis offences, (75% of those found guilty) 5,969 were fined over £20 and up to and including £50; 2,507 were fined over £50 and up to and including £100; and 975 were fined over £10 and up to and including £20.

It must be stressed that cannabis is categorised as a 'Class B' drug, and that the vast majority of police activity in relation to controlled drugs in fact relates to cannabis.

These figures do not take into account the thousands of dwellings that were raided where no cannabis was found, nor the many thousands of persons who were stopped and searched under the *Misuse of Drugs Act* power provided by Section 23 on "reasonable grounds", on whom no drugs were found.

Terra Incognita

"One of the major sources of conflict in areas where rioting has taken place springs from the raiding of premises for cannabis. As long as the law remains the same you will have bad blood. The legalisation of pot should be considered"

This statement was made in August of this year by Mr. Peregrine Worsthorne, the Editor of the *Sunday Telegraph*. Writing as far back as February 1970 in the same paper, he expressed the following views, which we feel to be of relevance to the issue:

"Drug-taking is the one social problem where the old have no right to pull rank, since it is no part of their experience. They cannot claim by reason of their years, to have had greater opportunities to imbibe the inherited wisdom of the ages, because on this subject in our society, there is no wisdom of the ages"

This is a far cry from the authorative moral attitude based on inherited experience of countless generations. It is a tentative, ambivalent authority, buttressed by books and reports and statistics, but not rooted in instinct and tradition.

Talking to the young about drugs one finds the beginnings of a folk-wisdom, of a knowledge based on experience, of a standard of values, of a genuine social attitude, which they are prepared to abide by and transmit. But the state does nothing to make it fructify, since the knowledge which the young are gaining about drugs through personal experience is strictly stolen knowledge which they are officially forbidden to lay their hands on.

It is as if a generation, which had never driven a motorcar sought to lay down the law about road safety simply by studying the statistics of road accidents, and refused to allow the next generation to experiment on the roads because it is too dangerous.

My plea is that responsible members of society should be allowed and assisted to join in this search for a social attitude to drugs based on the authority that only direct experience is likely to induce, instead of the hotchpotch of fear and prejudice based only on what people have read and heard."

A Political Judgment

Parliament has been a little light-hearted in recent years in creating offences in fields in which it is anxious to control particular activities but in respect of which no element of moral guilt appears to rise. If we want the law to be respected, however much we wish to control an activity and however much we are afraid of bogus defences, we must be careful not to exclude the element of conscious guilt from criminality.

To include deviant acts amongst criminal acts, for the possession and smoking of cannabis is no more than so, is to impugn moral undertones on the relative nature of law and go beyond the customary bounds of a legal definition of crime in a society that professes to be free and to adhere to democratic principles.

Could it be that the negative and counter-productive stance adopted over the years to cannabis law-reform springs from people without the clearest knowledge of where muddle-headed thinking on their part may lead other people? For what is ultimately at stake is a social and political judgement as Lord Hailsham (the Lord Chancellor in the present Conservative government) pointed out when summing up in his speech in Parliament on the Wootton Report in January 1969 (when he was Mr. Quentin Hogg):

> "This country owes a duty to the other countries of the world not to permit within these boundaries the spread of this vice. We have not suffered from it very badly yet. But if we were to go back on the policy, which we have deliberately adopted for more than forty years we should be breaking our pledged word. What is more, we should be interfering vitally with the struggle of some of the developing countries to lift their population from squalor, poverty and ignorance to which this particular drug is an important contributory cause, worse; we should be importing here another source of misery, crime and unhappiness."

After the riots?

Ultimately, cannabis prohibition has created more problems in our society than it has solved. It is maintained at great cost to the public purse, not to mention the cost in human terms of the searches, raids and consequent arrests and court appearances of thousands of usually law-abiding citizens, whose jobs and family life are put at risk. It is not cannabis but it's prohibition that has become an important cause of the riots, inflicting grave social damage on community relations, causing suspicion and deep resentment against the police, and thereby creating an uneasy and paranoiac social environment, especially in the inner city areas.

"When the wind blows, the grass bends" Confucius is reputed to have said. It is a sad reflection on our present society with its bureaucratic structure that it has not seen fit to move with the times and adopt more workable options for control, for the present system is held in disrepute by large sections of the community, and is seen to be enacted in an arbitrary and random fashion, creating a feeling of oppression.

We would go as far as to predict that the police, whatever their formal powers may be, will have no alternative but to severely restrict the use they make of the powers of search provided by the Misuse of Drugs Act, if the inner-city areas are to know any peace at all. It would be very much better if it were abolished.

In this connection, we feel that it is most unfortunate the Commission has recommended substantial extension of powers to stop and search, and believe that such recommendations should not be considered now in the light of the recent rioting.

In conclusion, let us say discussion legitimises, even if it does not authorise. It makes a subject respectable, if not legal.

Lee Harris

Ginseng: the Root of Being

Home Grown Magazine Volume 1 No. 9, 1981:

"Come to Ginseng with an open heart, for its enigmatic qualities have baffled man long before our time" I wrote in the *Alchemical Almanac* and *Handbook of Herbals Highs*, published in the winter of 1972. In those heady days we were a small, select band of devotees to whom Ginseng was a magical root that held within it the secret of eternal youth. Dating back to antiquity the 'Man-plant', 'Man-essence' was first recorded by Emperor Shen-nung 5,000 years ago as the highest, most potent herb amongst the thousands mentioned.

There is a rich history and mythology surrounding this 'Root of life', and we seekers felt a certain kinship to this inscrutable herb that had evaded man in his quest to understand its hidden secrets.

On a winter night in that same year ('72), a young Oxford graduate Stephen Fulder, a Ph.D. in biochemistry, was sitting in a library of the *National Institute for Medical Research* in London, doing a routine survey of scientific journals when he came across an article describing the discovery that an Oriental plant, ginseng, when added to human cells that were growing in the laboratory could preserve them and prolong their life. This intrigued him, as he was involved with research into the aging process, and also happened to be growing human cells in the laboratory at the time.

Here was a plant which he had never heard of before, which could not only prolong the life of cells, but was apparently used as 'A tonic and preventative of old-age debility'.

Shortly afterwards, Stephen Fulder and I, who were old friends, ran into each other and discovered that we both had an interest in ginseng, though mine was alchemical and his biochemical. He begins his book, '*The Root of Being; Ginseng and the Pharmacology of Harmony*', the first full and critical exploration of the remarkable healing properties of ginseng, with that meeting:

"It was shown to me reverently by a long-lost friend of mine. He was now trading in herbs, knick-knacks and strange discoveries. Ginseng was his prize find. At the back of his shop, amidst the old sweet jars full of aromatic herbs, was a balsa-wood box containing the ginseng. It was a root, maroon gnarled and crusty, as if aged by the elements. Yet it was also crystalline and peculiarly translucent. I could even see light through it when I held it up to the light bulb. I tasted some. It was extremely hard and its flavour evoked the sweetness of the liquorice, the bitterness of orange peel and the dryness of dust. My friend bubbled with enthusiasm about it. 'It is quite unique, the potion of the Emperors. The Chinese take it whenever they can, especially the old people. They say that it gives them strength and energy, you know, to keep them going, and that it is useful against impotence too. I take it every morning with my tea. It makes me feel buoyant, almost sparkling, and very positive. But it is also mysterious. It doesn't work in the same way for everybody. The Chinese say its effect is related to your inner state. Why not do some research on it?"

Reminding him that it took seven years for the ginseng root to grow to maturity, he began his quest, which eventually flowed from the meeting of the concepts of Oriental medicine and the practice of science, into the understanding of a new generation of subtle, non-toxic medicines which may well change the face of pharmacology.

The harmony remedies, Adaptogens, are biologically active substances of plant or animal origin that achieve their effect by improving inner equilibrium and increasing human capability. The ancient medical system built upon the Taoist view of health taught that the primary activity should be to establish harmony so as avoid disease, and this art of prevention was consequently developed to an unparalleled degree. East and West were coming together in a great current of cross-fertilization and Panax ginseng came under the microscopic and analytic eye of scientific man. By clinical trial and error, by discovering its chemical structure and active constituents, the gurus of science have prized open some of its secrets, revealing ginseng's enigmatic nature.

The 'Grand old man' of ginseng research is Prof. I. Brekhman of the *Institute of Biologically Active Substances* in Vladivostock, in the far east of the U.S.S.R.

I attended a scientific symposium on ginseng in Lugano in

Switzerland in 1976 and heard him read a paper summing up his findings after thirty years of study. In carrying out tests on mice and men he discovered that it helped the body adapt to changing conditions, intensified the stamina effect and seemed to be cumulative. He coined the term 'Adaptogens', to cover similar substances, such as 'Pantui' from the antlers of the deer, that had this harmonizing effect. In the Soviet Union millions of people whose tasks require fast physical actions, mental concentration and co-ordination now take the harmonizers.

Also at the symposium was the eminent behavioral scientist, Prof. W. Petcov, head of the *Faculty of Pharmacology in the Institute of Specialized and Advanced Medical Training*, Sofia, Bulgaria, who has presented scores of scientific publications on ginseng using the classical conditioning methods of Pavlov, but with rats instead of dogs.

Petcov discovered that ginseng stimulated the cerebral cortex of the central nervous system, the information-processing area of the brain "Through simultaneous reinforcement of the process of excitation and inhibition". In Pavlovian terms the healthy ability to depress one centre and light up another, to excite and inhibit, constitutes the adaptability of the individual. He concludes that ginseng is the first truly balanced stimulant, which does not cause excitation, insomnia or discord.

In Tokyo, Japan, Prof. Shibata broke through the pure form of ginseng and cracked its saponin or glycoside code, identifying its active constituents and structure. Some of its components were found to stimulate, while others had a sedating quality, effecting a complex balanced arousal.

As the devotees of science persevere still further, discovering many of the healing properties of the root ginseng, I wonder when we'll reach the stage when Western medicine will drop the folly of synthetic drugs and search once more among the plant kingdom for remedies that bring us into closer harmony with our natural environment. It was Emperor Shen-nung who wrote many thousands of years ago about the ginseng plant; that it was:

> "a tonic to the five viscera, quieting the animal spirits, strengthening the soul, allaying fear, expelling evil effluvia, brightening the eyes, opening the heart, benefiting the understanding and, if taken over a period of time, will invigorate the body and prolong life".

Maybe science will reach the same conclusions as the ancient sage. Meanwhile the Russians are giving their cosmonauts adaptogens for that ultimate in human adaptability and stress experiences, the journey into space. Stephen Fulder, in *The Root of Being* acknowledges me for first awakening his interest in ginseng and keeping the ginseng bottle boiling thereafter. I would like to acknowledge him for his magnificent effort, using the skills of science and the ancient teachings of the East, in deciphering much of the puzzle that is ginseng, and by doing illuminating a way towards a more refined relationship with the medical substances of our environment. "Ginseng doesn't just go to your head, it gets everywhere," we used to say.

A Footsoldier's Tale

Previously unpublished, September 1999:

It all started in the magic theatre in the mind of J. Henry Moore, a small bespectacled gnome-like character in his early thirties, sporting a shaggy beard and long hair. What Jack, as he was called, visualised as theatre, his great friend Jim Haynes would find a space for. It was part of the Jim and Jack show.

In physical appearance and personality they could hardly have been more different. Jim was a tall, genial bear of a man, with trim-cut beard and neat dark hair, who warmly hugged you. Jack was secretive and evasive, avoiding the limelight that shone so brightly on Jim. They were part of the American expat crowd that made the counter-culture sparkle in the London of the late Sixties.

I first met up with them in the autumn of 1966 when they were part of the collective who brought out the early issues of *IT, International Times*, the voice of the seminal underground movement. We teamed up on my Theatre of Action idea, *'The Fletcher File'*, based on a transcript of a murder trial. Jim hired the vast cold and empty former railway shed in Camden, called 'The Roundhouse'.

This was the early days and it had only been used for two parties before. I edited and adapted the script (not for the stage) and the presentational supervision (not direction) was by J. Henry Moore. This event took place on Sunday the 5th of February 1967. We called for the release of Roy and Alice Fletcher and the arrest of the Home Secretary. By the end of that year they were let out after serving six years of a life sentence, and the case became an underground cause celebre.

At that time I used to visit them in the flat they shared in Long Acre in Covent Garden. Jim had come down to London from Edinburgh, flushed with success and adoration, having founded the *'Traverse'* fringe theatre club. He had brought Jack down with him and they had found an empty warehouse in Drury Lane and converted it into an experimental multi-media centre called *The Arts Laboratory*, containing a theatre, cinema, art gallery, restaurant and open space.

The chemistry was right, the scene was set, and Jim and Jack's dream warehouse became the centre where many avant-garde works took place. Jim was a catalyst that brought creative types together, an underground entrepreneur who could make things happen with shoestring budgets and the love and sweat of an army of devoted helpers. I was one of them. In its short heyday it catered to the celebrity crowd and was the place to spend an evening with the 'Counter-culture'.

In the autumn of 1967 I sojourned abroad. I travelled to South Africa to see my dying mother, then on to Kenya and Israel. I used the time to finish writing *'Love Play'*, an LSD-induced lyrical fantasy for the theatre. My characters had no life-careers, only life-rhythms; there was no exposition, only explosion, and no narrative, only patterns. I was inspired by the mad visionary and surrealist Antonin Artaud, who wrote of the theatre as "the truthful precipitate of dreams."

I came back to London in the late summer of 1968. It was a strange time, altogether. The spirit of the time was rampant with discord and mayhem. Chairman Mao's *'Little Red Book'* jostled with the embryonic reality of a cybernetic age. Angry anarchists vied with whacked-out weirdos, reality-freaks versus space cadets. Pass the liberation and blow your mind. We were on a freewheeling roller-coaster veering from sexual liberation to spiritual upsurges; helter-skelter from drugs and rock and roll to macrobiotics and yoga.

It was the moment to smash the clocks and arrest time. Revolutionary fervour was running amok. Radical *Situationists* were storming the barricades in Paris, students and the dropout homeless were squatting empty properties in London. There were violent demonstrations against the war in Vietnam in Europe and elsewhere. In the U.S.A. *Black Power* erupted into race riots. At the end of August the Soviet invasion of Czechoslovakia laid waste to the dream of the *'Prague Spring'*.

Wearing a flower in your hair and saying "Far out, man," as sure as hell didn't endear you to heavy political heads. Nevertheless, it was so good to be back at the *Arts Lab* after all those months away and to see my good friend Jim Haynes. The Lab had drifted towards being a people theatre, where we were all performing artists just by virtue of being there. The nice thing about the place was that all sorts of interesting people would pop in. Through Jim's largesse I worked as a make-up artist for Frank Zappa, went down to Stonehenge on a red double-decker bus with *'The Fugs'* and sat on the floor cross-legged rapping with Mama Cass.

That September, just a stone's throw from the Arts Lab, the hippy musical *'Hair'* opened and let the sun shine in with numbers like 'Sodomy' and 'Hashish'. We would rush through the auditorium as the show ended and dance on the stage with the actors and audience. The Lord Chamberlain's powers of theatre censorship had just been abolished after hundreds of years. Later that month I went to Amsterdam in search of a roving street-theatre group called *'The Human Family'* which was the creation of the "mother" of the family, my old friend Jack. They had just toured the hip capitals of Europe during the summer creating their spontaneous happenings at festivals. I met up with them at the Fantasia in Prins Hendrikkade, now the Kosmos.

It was like setting foot on some strange film set, watching a surreal movie being made of this new utopia where long-haired tourists lounge on carpeted platforms, sipping Mu tea and smoking dope. It was the first of its kind and Amsterdam was the magnetic centre of the new Stoned Age. That night I joined them in their wood-beamed attic above some artists' studios, this troupe of ragged wild-eyed poets and gentle blissful dreamers in their faded hippy finery. We squatted in a circle eating quietly our beggar's banquet of rice, fried beans, onions and carrots. We were a motley crew, some twenty of us from many countries, sleeping in our loused-up bags and blankets.

Then it happened. Early one morning we were raided and bundled off to the central police station. One by one we were searched; our belts and personal belongings taken away and locked up in solitary confinement. After the initial outraged excitement, the perverse pleasure of an absurd situation, I felt calm and relaxed. The endless banging and prolonged screams of my brothers and sisters had subsided in exhaustion. Long hours of random thoughts and growing claustrophobia passed by. Then I heard Sandos, our Italian brother, banging against his cell door and letting out a strange terrible cry that ended up in uncontrollable weeping. Then there was a deep silence.

That night I was taken to the Hoek of Holland, where I was deported, without having committed a crime, nor being charged for one. "Dutch police deport London theatre group," was the headline in a Sunday newspaper. That was my rite of passage to The Human Family. I arrived back at the *Arts Laboratory* at the end of September.

As the cold winter loomed, the casualties of the Love generation mounted. The warm glow of the *Arts Lab* provided shelter for the shoddy array of the dispossessed and unloved. The walking wounded were turning this once-derelict warehouse into a communal dosshouse. Its proximity to nearby Piccadilly Circus attracted the flotsam of the lonely streets. Lost denizens looking for a place to go, to belong. The first devotees of the *Hare Krishna* movement arrived from America and set up a temple just around the corner. I remember the first ecstatic chanting sessions held at the Lab with Guru Das and Mikunda in their flowing saffron robes and shaven heads.

The magic of the place was that it often came alive with spontaneous events and the rich camaraderie of shared ideals.

On one occasion, when we were sitting about and nothing in particular was happening, a white Rolls Royce stopped outside the entrance and in walked a sombre-looking gaunt young man wearing a Maoist-style blue denim outfit and cap.

This was the time of the Chinese Red Guard and the Cultural Revolution. At his side was a petite Japanese woman with long hair, draped in an ankle-length black cape. It was John Lennon and Yoko Ono. They joined us and crouched on the floor with their knees up. One of us went up to them and whispered. John nodded and they got up and went to a backroom. Later I asked my friend what had he said to Lennon. He replied, "I asked them if they would like to share a joint with me."

John and Yoko became frequent visitors to the Lab, the white Rolls would arrive and take Jim and Jack to their Surrey mansion, or they would go to the newly opened *'Seed'* macrobiotic restaurant in Bayswater where they would dine sitting on cushions. Jack Moore was a wizard with gadgets and an early exponent of video technology. John was so interested in what they planned to do that he had given them a gift of some video equipment.

At the Arts Lab all was not well. On November the 15th a notice was posted informing the Lab staff that *'The Human Family'*, comprising thirty people plus equipment, would be arriving on December 10th. The notice read: "They will stay at least until the day after Christmas. During this period Jack will make the schedule and policy decisions", It was signed by Jim Haynes and Jack Moore. It caused outrage and a group of artists broke away in an acrimonious split. I loyally stuck by my two friends and in a statement of support published in *'I.T.'*, I said: "The Arts Lab is alive and well - evolving in a freer form. The space in the building is to be given over more to the people who use it." And I attacked "titular heads and control freaks".

The first intimation I got that something was afoot was when Jack told Jim to book the *Royal Albert Hall*, that vast circular space crowned by a dome, for a night in December. All we footsoldiers were told was that Leonard Cohen, the balladeer and poet who wrote melancholic songs to commit suicide to, would be heading the bill. The event was to be called *'The Alchemical Wedding'*, a poster was designed by Jack and Bill Levy, another American underground mover. It was a medieval-type drawing of a head with the skin peeled back over the skull, denoting a blown mind, and a finger over the mouth making the sign to be silent.

To cap it all, one evening in early December, a group of heavy dudes, looking like wild-west frontiersmen, walked into the Lab. It was Ken Kesey and the *'Pleasure Crew'*, some Deadheads and two bikers from the *Hell's Angel* chapter in San Francisco. I spent the night sitting and rapping with them, and in the morning I rode pillion on one of their bikes to the Beatles' plush *Apple* offices in Savile Row.

The group occupied an office suite, and we had a great party where all sorts of people popped in during the day. Time seemed to have slipped by, for it was late in the evening when a figure loomed at the office door. There was a silence as he calmly said, "It is nice of you to invite me to your home," reversing the situation. "Are you asking us to split"? said one of the Pleasure Crew. "Ying yang, yes, no", answered George Harrison enigmatically. At the time Ken Kesey had crashed out on eggnog and was sleeping in the basement stairwell.

The revolution is over and we have won, was the mantra. At last it was the day of the *Alchemical Wedding*. We footsoldiers had rushed about beforehand doing all the little things that had to be done, like spreading the word and seeing that flyers were distributed all over the place.

I slept at the back of the Lab when I could and one night I collapsed from exhaustion, puking up the Indian curry I had hastily eaten earlier. Nevertheless, here I was on the night of the 18th December '68, travelling in a taxi with Jim's secretary from the Lab to the Royal Albert Hall, resplendent in my paisley kaftan. We sat back and gave a sigh of relief as we crawled through the rush-hour traffic.

By the time we arrived backstage, the well of the large hall was beginning to fill up. Although nothing was, to my knowledge, planned, a couple of rock groups had set up in case they were asked to play. I could see John and Yoko sitting on the side of the stage. Ken Kesey and his merry crew were hanging around. There were the Hare Krishna devotees and about four thousand of the most beautiful heads that the underground could muster, waiting in anticipation for this most auspicious event to begin.

The hour had come, the crowd buzzed with excitement, but nothing happened. The audience started to fidget in their seats, there was an air of anxiety about. Then I noticed the small bedraggled figure of Jack Moore walking slowly through the crowded well of the hall, his finger to his lips beckoning silence.

By the time he had reached the front of the stage there was a silence only broken by the odd nervous guffaw or raucous catcall from the back. The silence became long and deep and seemed to engulf us. Then, almost out of nowhere, someone banged a drum, there was an ecstatic cry of joy, the Krishna devotees began to chant and I found myself swept off my feet by the momentum. The space in front of the stage filled with swaying, swirling bodies high on the energy created out of the silence. It was J. Henry Moore's finest moment.

This was the culmination of what *The Human Family* was about. Theatre in its highest form, it was an act of communal magic that could transcend earthbound reality.

Musicians played, poets ranted, and John and Yoko crept into their white sheet-like bag on the stage and stayed there out of sight for what seemed like ages. I watched a baby crawl slowly by. And that was the bag happening. All mayhem broke out when a young female member of the audience stripped off her clothes and danced in naked delight.

When the police were called and attendants tried to remove her, groups of people started stripping off their clothes in solidarity. There was a retreat and a truce was worked out, and no one was arrested. The nude girl incident, with accompanying photo, made the front pages of the London evening papers.

The *Alchemical Wedding* had a profound effect on many of us who were there that night. It touched our lives and helped bring about changes. There is a difference between what a person does and what happens by itself. You will set yourself a task with determination and tenacity and then, suddenly, a gust of wind will come from another world and everything changes. You seem to be used by the gods, and, in spite of yourself, you are part of the Myth.

Afterword

Shine on

In time of terror, in time of strife
My inner soul bequeaths life
To flow and grow and overthrow
The dark forces that beckon and threaten
My vibrant existential equilibrium

There lies the warm glow in the dark
That feeling of calm as the brightness banishes
The ebbing tide of negativity and downside
Giving it a berth far and wide
Be calm; don't set off the bells of alarm
Radiate the gracious beam of light
That illuminates the black holes that blow away

There lies the warm glow in the dark
Like a spark at the dawn of the rising sun
Shimmering and glimmering tremulously so
Shining into the zone of love
Just above the parapet to be
Untouched by the nebulous forces
That disappear in the twilight

To turn darkness into light as day follows night
Guided by the goodness of the heart and mind
Who else but you to be kind,
Forgiving and living in the here and now
My compassionate soul brother
Will lead you to that place where
There's a warm glow in the dark
That shines from my open mind
To a terrain that is serene and sublime.

Shine on

Lee Harris

About The Author

Extracts from Wikipedia article:

Lee Harris (born 1936 in Johannesburg) was one of the few white members of the African National Congress, where he helped with the *Congress of the People* and met Nelson Mandela. He acted with Orson Welles, Dame Flora Robson, wrote for the British underground press including *International Times*, helped found the Arts Lab and has been an instrumental figure in the British counterculture movement since the seventies when he published *Brainstorm Comix* and *Home Grown* magazine.

The Arts Lab (1967-69) was hugely influential and saw Lee working as a make-up artist for Frank Zappa and travelled to Stonehenge with folk rock group The Fugs.

During this time Harris also wrote various articles and reviews for many underground publications such as *IT* (*International Times*) including an interview with San Francisco beat poet Michael McClure. In IT issue 52 Lee Harris reported on a new play by Jane Arden at the Arts Lab. He also wrote various pieces for magazines *Oz* and *Frendz*.

In 1977 to 1982 Harris started and edited Britain's first counter-culture and drug magazine. *Home Grown* was a breakthrough magazine that represented a defining moment in British underground culture. Lee was reporting on psychedelic happenings and *Home Grown* magazine was one of the few publications to support the Operation Julie defendants which included work from Timothy Leary, Michael Hollingshead, Harry Shapiro, Brian Barritt, Mick Farren, Bryan Talbot, Julie Burchill, Peter Tosh and Tony Parsons.

In 1972 Harris opened a shop in the Portobello Road, London called *Alchemy* - named after *The Alchemical Wedding*. The shop currently sells items such as incense, postcards, pipes and smoking accessories, liquorice as well as others. It remains a focus and gathering point for alternative Londoners to the present day and is London's oldest 'counter-culture' shop.

It was at this time in the first year, when Lee met Bryan Talbot. After reading his work Harris decided to publish Bryan's first work

Brainstorm Comix which followed the protagonist Chester P. Hakenbush on his psychedelic cerebral journey. It is regarded as the last major British Underground Comic and garnered compliments from *Marvel Comics* creator Stan Lee; "I got a kick out of it and turned it over to the bullpen so they could bask in its magnificence, just as I did".

The *Chester P Hakenbush* trilogy was then republished in one volume in 1982 and then another edition in 1999 titled *Bryan Talbot's Brainstorm: The Complete Chester P Hakenbush and Other Underground Classics* which has now been translated and sold in Italy.

Bryan Talbot has gone on to become one of the worlds renowned graphic novelists, creator of *The Adventures of Luther Arkwright*, *The Tale of One Bad Rat,* and his latest work *Grandville*. There was also *Brainstorm Fantasy Comix* which had one issue published in 1977 which was a new direction and included work by Brian Bolland, Hunt Emerson, Angus McKie and the first-published work of John Higgins.

In 2005 Lee decided to release a celebration of his thirty years of counter-culture in the form of a compilation album including many of the artists, producers and musicians he had met along the years such as acclaimed producer Youth also Raja Ram & Simon Posford collectively known as *Shpongle,* Howard Marks, *The Mystery School Ensemble,* JC001, *Bush Chemist* and more. This culminated in an event at *Subterrania* in Ladbroke Grove to celebrate the album's release.

During this period he met Hicham Bensassi, who had also performed at the event. A few years later Hicham invited him to record something for a project he was working on and quite organically the album *Angel Headed Hip Hop* was born.

They brought in special guests such as writer Brian Barritt, rapper JC001 and Hicham Bensassi wrote the music, performed vocally on four of the album's songs and remixed the song "Three men in a boat" with Howard Marks originally released on the previous album *30 Years of Counter-culture*. The album was released in 2009 on Arkadia Productions and was distributed by Gene Pool/Universal Music Group.

Harris and Bensassi travelled the UK and Europe on the *"Don't Hate, Create Tour"* which included a special performance in Paris for the 50th Anniversary of the publication of William S. Burroughs' seminal work *Naked Lunch* which was organised by Oliver Harris, Andrew Hussey and Ian Macfadyen accompanying the *Naked Lunch @50: Anniversary Essays* edited by Oliver Harris & Ian Macfadyen.

ABOUT THE AUTHOR

This was the inspiration for Lee Harris & Hicham Bensassi behind the experimental piece *Hunterland*.

Lee also features in two recorded albums; *'Alchemy: 30 years of Counter-culture'* (2002) and *'Angel Headed Hip Hop'* in (2009) and the documentary *'Echoes of the Underground'*.

More information on Lee Harris can found on his personal website here: www.leeharris.co.uk. The companion website to this book can be found here: : www.echoesoftheunderground.com.

BARNCOTT PRESS.COM

Made in the USA
Charleston, SC
07 February 2016